Theory, Development, and Strategy in Transmedia Storytelling

This book explores transmedia dynamics in various facets of fiction and nonfiction transmedia studies. Moving beyond the presentation/definition of transmediality as a field of study, the authors examine novel advancements in the theory, methodological development, and strategic planning of transmedia storytelling.

Drawing upon a theoretical foundation grounded in Peircean semiotics and reflected in the methodological approaches to fiction and nonfiction transmedia projects, the chapters delve into diverse case studies, such as *The Handmaid's Tale* and mega sporting events like the Olympics and FIFA World Cup, that illustrate the applications of our own methods and the implications of the logic behind transmedia dynamics. Expanding upon their own scholarship, the authors tackle the relevant topic of transmedia journalism, and present new approaches to transmedia strategic planning around educational initiatives in developing countries.

The book is an important reference for scholars and students of media studies, education, journalism and transmedia, and those interested in comprehending theory, methodological development, and strategic planning of transmediality.

Renira Rampazzo Gambarato is Associate Professor in Media and Communication Studies at Jönköping University, in Sweden. Her area of expertise revolves around fiction and nonfiction transmedia studies. She is the co-editor of the recent books *The Routledge Companion to Transmedia Studies* (2019) and *Exploring Transmedia Journalism in the Digital Age* (2018).

Geane Carvalho Alzamora is Associate Professor in Social Communication at Federal University of Minas Gerais, Brazil. Her area of expertise revolves around transmedia studies, semiotics and digital journalism. She is the co-editor of the recent books *Exploring Transmedia Journalism in the Digital Age* (2018) and *Textualidades Midiáticas* (2017).

Lorena Tárcia is Associate Professor in Social Communication at University Center of Belo Horizonte, Brazil. Her area of expertise revolves around transmedia studies, education, and journalism. She is the author of several articles published in peer-reviewed journals, such as *Journalism Studies*, *International Journal of Communication*, and *Global Media and Communication*.

Routledge Advances in Transmedia Studies
Series Editor: Matthew Freeman

This series publishes monographs and edited collections that sit at the cutting-edge of today's interdisciplinary cross-platform media landscape. Topics should consider emerging transmedia applications in and across industries, cultures, arts, practices, or research methodologies. The series is especially interested in research exploring the future possibilities of an interconnected media landscape that looks beyond the field of media studies, notably broadening to include socio-political contexts, education, experience design, mixed-reality, journalism, the proliferation of screens, as well as art- and writing-based dimensions to do with the role of digital platforms like VR, apps and iDocs to tell new stories and express new ideas across multiple platforms in ways that join up with the social world.

Transmediality in Independent Journalism
The Turkish Case
Dilek Gürsoy

Theory, Development, and Strategy in Transmedia Storytelling
Renira Rampazzo Gambarato, Geane Carvalho Alzamora, Lorena Tárcia

Theory, Development, and Strategy in Transmedia Storytelling

Renira Rampazzo Gambarato,
Geane Carvalho Alzamora,
Lorena Tárcia

Routledge
Taylor & Francis Group

LONDON AND NEW YORK

First published 2020
by Routledge
2 Park Square, Milton Park, Abingdon, Oxon OX14 4RN

and by Routledge
52 Vanderbilt Avenue, New York, NY 10017

Routledge is an imprint of the Taylor & Francis Group, an informa business

British Library Cataloguing-in-Publication Data
A catalogue record for this book is available from the British Library

Library of Congress Cataloging-in-Publication Data
A catalog record has been requested for this book

ISBN: 978-0-367-34304-0 (hbk)
ISBN: 978-0-367-51001-5 (pbk)
ISBN: 978-0-367-34305-7 (ebk)

Typeset in Sabon
by codeMantra

Contents

Illustrations

Figure

Tables

Acknowledgments

The process of writing this book has been highly valuable to us as we have had the opportunity to revisit and, moreover, to develop further our understanding of transmedia dynamics. In the past decade, we have been dedicating our scholarly work to various facets of transmedia studies and we are not alone. We would like to acknowledge with gratitude the involvement of Amanda Chevtchouk Jurno, Adriano Austeclínio Pádua dos Santos, and Sergei Andreevich Medvedev in the data collection for our studies dedicated to the Olympic Games and the *Fédération Internationale de Football Association* (FIFA) World Cups in Brazil and in Russia. And an even bigger thank-you must go to Dr. Luciana Andrade Gomes Bicalho, who has been actively collaborating with us in different capacities already for several years. Her insightful contributions to our research are visible throughout the book, especially in Chapter 5.

Introduction
Transmedia dynamics

The purpose of this book, based on a decade of research, is to present our theoretical-methodological vision of transmedia studies, understood here as a contemporary communication dynamics. This book expands on the previous studies and original writings of the authors of this book (Renira Rampazzo Gambarato, Geane Carvalho Alzamora, and Lorena Tárcia) regarding transmedia dynamics in various facets of fiction and nonfiction experiences. To understand the dimensions of the aesthetics, ethics, and logics of transmedia dynamics (Chapter 1), we start from the pragmatics conception of semiosis, proposed by Charles Sanders Peirce (1839–1914). Additionally, we utilize systems theory to understand transmedia dynamics as a supersystem composed of a set of subsystems of signs (Chapter 2). This theoretical perspective results in our methodological proposals for planning and analyzing transmedia dynamics (Chapters 3–5).

We understand transmedia storytelling as logic, similar to Jenkins (2017), but we adopt the Peircean conception of logic, or semiotics, as explained in Chapter 1 of this book. In our view, transmedia storytelling is a contemporary communication logic that permeates the most varied social practices in specific communication dynamics. Transmedia logic manifests as a communication process characterized by the multiplatform distribution of information and collective action for creative expansion of information.

According to Scolari, Bertetti, and Freeman (2014), there are at least two possible modes of transmedia expansion: media expansions and narrative expansions. They claim that transmedia storytelling can be considered a specific case of general transtexual storytelling. "The expansion of the narrative is thus at the same time a social, commercial and semiotic necessity of certain tales" (Scolari et al., 2014, p. 2).

In this regard, transmedia dynamics is a communication process that normalizes the course of actions through various mediating instances (institutional, technological, semiotic, commercial, social, political, cultural, etc.), configuring that the more robust the social practices are, the more associations they are able to make in online/offline connections. Thus, as a communication process, transmedia dynamics is also a complex mediation process that propagates in conjunction with vertical communication processes (triggered by media industries) and horizontal communication processes (based on collective citizen actions).

The studies reported here configure a specific approach to transmedia logic, understood as communication dynamics based on semiotic and pragmatic principles that specify mediation and engagement processes. Transmedia logic, according to our approach, is sufficiently malleable to adapt to the empirical specificities involved in diversified transmedia processes. In addition, each transmedia dynamics presents itself as a specific system of signs, as explained in Chapter 2 of this book.

For Giovagnoli (2011), "presetting the shape of a communicative system is a fundamental operation in the creative and editorial process of distributing a story in new media" (p. 24). He claims that one must consider the complexity of the communicative processes—both simultaneous and asynchronous—which are used today by transmedia producers:

> In fact, thinking transmedia doesn't mean just distributing parts of the story in different media, then strictly putting publishing restrictions and dealing with the shuffled parts on the table, as in a charming solitaire game. On the contrary. *Condicio sine qua non* for a transmedia tale is the continuous dialogue between the involved publishing platforms and the consideration of creative and consumer spaces that belong to each of them, necessarily starting from the audiences, at all times.
>
> (Giovagnoli, 2011, p. 10, original italics)

Transmedia dynamics particularizes the communication process in each empirical context, although it refers to the generic characteristics of transmedia logic. Therefore, understanding, describing, and analyzing the communication form of transmedia dynamics are necessary, based on theoretical and methodological perspectives that can support transmedia strategic planning proposals compatible with the various collective tactics of transmedia creative expansion.

According to de Certeau (1984), "a strategy is the calculation (or manipulation) of power relationships that becomes possible as soon as a subject with will and power (a business, an army, a city, a scientific institution) can be isolated" (pp. 35–36) and "a tactic is a calculated action determined by the absence of a proper locus" (p. 37). De Certeau (1984) considers that the space of the tactic is the space of the other. From this viewpoint, a tactic is an art of the weak that creates surprises, and it can be where it is least expected. In contrast, the notion of strategy presupposes a localized center of power.

> In sum, strategies are actions which, thanks to the establishment of a place of power (the property of a proper), elaborate theoretical places (systems and totalizing discourses) capable of articulating an ensemble of physical places in which forces are distributed.
>
> (de Certeau, 1984, p. 38)

On the one hand, the strategy outlines transmedia planning. On the other, the tactic can not only increase transmedia dynamics by collective actions but also redefine its course, interfering in the trajectory of transmedia strategic planning. The notion of trajectory is also very important in this scenario because it is related to the strategic planning of the communication and the social practices, or tactics, that "circulate, come and go, overflow and drift over an imposed terrain" (de Certeau, 1984, p. 34). These tactics remain heterogeneous to the systems they infiltrate, which are strategically planned.

The trajectory of transmedia dynamics is strategic (because it is directed toward a certain goal) and tactical (which makes it unpredictable to a certain extent). Thus, the trajectory of transmedia dynamics points simultaneously to the strategy (transmedia planning) and to the tactics (creative extensions through collective actions). In this sense, the definition of trajectory proposed by de Certeau (1984) is illuminating, as it highlights the impossibility of accurately tracing the path of a transmedia trajectory, even if it has been strategically planned:

> In order to give an account of these practices, I have resorted to the category of 'trajectory.' It was intended to suggest a temporal movement through space, that is, the unity of a diachronic succession of points through which it passes, and not the figure that these points form on a space that is supposed to be synchronic or achronic. Indeed, this 'representation' is insufficient, precisely because a trajectory is drawn, and time and movement are thus reduced to a line that can be seized as a whole by the eye and read in a single moment, as one projects onto a map the path taken by someone walking through a city.
>
> (de Certeau, 1984, p. 35)

In the Peircean semiotic viewpoint, the trajectory is related to the path of semiosis, or sign action. The Peircean sign is a triadic entity (sign-object-interpretant) that unfolds continuously according to a purpose. In this approach, the object determines an effect (interpretant) in a mind, human or not, through the mediation of the sign (representamen), whereas the interpretant represents the object that serves as a reference through the mediation of the sign (representamen) in association (collateral experience) with adjacent signs to this semiosis. Thus, the path of the sign action is an entangled trajectory because it involves adjacent sign associations. In addition, the sign trajectory is pragmatically oriented toward an end (final causation), as is argued throughout Chapter 1 of this book:

> The insight that the trajectory does not connect its source and its goal in the form of the geometrically more economic straight line, but in the longer trajectory of a curve is reminiscent of Charles S. Peirce's conception

of semiosis as a process in which signs have a 'final cause or end.' The final cause or purpose of a sign is to produce an interpretant in its interpreter. In contrast to an efficient cause, which operates immediately or mechanically, a final cause may reach its goal by detours. The sign's trajectory from their source in the object to their goal in the interpretant does not need to be direct.

(Nöth, 2019, p. 5)

According to Nöth (2019), the trajectory that the Peircean sign describes from its source to its goal is not the trajectory of a message that has its source in the mind of a sender and reaches its goal in the mind of a receiver but the sign trajectory in which the object determines the sign to represent it and to create an interpretant. This sign trajectory is a pragmatic dynamic of signs. Nöth (2019) stresses that sign processes are dynamic processes. In this regard, transmedia dynamics is a pragmatically oriented sign process but is contingently configured by the imponderable adjacent sign associations. The Peircean model of semiosis is useful therefore to better understand the limits and potential of strategies and tactics in the trajectory of transmedia dynamics.

This subject is explained in Chapter 1, in which we describe the transmedia dynamics of mobilizations mediated by hashtags based on the Peircean model of semiosis. The impossibility of ascertaining the complete path of a hashtag is explained in this chapter based on the productive incompleteness of the interpretant, which always triggers new connections by sign association. Despite the uncertainty, it is possible to apprehend the semantic universe of the hashtag by tracing its semiotic trajectory, which constitutes fluid and fragmented transmedia dynamics.

For Alzamora and Andrade (2019), hashtags operate as mediating signs that connect one instance of meaning to another through sociotechnical connections and social use outside digital media environments. Because of this, hashtags can configure transmedia dynamics. In their study about transmedia mobilization mediated by hashtags, Alzamora and Andrade (2019) explain that activist hashtags promote mediation between a common sociopolitical position that serves as a reference (the logical place of the object) and a sociotechnical link that triggers a socio-communicative context (the logical place of the interpretant). However, hashtags connect one instance of meaning to another through the logical chain of hashtags, creating a transmedia dynamic that can legitimize or reconfigure its initial meaning by sign association.

According to this approach, transmedia dynamics involves all media environments, from digital to analog, online to offline, and vice versa. In this sense, transmedia dynamics is not restricted to the multiplatform narratives outlined by media industries because they also encompass alternative and circumstantial media configurations. Thus, any media-centered connotation of transmedia dynamics is removed, in favor of the broader notion of sign mediation.

This understanding influences the empirical-conceptual and the theoretical-methodological singularities of our research on transmedia dynamics, as described throughout this book, especially in Chapter 5. In this chapter, we present our proposal for communication planning in transmedia education for public schools in developing countries, where hegemonic media arrangements vary and digital connections are not always predominant.

The prefix trans-

In Chapter 2, we remind the reader that the term "transmedia" is a relatively new concept. This term is usually used to describe contemporary communication processes, markedly related to digital contexts. However, the adjective transmedia can also refer to older communication phenomena. Although digital connections are common in transmedia dynamics, they do not necessarily characterize the transmedia phenomenon. We present the characteristics of the transmedia phenomenon in Chapter 3.

According to Scolari et al. (2014), as transmedia storytelling emerges from a cultural convergence between media industry and collaborative practices, the archaeology of transmedia should start with the transmedia productions created before the introduction of the concept in the 1990s and its subsequent popularization in the 2000s. The authors consider that as early as the 1930s many popular narratives, such as Batman and Mickey Mouse, had been expanded to different media. At the same time, the fan communities were very active and participated considerably in the expansion of these fictional worlds. As a result, these productions could be considered a transmedia phenomenon, although the concept had not yet been formulated.

These examples demonstrate that it is necessary to take into account an expanded conception of media to reach the wide variety of social connections that transmedia dynamics encompasses. If we consider the transmedia phenomenon as a contemporary logic of communication, we must consider the different modalities of media today, in addition to digital connections and traditional mass media.

According to Huhtamo and Parikka (2011), media are not only related to the established institutions of modernity. The authors stress that media archaeology rummages through textual, visual, and auditory archives as well as collections of artifacts, emphasizing the discursive and material manifestations of culture. The broad conception of media therefore encompasses different textual, material, discursive, and cultural aspects.

We understand media as a kind of interaction environment that establishes dispositions and configures ways of acting through the network that media environment constitutes. This conception assumes that one media environment is intertwined with others, in a dynamic of reciprocal affectation that contaminates the circumstantial configuration of each media materiality (Alzamora, Ziller, & D'Andrea, 2017). The dynamics of mutual affectation between media environments, regarding the notions of intermedia and transmedia practices, is presented in Chapter 1.

The notion of media that underlies our idea of transmedia storytelling permeates the book, especially throughout Chapters 1, 3, and 5. The Peircean foundation of the notion of media is developed in Chapter 1. We consider any means of communication, digital or analog, that allows individual or collective expression of ideas, social interaction, and cultural exchange as a media environment. Based on this media perspective, we take into account the most varied media outlets in our communication planning in transmedia education for public schools in developing countries, as detailed in Chapter 5. However, as presented in Chapter 3, transmedia extensions are discussed in the scope of a transmedia supersystem, in which the idea of the media platform is stressed.

Platforms have penetrated the heart of societies, in a comprehensive view of a connected world according to Van Dijck, Poell, and De Wall (2018). In their view, a platform is a programmable digital architecture designed to organize interactions between users. The authors coined the term "platform society" to emphasize that platforms are an integral part of society today. They also coined the term "platform ecosystem" to designate the "assemblage of networked platforms, governed by a particular set of mechanisms that shapes everyday practices, once a single platform cannot be seen apart from each other but evolve in the context of an online setting that is structured by its own logic" (Van Dijck et al., 2018, p. 4). Thus, although digital connections are not essential to transmedia dynamics, they are very important in the social dissemination of transmedia logic in contemporary times.

In Freeman and Gambarato's view (2019), there is a consistent and clear emphasis on understanding transmediality as an experience permeated by technology, and intrinsically related to the creativity of audiences, particularly in the context of strategically motivated and democratically augmented media. They posit that only by embracing the multiplicities and pluralities of transmediality as a cross-disciplinary phenomenon can one fully grasp its prominence:

> Revising, refining, and clarifying our understanding of what does—and therefore what does not—constitute a form of 'transmedia' is indeed crucial, both to the future of this avenue of study but more importantly to our collective abilities to make sense of how, why, and when media content flows, expands, and moves across multiple media platforms in particular ways, for particular reasons, and with particular effects.
>
> (Freeman & Gambarato, 2019, p. 2)

For Jenkins (2019), the definition of transmedia is neither rigid nor static. According to him, each step along the way, we have had to expand and sharpen our understanding of what we mean by transmedia:

> To me, transmedia was about a set of relationships across media, not a single model for how different media might 'collide.' We need lots of different models for the forms that transmedia might take as different creative teams pursue different functions in relation to different stories for different audiences in different national contexts. When my students ask me whether something is or is not transmedia, I usually ask them in what ways it may be useful to read it as transmedia. So, there may be some circumstances where it makes sense to read fan fiction as part of a larger transmedia system while other times, it is important to maintain clear distinctions between canon and fanon, between continuity and multiplicity.
>
> (Jenkins, 2019, p. xxix)

In our view, to better understand what transmedia is, it is necessary to specify not only what media in the contemporary context means but also the way the prefix trans- qualifies it. In this regard, we first need to understand the differences among media concepts and then specify how the prefixes inter- and trans- qualify the relationships established among media environments. As explained in Chapter 1 and considered again in Chapter 2, the semantic universe of the term transmedia encompasses related terms, such as transtextuality, intertextuality, and paratextuality. This semantic universe also includes terms such as intermedia, crossmedia, and multimedia. Nonetheless, the prefix trans- singularizes a certain approach in this scenario.

According to Van Bauwel and Carpentier (2010), the prefix trans- refers to the leaping of codes and attempts to capture a series of connections that are transfigured into a specific connection between the text and the social and historical contexts. The authors consider that the prefix trans- oscillates between continuity and discontinuity, with a stronger emphasis on the process of change, on the simultaneous coexistence of what was and what has been transgressed, and on their fluid mergers.

For Alzamora and Tárcia (2012), when the prefix trans- is associated with media, it points to transgressive and original modes of interaction, language, and formats in multiple media contexts. According to Alzamora and Tárcia (2012), the transmedia perspective presupposes not only media complementation, although this is a relevant characteristic of the process, but also mainly the displacement of characteristics traditionally related to media environments. "It would thus constitute reticular zones for the mixing of genres and formats among digital media connections" (Alzamora & Tárcia, 2012, p. 30).

Therefore, the prefix trans- delineates a singular media trajectory, insofar as it strategically points to the deviations and transgressions that usually characterize the tactical resignifications of collective actions in the context of media. Throughout this book, we have sought to highlight the theoretical and methodological implications of this approach to the transmedia communication process in our own way.

In Chapter 2, we define system within the sphere of general systems theory and system of signs in the Peircean view. In this approach, complexity is a fundamental parameter not only for its relation with the intricate parts that compose a transmedia story but also for all the implications in the interplay between these parts and the social environment where they are inserted. We conclude the chapter by discussing the implications of what we call the "transmedia effect," that is, the expansion of storyworlds that are robust and exciting enough to function across multiple levels of interest, from audiences to producers to authors to financiers.

In Chapter 3, we present our transmedia design analytical model. We apply this model to the fictional transmedia project *The Handmaid's Tale*, which represents the idea of the transmedia effect discussed in Chapter 2. This transmedia design analytical model serves as the ground for the application of the same parameters to journalism, which are explored in Chapter 4. We describe how transmedia features are structured and implemented in the news coverage of mega sporting events, such as the Olympic Games (in Sochi and Rio) and the *Fédération Internationale de Football Association* (FIFA) World Cup (in Brazil and Russia).

In Chapter 5, we contextualize and analyze practices, strategic planning, and methodologies related to transmedia dynamics in education. We present our methodology in transmedia education developed for low-income communities in Portuguese-speaking countries, such as East Timor, Mozambique, and Brazil. The aim of our research in the transmedia education realm is to create educational actions across multiple platforms, integrating online and offline dynamics and highlighting the engagement and participation of the school community.

In the end, we return to the main theoretical and methodological discussions presented throughout the book to clarify our point of view on transmedia dynamics. Our intention is that this book, which discusses and analyzes various aspects of fictional and nonfictional transmedia dynamics, can be useful for transmedia researchers and producers. Currently, transmedia dynamics is a very relevant subject that requires an integrated research effort to develop it further. This book aims to contribute to this research scenario.

References

Alzamora, G., & Andrade, L. (2019). A dinâmica transmídia da hashtag #vemprarua: Mediação e semiose [The hashtag's #cometothestreet transmedia dynamics: Mediation and semiosis]. In I. Satuf & J. A. B. Prado (Eds.), *Comunicação em ambiente digital* [Communication in the digital environment] (pp. 171–191). Covilhã, Portugal: LABCOM.

Alzamora, G., & Tárcia, L. (2012). Convergence and transmedia: Semantic galaxies and emerging narratives in journalism. *Brazilian Journalism Research, 8*(1), 22–34.

Alzamora, G., Ziller, J., & D'Andrea, C. (2017). Medios y dispositivo: Una aproximación a luz de Michel Foucault. [Media and device: An approximation in the light of Michel Foucault]. In B. Leal, C. Carvalho, & G. Alzamora (Eds.), *Textualidade midiática* [Media textuality] (pp. 69–94). Barcelona, Spain: Editorial UOC.

de Certeau, M. (1984). *The practice of everyday life* (S. Rendall, Trans.). Berkeley: University of California Press.

Freeman, M., & Gambarato, R. (2019). Introduction – Transmedia studies: Where now? In M. Freeman & R. Gambarato (Eds.). *The Routledge companion to transmedia studies* (pp. 1–12). New York, NY: Routledge.

Giovagnoli, M. (2011). *Transmedia storytelling: Imagery, shapes and techniques.* Pittsburgh, PA: ETC Press.

Huhtamo, E., & Parikka, J. (2011). *Media archaeology: Approaches, applications, and implications.* Berkeley: University of California Press.

Jenkins, H. (2017). Transmedia logics and locations. In B. W. L. D. Kurtz & M. Bourdaa (Eds.), *The rise of transtexts: Challenges and opportunities* (pp. 220– 40). New York, NY: Routledge.

Jenkins, H. (2019). Foreword. In M. Freeman & R. Gambarato (Eds.), *The Routledge companion to transmedia studies* (pp. xxvi–xxx). New York, NY: Routledge.

Nöth, W. (2019, September). *Trajectory: A model of the sign and semiosis.* Paper presented at the 14th World Congress of Semiotics, Buenos Aires, Argentina.

Scolari, C. A., Bertetti, P., & Freeman, M. (2014). *Transmedia archaeology: Storytelling in the borderlines of science fiction, comics and pulp magazines.* New York, NY: Palgrave.

Van Bauwel, S., & Carpentier, N. (2010). The politics of the prefix: From "post" to "trans" (and back)? In S. Van Bauwel & N. Carpentier (Eds.), *Trans-reality television: The transgression of reality, genre, politics, and audience* (pp. 297–315). London, England: Lexington.

Van Dijck, J., Poell, T., & De Wall, M. (2018). *Platform society: Public values in a connective world.* New York, NY: Oxford University Press.

Part I
Theory

1 The semiotics of transmedia storytelling

Peircean communication model

Models articulate organization, prediction, measurement, and heuristic functions (Deutsch, 1952); therefore, models are relevant research instruments capable of illuminating intricate relationships in a given field of knowledge. Severin and Tankard (1979) suggest that the relevance of a model can be gauged by questions such as "How general is the model?" and "How does the model help in discovering new relationships, facts, or methods?" Based on these issues, we aim to characterize the communication model of transmedia dynamics.

According to McQuail and Windahl (1993), a model seeks to show the main elements of any structure and the relationship between these elements. They claim that in the most general terms, communication implies a sender, a channel, a message, a receiver, a relationship between the sender and receiver, an effect, a context in which communication occurs, and a range of elements to which the messages refer.

In social communication, over time different models show terms and relations in various theoretical-methodological aspects. Almost all emphasize aspects described by McQuail and Windahl (1993), including varied semiotic approaches, but "the diversity of the semiotic models of communication is by no means greater than the diversity which prevails in the field of communication theory in general" (Nöth, 2014, p. 115).

Our approach is based on Charles Sanders Peirce's (1839–1914) semiotic theory. Complex and very abstract, Peirce's thought, especially his semiosis model, has been recurrently used to understand general aspects of communication because "communication, according to Peirce, is a particular process of semiosis, that is, a sign process" (Nöth, 2014, p. 99). Our discussion focuses on the pragmatic relationship between semiosis and communication to characterize transmedia dynamics as a pragmatic offshoot of semiosis in media (Alzamora & Gambarato, 2014[1]). This perspective considers the pragmatic incompleteness of the interpretant.

Peirce is considered the forerunner of pragmatism—a philosophical movement that investigates the relation between thought and action. This movement emerged in the early 1870s, in Cambridge, Massachusetts (the United States), from a small group of scholars of philosophy, among them Peirce and William James. At that time, Peirce coined the pragmatic maxim, according to which the meaning of any concept is the total sum of its conceivable practical consequences. Later in this chapter, we will present how Peirce's pragmatic model of semiosis influences our transmedia approach. However, to understand how the Peircean semiosis model operates as a communication model of transmedia dynamics, we must explain the Peircean semiosis model.

As stated by Nöth (2014), Peirce's concept of sign corresponds roughly to that of message in communication theory. "Instead of mediating between an addresser and an addressee the sign mediates between the object, which the sign represents, and the so-called interpretant, the interpretative effect which it creates" (Nöth, 2014, p. 100). The interpretant is the third element of the sign triad: The interpretant is the mediator of the first element (sign or representamen) and the second element (object). Thus, the interpretant may represent the object, which determines the interpretant through mediated action of the sign and becomes itself the determinant of the subsequent triad (Short, 2007).

According to Peirce's later writings (under the influence of his pragmatism), mediation circumscribes the representation, that is, representation becomes an aspect of mediation. "Representation is now the purpose of the sign" (Nöth, 2011, p. 33). Thus, mediation configures the triadic sign relation and delineates the notions of sign and semiosis in Peirce's mature works. "In this semiotic model it is the sign relation itself rather than one element taken alone that reveals a triadic, synthetic, and mediational quality" (Parmentier, 1985, p. 38).

Peirce's conception of semiosis involves abstractness, and it,

> is partly purchased by abstracting from the interpreter of signs, whereas what counts as an object of any sign does so only in reference to the purpose of some agent and, thus, in connection with the role of some interpreter.
>
> (Colapietro, 2004, p. 22)

Colapietro (1989) emphasizes that the suffix "-is" in semiosis refers to an action or process. He clarifies that in semiotics there is an essential inheritance between an unqualified or issued process (utterance) and an activity in which the interpretant is captured as such (interpretation). In a similar perspective, Santaella and Nöth (2004) consider that semiosis, or mediation, is a communication model in which signs unfold continuously in the triadic relation established among the sign (the logical place of the message), its object (the logical place of the emission), and its interpretant (the logical place of the interpreter).

In this model, the object determines the sign to produce a real effect, the interpretant. The way that the object reveals itself partially on the sign characterizes the immediate object, as the dynamic object of the external determination to the sign (reality). Bergman (2009, p. 103) states that "a sign may represent its real object falsely by producing an erroneous immediate object." This is possible because "whenever signs can be used for asserting the truth, they can also be used to deceive. If they assert, they will be used as lies" (Nöth, 1997, p. 143).

The sign reveals its object to the interpretant in three ways: as an icon (the domain of firstness), an index (the domain of secondness), and a symbol (the domain of thirdness). All of Peirce's work is built on his three phenomenological categories: firstness (quality, monad, instance of chance), secondness (reaction, dyad, instance of action), and thirdness (mediation, triad, instance of purpose of action). The three categories are dynamic, interdependent, and universal (Santaella, 1992).

In the domain of firstness, the icon is a mere quality of feeling (CP 2.276) that communicates with analogy (CP 2.248). The index places physical contiguity with the dynamic object; that is, the index presents itself as an existential trace of the object (CP 2.299) and acts in semiosis as a replica of symbols, which are general signs. The symbol operates on semiosis by virtue of a law, that is, a convention (CP 2.276). The symbol is a hybrid sign because it encompasses the quality of the icon and the path of the index to produce an association of general ideas. According to Santaella (2003), the referential power of the symbol corresponds to its indexical ingredient, which makes the symbol capable of denoting its object by extension (breadth), while the symbol's connotation capacity corresponds to its iconic ingredient, which deepens the symbol's capacity for meaning by analogy (depth).

However, as the object always escapes of the sign representation to some extent, other signs join the sign triad by collateral experience (CP 3.14) to form the interpretant that represents the object in partial and incomplete sign mediation. According to Bergman (2010), the notion of collateral experience, related to previous familiarity with what the signs denote, is predominant in the mature phase of Peircean theory, when the concepts of semiosis and pragmatism are approached. Bergman (2010) considers that when the habits of action improve, the more sophisticated the collateral experience will be and consequently also the more accurate the semiosis.

The action of the interpretant, which involves several triadic subdivisions, is highly relevant in understanding the pragmatic logic of semiosis, which directs the flow of signs toward an ideal of truth (final interpretant) that would represent an ideal of reality (dynamic object), if it were possible to reach such a stage of semiosis. "The interpretant is nothing but another representation to which the torch of truth is handed along" (CP 1.339). Thus, the interpretant will necessarily generate another sign that acts as its interpretant, and so forth, *ad infinitum.*

Interpretant is a term that Peirce characterized as being the effect and the meaning of the sign, be it current, potential, or future (Bergman, 2003).

The diversity of interpretants, which range from mere interpretative capability to an ideal of understanding that relates to the notion of truth, was developed by Peirce in divisions that specify the term in functional and differentiated stages. One of the best-known classifications refers to the immediate interpretant (interpretative potentiality) inscribed in the sign, the dynamic interpretant (the concrete effect), and the final interpretant (the ideal effect), respectively, in the domains of firstness, secondness, and thirdness.

Peirce subdivided interpretants in another trichotomy into (1) emotional—"the first proper significant effect of a sign is a feeling produced by it" (CP 5.475), (2) energetic—"if a sign produces any further proper significant effect, it will do so through the mediation of the emotional interpretant, and such further effect will always involve an effort. I call it the energetic interpretant" (CP 5.475), and (3) logic—"the essential effect upon the interpreter, brought about by the semiosis of the sign" (CP 5.480).

Peirce identified the logical interpretant within the sphere of habits. "Therefore, there remains only habit, as the essence of the logical interpretant" (MS 318), and this, according to Peirce, participates vigorously in communicative processes (Johansen, 1993). According to Santaella (2004), identification of the logical interpretant with habit, in the light of Peircean late pragmatism, no longer makes semiosis an infinite abstract process but places the process in pragmatic connection with human action. For Colapietro (1995), habits play, in communication processes observed through the lens of Peircean theory, a similar role to codes in communication processes reviewed by authors within the Saussurean tradition. According to him, habits regulate conduct, just as codes regulate messages. Thus, the logical interpretant and its related habits lead the way to a dialogical association of ideas, resulting in communication.

Bergman (2009) relates the logical interpretant to habits and the ultimate logical interpretant, the third division of the logical interpretant, with changing habits. He suggests that "it does not seem too farfetched to maintain that he [Peirce] is suggesting that pragmatistic philosophers need to move beyond mere analysis towards a more active engagement in the makeover of habits" (Bergman, 2009, p. 165). This perspective is particularly relevant for understanding how transmedia dynamics can involve creative extensions that even subvert the source narrative. Just as habits are necessary to generate engagement with the narrative universe, changing habits is fundamental to absorb the necessary transformations for the creative expansion of transmedia dynamics.

As Santaella (2004) emphasizes, Peircean scholars differ regarding the location of semiosis regarding the divisions related to emotional (domain of firstness), energetic (domain of secondness), and logical (domain of thirdness) interpretants. We agree with the stream of scholars, among them Santaella (2004), who consider those three interpretants as a division of the dynamic interpretant, that is, as a concrete and particular way of mediating the meanings that emerge from the semiosis process. The incompleteness of semiosis itself, and consequently of interpretants, generated in this open-ended process, may correspond to the richness of the variability of interpretations that a sign-object-interpretant relationship can evoke. The dynamic interpretant is particularly prepared to produce variability of emotions and actions. It is experienced in each act of interpretation.

What then is the value of this variability of interpretation allowed by the dynamic interpretant? First, semiotics refers to signification, representation, reference, and meaning, and Peirce emphasized the importance of interpretation to signification, which differentiates his theory of signs. Second, in the realm of creative industries, the richness of communication possibilities lies in a sense of freedom, in the absence of conditioning, and in an elimination of the obvious. The ultimate logical interpretant, an interpretant that itself has no further interpretant (CP 5.491), evokes changing habits. "Peirce's dynamical interpretant designs the creative potentialities of signs" (Ponzio, 1990, p. 327). The creative diversity of the dynamic interpretant, related to the division of emotional, energetic, and logical interpretants, is very important in the communication dimension of semiosis.

In the division of interpretants specifically related to the dialogic communication process, Peirce stated that a communication intention comes from the mind of the issuer (intentional interpretant) to the mind of the interpreter (effectual interpretant), which should result in a "fusion" of the minds of the issuer and the interpreter (communication interpretant or cominterpretant) through some form of agreement that presupposes a common experience (common ground).

Peirce did not explicitly mention how this division of interpretants is related to other divisions of interpretants in his model of semiosis, but Johansen (1993) considers a clear relation between the intentional interpretant and the immediate interpretant, the effectual interpretant and the dynamic interpretant, and the cominterpretant and the final interpretant. This proposal finds resonance in Deledalle's (1997) proposal, which considers that "the interpretant is formally the sign. Just as the representamen is the sign of the sender, the interpretant is the sign of the receiver" (p. 58). In Bergman's (2007) view, common ground, despite being the prerequisite for communication in the Peircean framework, does not amount to a demand for identical experiences, once true communication exchange and development require experiential divergences.

Although this division of interpretants is the only one that is explicitly related to communication, we do not discuss it as an offshoot of semiosis but as a way of understanding semiosis in a communicational view. As the interpretant is the sign mediator between a previous and subsequent triad sign, we clarify how its productive incompleteness is a communication question within transmedia narratives. Thus, we must clarify what we call media in Peirce's approach to semiotics.

Media studies has been progressively permeated by several theoretical and methodological perspectives, including various semiotic approaches. Danesi (2010) emphasizes the preeminent position occupied by the Internet in the contemporary media studies and semiotics. In our approach, the notion of media that underlies transmedia dynamics derives from the Peircean notion of sign. In his mature works, Peirce uses the term medium instead of sign. "All my notions are very narrow. Instead of 'Sign', ought I not to say Medium?" (MS 339 cited by Parmentier, 1985, p. 23). In his view, a sign is a medium of communication. "A sign is plainly a species of medium of communication, and medium of communication is a species of medium, and medium is a specie of third" (MS 283, cited by Parmentier, 1985, p. 45).

Thus, media can be understood as an expressive form that materializes sign mediation according to its reference languages and the transformations related to the audience's repertoire and interest. The semiotic mediation process involves determination arising from a preceding sign, its object, and the representation by association (collateral experience) of a posterior sign, its interpretant. According to Bergman (2009), collateral experience is an adjacent process of semiosis, based on approximate knowledge of the meaning context in which the sign is inscribed. Consequently, the composition of the sign changes as social practices affect it intensely and cumulatively. In this sense, media specificity derives from (1) the relationship that the medium (sign) establishes with its reference languages (object); (2) the way the medium (sign) particularizes and materializes this influence, that is, its expressive form; and (3) the transformations (semiosis) arising from the audience's repertoire (collateral experience) based on their interests (emotional interpretant), dedication (energetic interpretant), and purposes (logical interpretant).

The process of semiotic mediation occurs on two levels: between the object and interpretant (through the mediation of the sign) and between one triadic sign (sign, object, or interpretant) and another, through the mediation of the interpretant. Therefore, semiosis is a double, nonlinear, reticular process because the two semiotic levels deal with the associated action (collateral experience) of the sign. According to Bergman (2009, p. 102), Peirce outlines how a sign may acquire a meaning and reference in a system of signs, in which "the object seems to be intra-systemic" through the immediate object in the sign, and the collateral experience is a semiotic extra-systemic movement. "This grounding is extra-systemic, which is why Peirce speaks of additional or collateral experiences and observation" (Bergman, 2009, p. 140). The interpretant, which results from the associated sign action of the collateral experience in the first semiotic level of semiosis, becomes a mediating sign in the subsequent triadic sign, that is, in the second semiotic level of semiosis.

Our transmedia dynamic approach involves articulating two levels of semiosis: (1) Intermediality presents on the first level of media semiosis, and (2) transmediality presents on the second level of media semiosis, which is derived from the first level. Both configure intra- and extra-semiotic systems, although intermediality predominates in the intra-semiotic system and transmediality predominates in the extra-semiotic system.

Transmedia communication model

The adjective "transmedia" usually describes how contemporary media content propagates in the intersection of media environments, albeit each textual media configuration presents semiotic autonomy and the content could be continually expandable by the integrated actions of the producers and consumers (Alzamora, 2019). Based on the Peircean semiotic model of communication, transmedia dynamics may be understood as a mediation sign process that involves semiotic processes of determination and representation integrated in two semiotic ways: (1) at the first level of semiosis, related to the textual arrangements based on diversified media environments, through intertextual references (the domain of determination); and (2) at the second level of semiosis, related to the intersection between two or more media platforms, through transtextual association (the domain of representation) built on the experiences of the sign user. Bergman (2009) emphasizes that the sign user is not necessarily human and states, "the dynamical interpretant is closely connected to the concrete sign user, situated in semiosis" (p. 120).

In this respect, digital media semiosis mixes aspects of human and non-human sign users because algorithm actions interfere in the sphere of human actions in this context and vice versa. Thus, the sign user of digital media, who may be human or not, acts on the course of transmedia semiosis in a heterogeneous and creative way (dynamic interpretant) with different kinds of sign association (collateral experience). The dynamic interpretant is the concrete face of the sign user's action in transmedia semiosis and therefore constitutes sign mediation in the next stage of transmedia semiosis.

Sign mediation configures the semiotic communicational system of transmedia dynamics intertwining the intertextuality from the domain of semiotic operation of determination and transtextuality from the domain of semiotic operation of representation. Thus, the semiotic process of determination belongs to the narrative universe of the reference (object), and the semiotic process of representation emphasizes the creative capability of the interpretant, which promotes meaning diversity in the transmedia dynamics by sign association (collateral experience).

Intertextuality marks the influence of one set of texts on another (Nöth, 1995), and transtextuality refers to a narrative created through accretion across multiple texts rather than within a single work (Bertetti, 2014). According to Alzamora (2019), the importance of intertextuality in the notion of transmedia is endorsed by Jenkins (2009, cited by Delwiche, 2017, p. 35), for whom "a work needs to combine radical intertextuality and multimodality for the purpose of additive comprehension to be at transmedia storytelling." Although Marsha Kinder (1991) first described the notion of transmedia as transmedia intertextuality in media-related products, intertextuality is often associated with intermediality.

As claimed by Herkman (2012), the intermedia flow is intertextual, based on the continuity and variation of media arrangements in a particular context of meaning. He emphasizes that each media environment is differentiated by historical, social, cultural, aesthetic, and institutional aspects, and these aspects persist, to a greater or lesser extent, in the intermedia dynamic. Thus, intertextual references evoke the intermedia process of communication, which refers to the context of mutual affectation in which one media environment shares aspects of language with another.

For Elleström (2010), the intermedia process should be understood based on a complex network of materially tangible qualities that constitute the fundamental conditions of each medium, and in tune with the perceptive and interpretative operations performed within the reception. According to Elleström, the intermedia approach presupposes the conditions of production, circulation, and media consumption, as well as the material interfaces linked to social, cultural, historical, communicative, and aesthetic circumstances. Although intermedia and transmedia dynamics usually appear intertwined in digital media connections, each dynamics refers to distinct communication processes. In general, transmedia dynamics involves some aspects of intermediality, but not all intermediate dynamics culminate in transmediality.

In Evans' (2020) view, transmediality is inherently about expanding the time frame of the content and the audience experiences of the content. According to Evans, as transmediality becomes increasingly widespread, the same engaging experience may encompass multiple distinct but integrated experiences. Freeman and Gambarato (2019, p. 2) point out that "transmediality remains an important concept for understanding the fundamental shifts that digital media technologies have brought on the media industries and their audiences." For Elleström (2020), transmediality refers to different types of media that share basic traits and that can be described in terms of material, or physical, properties. Elleström differentiates transmediality from transmediation related to repeated mediation of equivalent sensory configurations by another technical medium. Elleström (2020) places transmediation within the broader frames of intermediality, that is, relations among different types of media products.

The challenge for communication processes based on intermedia dynamics is to adapt to contemporary content production and circulation, such as multiplatform distribution and interactional practices in material conditions of participation, appropriation, and content sharing in digital media connections. These conditions, often associated with transmedia dynamics, derive from the specificities of digital media, which operate by permeability and compatibility based on flexible and porous limits. Freeman and Gambarato (2019) emphasize the role of the Internet in transmedia dynamics:

> The Internet and all digital technologies unequivocally play a crucial role in (1) disseminating transmedia content, (2) making content easily available worldwide, (3) reaching a diversified range of audiences, (4) enabling audience engagement, and (5) contributing to a participatory culture, for instance. But the possibilities to enrich the audience experience via online activities, live events, and analogue initiatives, are immense because they can dramatically contribute to (1) the feeling of immersion, (2) the sense of belonging, and (3) the emotional response of audiences, as discussed in the afterword of this collection.
>
> (p. 3)

From the perspective of the Peircean semiosis model, ambivalence defines transmedia dynamics because it is configured in the relation between the reference (object) and creativity (interpretant). Thus, although transmedia planning suggests a specific course of collective action, this is always relatively imponderable because some form of indetermination often predominates in transmedia semiosis. Bergman (2009) states that some aspects of indeterminacy, such as ambiguity, vagueness, and generality, are important in the Peircean approach to communication processes because they are not divorced from the experience and habitual practices. In this way, "ambiguity implies doubt between two or more clearly distinct alternatives" (Bergman, 2009, p. 150). This outlook is decisive in creative expansion of transmedia storytelling because it presupposes choice, creativity, and boldness—aspects often related to the agency of sign users in semiosis.

According to Jenkins (2006), transmedia storytelling propagates in the intersection of vertical communication processes (triggered by media industries) and horizontal communication processes (based on citizen actions, which are varied and unpredictable). Strategic planning of transmedia dynamics is proposed vertically, while its contingency is horizontally configured. This tension characterizes transmedia dynamics.

Transmedia distribution strategies are an example of strategic planning for transmedia dynamics. Evans (2019, p. 242) considers that distribution has "historically been an often-overlooked part of media scholarship, with a greater amount of attention being paid to the process of production, reception, and occasionally exhibition." Evans states that transmedia distribution strategies continue the traditions of vertical integration and conglomeration because established media industry organizations have used transmedia distribution strategies to maintain control over how, where, and when their audiences access content. However, "the emergence of transmedia logics is reshaping the media landscape, and distribution sits at the very heart of that process" (Evans, 2019, p. 250).

Evans believes transmedia logics therefore resignify all stages of the communication process because it alters the traditional semiotic functions of the sender and interpreter around a continually and collective building message.

The specificity of transmedia dynamics is seen by Jenkins according to the seven principles of the transmedia narrative, which he proposed in 2009 and revised in 2010: (1) spreadability vs. drillability, (2) continuity vs. multiplicity, (3) immersion vs. extractability, (4) worldbuilding, (5) seriality, (6) subjectivity, and (7) performance. From a Peircean semiotic point of view, the seven principles can be related to each other in mediation, according to the domains of the semiotic operations of determination and representation (Alzamora, 2019). For example, transmedia dynamics operates on drillability, under the semiotic operation of determination, and spreadability operates under the semiotic operation of representation. For Jenkins (2010, para. 14), "drillability refers to the ability to dig deeper into something which interests us," and "spreadability refers to a process of dispersal." The former is predominantly related to the intra-semiotic system, and the latter is predominantly related to the extra-semiotic system.

In the Peircean perspective, drillability is related to the way in which storytelling may delineate different kinds of interaction around itself without losing its reference, and spreadability emphasizes the variability of splits derived from the sign user. In this sense, drillability and spreadability together shape the complex mediating process of transmedia dynamics, which broadens the narrative of origin in varied contexts of meaning. Bergman (2009) points out that "semiosis is not only a process of determination in the sense of delimitation and constraint" (p. 108) but also "the contribution of some sign-interpreting agency" (p. 112).

As Jenkins (2010) states, the media industry often talks about continuity in terms of canons, that is, information accepted as part of the definitive version of a particular story. In contrast, multiplicity is related to multiple alternative versions compared to the established canon. In the Peircean approach, continuity is related to the endless process of semiosis, which incorporates multiplicity by the variability of interpretants. Thus, continuity delineates the expansion of transmedia dynamics based on references from canon storytelling (object) associated (collateral experiences) with contributions of social participation (interpretant agency). This semiotic approach, which emphasizes the purposiveness of semiosis derived from the sign user without losing the message reference, also refers to the other principles of transmedia storytelling:

> The purposiveness of semiosis is ultimately derived from the sign user, a living being that acts interpretatively. In itself, a sign is not necessarily teleological; proper semiosis requires at least the contribution of some sign-interpreting agency. However, this does not mean that the semiotic development could be entirely attributed to the interpreter.
>
> (Bergman, 2009, p. 112)

The interpretant's varied agency impacts the course of semiosis and consequently the configuration of transmedia dynamics. Thus, understanding how semiotic agency promotes the formation of new meanings in semiosis through engagement and the availability of action is crucial. However, one wonders what characterizes engagement in transmedia dynamics from Peirce's semiosis point of view.

The term engagement encompasses various meanings, but the notions of emotional involvement, motivation, and willingness to act are often associated with the term. According to Dahlgren (2013), engagement is conditioned to rational and affective aspects of mental dynamics, incorporating modes of cultural expression that are mediated by the media. From this perspective, engagement combines affective (emotional interpretant) and rational (logical interpretant) aspects based on incorporation (energetic interpretant) modes of cultural expression mediated by the media (collateral experience). Thus, this concept of engagement fully conforms to the mediating action of the dynamic interpretant. The notion of collateral experience is particularly important in understanding social engagement because it emphasizes the inclusion of the audience repertoire in transmedia dynamics according to the variety of their interests and purposes.

In Taylor and Kent's (2014) view, engagement is an orientation that influences interactions and the approach that guides the process of interactions among a group. The authors emphasize that "little evidence has emerged from social media research in public relations about exactly how engagement is created" (Taylor & Kent, 2014, p. 386). This perspective emphasizes the abstract dimension of engagement and its lack of specificity. The aspects Taylor and Kent discuss refer to the immaterial dimension of sign agency expressed in the mediation of the interpretant. Although the sign acquires the material form of the dynamic interpretant, it unfolds immaterially in various divisions of the interpretant toward an abstract purpose. Therefore, to comprehend how engagement is created, the broader process of communication in which the engagement emerges must be considered. In the Peircean semiotic view, engagement is related to the productive incompleteness of the interpretants, which enhances the composition of media signs through collateral experience.

According to Evans (2020), the contemporary complexity of the arrangements between different media environments demands a specific approach for understanding the audience transmedia engagement. Evans understands transmedia engagement more broadly as extending beyond the end point of the content that inspired the engagement. In this scenario, Evans considers that engagement is a discursive powerful term because she sees it as denoting a fundamentally positive experience and encompassing a set of relations among producers, texts, and audience. Evans understands engagement as consisting of four core components: (1) type of behavior, (2) form or response, (3) cost, and (4) value. In addition, Evans states that engagement also involves three potential forms of response: (1) emotional, (2) physical, and (3) cognitive. In the Peircean semiotic approach, these three potential forms of response correspond to the emotional interpretant, the energetic interpretant, and the logical interpretant, respectively. They are potential because each interpretant is a mental form, although it has a concrete manifestation, such as liking, commenting, or sharing a post on online social networks.

In contrast, Vieira (2013) considers that engagement manifests as social disposition for different practical effects in three basic forms in an integrated evolution: (1) adherence, (2) mobilization, and (3) activism. Adherence refers to mere thematic identification with the event. In the process of semiosis, adherence manifests as an emotional interpretant. Mobilization occurs when network propagation actions are triggered, which corresponds to the energetic interpretant. Activism, however, corresponds to the realization of previous strategies aimed at maximum involvement, concentrating forces and acting systemically in favor of the visibility of the cause, as the logical interpretant acts in semiosis (Alzamora & Andrade, 2019a).

In addition, Schaufeli (2013) points out that two approaches are predominant in engagement studies: Either engagement is defined narrowly as an experience (i.e., a purely psychological state), in which engagement's practical relevance is reduced, or engagement is defined in broader terms that include its behavioral expression, in which case the concept gets fuzzy. For Schaufeli (2013), "a pragmatical solution could be to consider engagement as a psychological state in conjunction with its behavioral expression" (p. 25). This idea could be developed in the Peircean pragmatism sense, which takes into account the practical effects of actions on the process of semiosis. We must first consider what constitutes transmedia logics from the Peircean pragmatic view. Evans (2020) states that the combination of multiple transmedia logics means that transmediality occurs across mundane and everyday screen experiences. Therefore, we seek to explore what constitutes transmedia logics and to what extent they can be characterized as contemporary communication logics.

Transmedia logics

Jenkins (2017) adopts the term transmedia logics to designate the intended interaction between consumers, producers, and texts in relation to the purpose of transmedia planning. "By transmedia logics, I mean two interrelated things: the goals a transmedia production is intended to serve, and the assumptions made about the desired relationship among transmedia consumers, producers, and texts" (Jenkins, 2017, p. 222). He considers that transmedia logics are related to the seven principles of transmedia storytelling.

In Jenkins's (2017) view, transmedia storytelling is one of a range of transmedia logics, which might also include transmedia learning/education, transmedia branding, transmedia performance, transmedia mobilization/ activism, and so forth. Jenkins considers transmedia a type of adjective that qualifies different social, cultural, and industrial contexts. However, despite having adopted the terminology "transmedia logics," Jenkins did not specify exactly what he meant by logics and why this notion is the best suited for his conception of transmedia.

For us, transmedia logics are contemporary communication logics that delineate different contexts of meaning. Transmedia logics are communication logics because any transmedia dynamics promotes social interaction, mutual affectation, and information exchange, which are crucial aspects of a communication view (Nöth, 2011). Moreover, our conception of transmedia logics is based on Peirce's semiotic approach, which is also related to his pragmatism view. Therefore, our conception of transmedia logics is pragmatic and semiotic, also understood as a contemporary communication logic.

In Peirce's view, logic is another name for semiotics: a normative science that investigates language and its processes of meaning, that is, semiosis. Because semiosis is also a communication model, semiotics can be understood as a communication logic, too. Along with ethics, which investigates the nature of action, and aesthetics, which turns to what is admirable in itself, logic (or semiotics) integrates the three Peircean normative sciences, that is, sciences guided by ideals.

Peirce's theoretical framework, including his cartography of sciences,[2] arises from his three phenomenological categories: (1) firstness, (2) secondness, and (3) thirdness. Thus, semiotics is a normative science guided by thirdness, ethics is guided by secondness, and aesthetics is guided by firstness. According to Kent (1987), the three normative sciences (the domain of secondness) are based on phenomenology (the domain of firstness) and provide principles for metaphysics (the domain of thirdness). Logic is a normative science that investigates languages on their practical dimension. Together, the three normative sciences investigate the logic route of actions toward an ideal of admirability *per se*. Because of this, they are closely related to the Peircean pragmatism approach.

Peirce conceived pragmatism, or *pragmaticism*,[3] as a special application of ethics (Kent, 1987). This normative science investigates the nature of actions in accordance with beliefs that delineate actions. According to Colapietro (2004), since 1903, under the influence of Darwin's evolutionism, Peircean pragmatism has emphasized the logical improvement of meaning, which presupposes the progressive improvement of the beliefs and habits of the action involved. Beliefs (the domain of secondness) are based on feelings (the domain of firstness) and spread by habits of action (the domain of thirdness), which are examined within the contexts of logic or semiotics. Habits, in their regularity, exist in the meaning of belief, and belief depends on what is admirable. Thus, Peirce's ethics is interested in the logical course of action toward an ideal of admirability.

Peirce's ethics involves exerting individual effort with the efforts of the extended community around the logical path of actions, according to Gambarato and Nanì's (2016) view. As a result, Peirce's ethics applies remarkably to transmedia storytelling because a core principle of transmedia experiences is creating communities around the story universe. The collective experiences created around the narrative universe promote the growth of ideas that make up the transmedia narrative and thus contribute to its expansion in varied contexts of meaning. Gambarato and Nanì (2016) state,

> In Peirce's view, the supreme ideal should always evolve, promoting the continuous growth of ideas. In the realm of transmedia narrative, this growth can be achieved with the constant generation of interpretants. The fact that the generation of interpretants belongs to the transmedia designer/writer and the audience, the productive incompleteness of interpretants contributes to maintaining the wheel of the story rolling through expansion of content within the story universe. In the midst of participatory culture, this expansion can be developed by the authors and co-created by the audience.
>
> (p. 154)

The productive incompleteness of the interpretants is a crucial aspect of the creative expansion of transmedia storytelling because each dynamic interpretant updates transmedia semiosis in a unique perspective that, in turn, integrates the entire transmedia universe. This process is outlined by transmedia logics, understood from the pragmatic perspective of semiosis. The concepts of semiosis and pragmatism are approximate because the more the habits of action are improved, the more sophisticated the collateral experience becomes and therefore the more accurate semiosis will be. In this regard, transmedia dynamics is a pragmatic sign process in permanent reticular expansion, which involves the diverse proliferation of interpretants.

From the Peircean perspective on semiosis, the medium is a process of mediation whose references are various languages and interactional practices. These references are part of media semiosis in a persistent but not necessarily perennial way. Thus, transmedia logics can be considered as pragmatic branches of media semiosis. In this sense, intertextuality is a kind of reference to transmediality, which operates as a pragmatic spread of intertextuality in media semiosis.

Moreover, semiotic regimes of determination and representation confirm sign mediation under the aegis of historicity and temporality, respectively. In the first case, media semiosis recursively points to the reference languages in its intermedia domain. In the second case, representation expands the media semiosis in the transmedia domain, articulating varied temporalities in social practices triggered by collateral experience (Alzamora, 2019).

However, media semiosis may do without transmedia dynamics but not without the semiotic representation operation, which describes transmedia dynamics predominantly. The semiotic operation of representation also can endorse the intermedia dynamics that serves it as a reference.

As a result, media semiosis is always intermedia but not necessarily transmedia, although the latter can function as a kind of logical enhancement of the former.

The intermedia condition arises from the media historical constitution, while the transmedia probability reflects the plurality of possibilities related to contemporary media. Representative plurality relates to the diversity of the interpretants, which acts variously in the temporal route of media semiosis in accordance with the collateral experiences that are triggered in each communication situation. Transmedia dynamics develops through the productive incompleteness of the interpretant, which acts in various ways to resignify media semiosis. Because of this, it is crucial to understand the variability in interpretants in transmedia semiosis.

The interpretative potential of the sign (immediate interpretant) may be understood in transmedia semiosis as a kind of invitation to participation that will become a new sign (dynamic interpretant) only through the associative action of signs (collateral experience) outlined by the semiotic operation of representation. The phenomenological variety of dynamic interpretants (emotional, energetic, and logical) is translated into different forms of representation that can differently resignify transmedia semiosis. Each dynamic interpretant mediates a sign between one triadic sign and another according to the degree of engagement of the sign user.

In a concrete way, each dynamic interpretant presupposes a form of creative extension in transmedia dynamics because it associates new signs with transmedia semiosis through collateral experience, without losing the language reference that constitutes the narrative universe. Consequently, transmedia logics refer to the route of collective action involved in the common construction of the narrative universe, considering the variability of the creative extensions based on the multiple repertoires and interests of the connected audience and the references of language from transmedia planning, which ensure cohesion of the fragmented and plural narrative universe.

The generation of dynamic interpretants is constantly updated, according to Gambarato and Nanì (2016); that is, the productive incompleteness of the interpretants can transform the overall experience offered within transmedia experiences. In this sense, the audience repertoire, expressed in the sign association (collateral experience), enhances the narrative universe and integrates transmedia semiosis. Moreover, transmedia dynamics expands in line with media consumption habits, and these habits improve as they best fit transmedia logics. Thus, transmedia logics, from the Peircean perspective argued in this book, are a communication pragmatic logic.

According to this view, we understand transmedia dynamics as a pragmatically oriented mediation process that involves action habits that can be continually refined because habits are effects of beliefs and beliefs can be modified by the scrutiny of doubt to reach some aspect of the ideal truth. In the Peircean approach, the pragmatic conception of truth is related to the pragmatic conception of semiosis, a logical process of the continuous improvement of meaning. This perspective presupposes the understanding that the more refined the mediation processes involved in transmedia dynamics are, the more vigorous the engagement processes it engenders will be.

Mediation therefore promotes connections that foster temporary engagement motivated by shared beliefs. The doubts that permeate this process provide the change of habit needed to improve the belief, and it will be expressed in new actions of engagement.

Transmedia dynamics

Because transmedia logics are also a contemporary logic of communication, the variety of transmedia dynamics is enormous. To demonstrate our argument, we present two examples of transmedia dynamics related to social mobilization around hashtags in Brazil.

Hashtags can boost the visibility of a certain political position in online and off-line connections to gauge the consensus regarding a collective cause. This is what happened with the transmedia dynamics of the hashtags #vemprarua [come to the street] and #cadêaprova [where is the proof]—the first used in street protests in Brazil and the second in contexts of political polarization in the same country. Both may be characterized as transmedia dynamics because they permeate cross-media and acquire varied meanings over time based on social participation. We relate the idea of dynamics to the Peircean pragmatic notion of semiosis and transmedia to the incompleteness of the interpretants, as discussed below.

Hashtags were created in 2007 on Twitter to aggregate related content and have been widely used to demarcate political positions in different social mobilization contexts, especially since 2009, when they came to be used as a ranking of the most popular topics among Twitter's trending topics. They are a kind of new media agenda because trending topics define the relevance of everyday subjects by the number of keywords and hashtags on the platform over a short period of time (Groshek & Groshek, 2013).

Activist groups have invested heavily in communication strategies to reach trending topics as a way of interfering in the public debate. In a study on audiovisual content on Twitter related to terrorist attacks in Paris and Brussels in 2015 and 2016, respectively, Bruns and Hanusch (2017) consider that nonhuman actors, especially bots, can play a crucial part in the content dissemination patterns on Twitter. A bot is a software application that is programmed to do certain tasks, such as replacing human user behavior on social media. Bruns and Hanusch's work (2017) exemplifies the relevance of algorithms in Twitter communication strategies to boost collective actions oriented by a common cause.

The communication function of hashtags has been enhanced from a cross-media perspective since they began to be used across multiple social media platforms in different but complementary ways, such as Instagram since 2010 and Facebook since 2013 (Andrade, 2019). Zappavigna (2015) considers that the relational exchanges through hashtags happen under affiliation with the media environment; although users have never interacted off-line, they create a commonsense network when they use a common hashtag.

However, regardless of the social media platform, hashtags are always used to synthesize a certain common semantic universe. Hougaard (2016) argues that the communication function of hashtags is to operate as contextual markers in the generation of networks of common interests. Because of this, Hougaard (2016) considers hashtags "transmedia connectors," as they function as a medium whose meaning depends on the context to which the medium is linked. For Laucuka (2018), hashtags are semiotic resources capable of interpreting various meanings in online social networks.

These ideas dialogue with our proposal of transmedia logics, which are also communicational, semiotic, and pragmatic logics. In this approach, a hashtag is sign mediation that articulates collective arguments based on social use (sign or representamen) in reference to the alluded empirical context (object) to promote a specific interpretation of reality (interpretant) in a web of endless connections. Thus, from the pragmatic perspective of Peircean semiosis, transmedia dynamics may be considered as a sign process in continuous reticular expansion, involving a wide range of interpretants articulated by human and nonhuman interconnected users.

Hashtags act as argumentative terms for social and political issues (Husson, 2015) in the social mobilization context. Yang (2016) emphasizes the growth of hashtag activism to give mediatic visibility to activist causes and then influence the public agenda. "I consider narrative agency in hashtag activism as the capacity to create stories on social media by using hashtags in a way that is collective and recognized by the public" (Yang, 2016, p. 14). The growth of hashtag activism depends on the expansion of social use and the strengthening of its mediating role in online and off-line interactions. Thus, hashtag activism could be characterized as transmedia activism or transmedia mobilization.

Transmedia activism, a term coined by Lina Srivastava (2009), designates how activists use media platforms to expand local narratives through collaborative work to produce social change. The term refers to the complex production of content aiming at raising awareness, engagement, and action to promote change. According to Srivastava (2009), transmedia dynamics offers important possibilities for social change movements. Thus, the transmedia activism process is related to collective actions in media connections that foster awareness, engagement, and social change (Alzamora & Andrade, 2019b).

Nonetheless, as the term *activism* may refer to a very diverse context, which includes even art and games (Silveira, 2009), some authors, such as Jenkins (2016), prefer the term *transmedia mobilization* to designate collective online and off-line contexts aimed at promoting social change. Jenkins (2016), for example, argues that the concept of transmedia mobilization broadens the idea of participation by integrating online and off-line media connections to diversify strategies and share a social agenda. Transmedia mobilization therefore integrates the culture of participation with contemporary political and civic aspects.

In the social mobilization contexts, hashtags articulate related political positioning, forming symbolic links that highlight collective processes of meaning. The hashtags form hyperlinks that bring together various publications, in specific media contexts and in different temporalities, from a common meaningful form in an index (Alzamora & Andrade, 2019b).

This is what happened with the #*vemprarua* [come to the streets] transmedia dynamics in Brazil. Since 2013, when people started regularly taking to the streets in Brazil to demand social and political changes, this hashtag has appeared recurrently on Twitter's trending topics list in different contexts. However, tracking a hashtag's mediation operations is no simple task because any clipping suggests nonexistent linearity that camouflages its fragmented and continuously expanding mediating nature in online and off-line connections. According to Malini et al. (2014), the expression "come to the street" has been used in Brazil since the early 2000s as part of the *Movimento Passe Livre* [Free Pass Movement] organized around issues concerning urban mobility. Therefore, the social use of this expression, which has become one of the most widely used hashtags in Brazil (Malini et al., 2014) in contexts of transmedia activism, predates the emergence of social media platforms.

The #vemprarua hashtag, one of the most commonly used hashtags by demonstrators who protested during the FIFA Confederations Cup in 2013, in Brazil, illustrates the dynamics of entanglement between streets and social media that distinguished the June Journeys, as the June protests in 2013 in Brazil became known. The June Journeys occurred during the FIFA Confederations Cup, an event that preceded the 2014 FIFA World Cup in Brazil. The premise is that the Brazilian protests in June 2013 functioned as networked events that influenced social media and the streets, without being simplistically reduced to either one (D'Andrea, Alzamora, & Ziller, 2015, p. 117). The 2013 June Journeys foreshadowed the protests that culminated in the impeachment of Brazilian President Dilma Rousseff in 2016.

In a way similar to that adopted by citizens in other countries, such as Spain (during the 15M movement in 2011), Egypt, Tunisia, and other Arab countries (during the Arab Spring in 2010–2012), Brazilian citizens planned and exchanged communications about street protests primarily through online social networks such as Twitter, Facebook, and Instagram, thus evincing complex interconnections between urban space and cyberspace. This connection between the streets and the online social media networks is exemplified by the most popular hashtag #*vemprarua* during the June Journeys. "This hashtag created hybridity between urban space and the Internet by using online social networks to nudge Brazilians to abandon their 'slacktivism'" (D'Andrea et al., 2015, p. 115).

The expression *vem pra rua* [come to the streets] was also part of a car manufacturer's TV advertising created for the FIFA Confederations Cup. On TV and radio, the commercial jingle invited Brazilians to "come to the streets because the streets are actually Brazil's biggest bleacher [stadium seats]."[4] During the 2013 June Journeys, protesters sang this jingle in the streets, which illustrates intermedia articulations among commercial mass media and social media activism. The overlapping political semantics surrounding advertising hashtags, which, in turn, have appropriated hashtags disseminated by protesters, emphasizes the increasingly intense political dynamics of sharing that integrate social media with the Brazilian streets (D'Andrea et al., 2015).

In this sense, the reference of the TV advertising created for the FIFA Confederations Cup operates as intermedia dynamics for the street protests. In that political context, the social use of the hashtag *#vemprarua* referred to the sign associations that redirected the intermedia semiosis route to an activist transmedia dynamics. Since then, this hashtag has been recurrently used in Brazil, especially for political mobilizations, but also in entertainment contexts, such as the Pokémon Go game, which has brought together players in urban areas of the country since 2016. Thus, we consider the transmedia dynamics of the hashtag *#vemprarua* as a case of transmedia activism.

Based on the theoretical-methodological perspective of Peirce's semiosis, Alzamora and Andrade (2019b) investigate the route of transmedia dynamics of *#vemprarua* in Brazil between 2013 and 2017. In this investigation on social networks, automated collection procedures were used to reproduce possible trajectories of the hashtag under study. The Hashtagify. Me digital monitoring tool made it possible to view the hashtag network generated around *#vemprarua* over time on Twitter and Instagram. The results pointed to a form of transmedia activism that operates with successive resignifications. The hashtag has been often used by groups with different interests and positions, which stresses the variety of mediation processes that permeate the semiosis of *#vemprarua*.

Alzamora and Andrade (2019b) report new signs (dynamic interpretants) associated with the hashtag *#vemprarua* formed especially during the 2014, 2015, and 2016 period marked by intense social mobilization in Brazil. According to Alzamora and Andrade, the semiosis of the hashtag *#vemprarua* changed whenever other hashtags were associated with it (collateral experience), which strengthened the hashtag's symbolic presence in online and off-line connections.

In that investigated context, the hashtag *#vemprarua* was predominantly linked to hashtags for political groups favorable to Dilma Rousseff's impeachment, which took place in 2016. It is the case of the associated hashtags *#foradilma* [out Dilma], in reference to the then president of

Brazil, Dilma Rousseff, and *#foraPT*, in reference to the Workers' Party—Rousseff's political party—which had been in power since Luíz Inácio Lula da Silva assumed the presidency of Brazil in 2003.

However, there was also an association, to a lesser extent, with the hashtag *#mudamais* [change more], used by Dilma Rousseff's supporters in reference to the social changes that would have been implemented in her government. This association with the hashtag *#mudamais* demonstrates the heterogeneous nature of sign contexts that reference the *#vemprarua* hashtag. Over the period analyzed, this hashtag was also linked to football games, augmented reality games, and in-store advertising. In this example, we can identify transmedia dynamics notably characterized as transmedia activism.

The case of the hashtag *#cadêaprova* [where is the proof] is a little different, as it is clearly characterized as transmedia mobilization because the social use of this hashtag referred only to transmedia dynamics embedded in the context of political polarization. Both political sides (for and against the former Brazilian President Luiz Inácio Lula da Silva) used this hashtag with different meanings in each communication context.

The hashtag *#cadêaprova* was created during the trial of Luiz Inácio Lula da Silva in January 2018 to question the veracity of the accusations against the former president. However, during the presidential election in Brazil in October 2018, this hashtag was appropriated by supporters of Jair Bolsonaro's candidacy to refute the alleged WhatsApp illegal mass text messaging scheme (Mello, 2018) against *Partido dos Trabalhadores* (PT) [Workers' Party], reported by *Folha de S. Paulo* newspaper. The process of appropriation and resignification of this hashtag demonstrates how transmedia logics work in setting up collective arguments in online social networking connections.

The former president was arrested on April 7, 2018, and after being convicted of passive corruption and money laundering was sentenced to 12 years and 11 months in prison. During the second trial, which took place on January 24, 2018, the hashtag *#cadêaprova* [where is the proof] competed with *#molusconacadeia* [mollusk in jail] and *#lulanacadeia* [Lula in jail] for first place in Twitter trends in Brazil and worldwide (Alzamora & Andrade, 2019b). These hashtags, which allude to the name of former president Luís Inácio Lula [squid] da Silva, were mainly used by supporters of the former president to question the validity of the alleged evidence analyzed for his conviction.

On October 18, 2018, ten days before the second round of elections in Brazil, the journalist Patrícia Campos Mello of *Folha de S. Paulo* newspaper published a report denouncing alleged illegal messaging against PT [Workers' Party] on WhatsApp. According to Mello's report (2018), businesspeople who supported Bolsonaro bought bundles of millions of messages, which would be triggered using the candidate's own database and digital agencies. The practice would violate electoral legislation that prohibits unreported donations, the purchase of third-party databases, and the promotion of messages under these conditions. In 2019, "WhatsApp admits illegal mass text messaging in the 2018 elections" (Mello, 2019).

On the morning of October 18, the hashtag *#caixa2dobolsonaro* [Bolsonaro's slush fund] reached first among the national trending topics on Twitter. On the same day, Bolsonaro's allies used the *#cadêaprova* [where is the proof] hashtag to question the legitimacy of the *Folha de S. Paulo* report. This hashtag ranked second among the national Twitter trending topics, alongside *#marketeirosdojair* [Jair's marketer], both used by President Jair Messias Bolsonaro's supporters. The next day, the hashtags *#cassaçãodobolsonaro* [Bolsonaro's impeachment] and *#folhafakenews* [in reference to the *Folha de S. Paulo* newspaper] vied for the ranking by explaining the political polarization context. The first hashtag called for the cancellation of Bolsonaro's presidential term, and the second stated that the *Folha de S. Paulo* report was fake news (Alzamora & Andrade, 2019a).

The social appropriation of the hashtag *#cadêaprova* by Bolsonaro's supporters altered its production of meaning, initially linked to the figure of former President Lula. As a result, on November 14, 2018, the defense campaign created by the Workers' Party presented the hashtag *#cadêaprovacontralula* [where is the proof against Lula]. This hashtag trended nationally on Twitter and was used in association with *#cadêaprova*. In a clear communication strategy for transmedia mobilization, supporters of former President Lula created t-shirts, posters, and printed materials with the new hashtag, also used in connection with *#LulaLivre* [free Lula] in online and off-line contexts.

According to Alzamora and Andrade (2019b), *#cadêaprova* [where is the proof] could aggregate opposite meanings because it operated semiotically in symbolic predominance, that is, maintained with its varied references (object) a relation of abstraction and aimed to generate regularity of interpretative action (interpretant) in line with the intended meaning in each communication context.

Referring to similarities, analogies, and metaphors (icon), the symbol triggers the intended meaning by connotation, altering the meaning previously established by the hashtag. This semiotic process is consolidated by collective actions of sharing in digital contexts, which reinforce the meaning intended by denotation (index). The use of bots is particularly important in this indexed semiotic process, as it ensures visibility of the intended interpretation in Twitter's trending topics with a view to consolidate common meaning on a large scale.

In Alzamora and Andrade's (2019b) view, the transmedia expansion of *#cadêaprova* cannot be understood only by what is visible through the mediation of this hashtag because the redirection of its semiosis was driven when these hashtags were linked to others of similar meaning. In this case, complex semiotic systems are formed, with expanded and diversified semiotic capacity. We approach this subject in Chapter 2, in a different empirical context.

Notes

1 This chapter is based on Alzamora and Gambarato (2014), first published on Ocula (see references).
2 Peirce rated the sciences of his time relating them according to their three phenomenological categories, placing them in a kind of cartography at different levels of generality, abstraction, and application (see Kent, 1987).
3 Around 1905, Peirce adopted the term *pragmaticism* aiming at differentiating his perspective from other pragmatisms. Among the differentiating aspects, we highlight Peirce's emphasis on meaning and not on truth. See Ketner and Kloesel (1986).
4 *Vem pra rua* [Come to the street] Fiat campaign. Retrieved from https://www. youtube.com/watch?v=3AFMybxWiF0

References

Alzamora, G. (2019). A semiotic approach to transmedia storytelling. In M. Freeman & R. Gambarato (Eds.), *The Routledge companion to transmedia studies* (pp. 438–446). New York, NY: Routledge.

Alzamora, G., & Andrade, L. (2019a, June). *Transmedia activism in the 2018 elections in Brazil: The semiosis of #cadêaprova [#whereistheproof]*. Paper presented at the XXVIII Encontro Annual da Compós, Porto Alegre, Brazil. Retrieved from http://www.compos.org.br/biblioteca/trabalhos_arquivo_VVK25NUA6K T6GLG2ZYMD_28_7744_22_02_2019_06_24_41.pdf

Alzamora, G., & Andrade, L. (2019b). A dinâmica transmídia da hashtag #vemprarua: Mediação e semiose [The hashtag's #cometothestreet transmedia dynamics: Mediation and semiosis]. In I. Satuf & J. A. B. Prado (Eds.), *Comunicação em ambiente digital* [Communication in the digital environment] (pp. 171–191). Covilhã, Portugal: LABCOM.

Alzamora, G., & Gambarato, R. R. (2014). Peircean semiotics and transmedia dynamics: Communication potentiality of the model of semiosis. *Ocula: Semiotic Eye on Media*, *15*, 1–13. Retrieved from http://www.ocula.it/files/ OCULA-15-CARVALHOALZAMORA-RAMPAZZOGAMBARATO-Peircean-semiotics-and-transmedia-dynamics.pdf

Andrade, L. (2019). *A função mediadora das hashtags no processo de impeachment de Dilma Rousseff: Semiose e transmídia* [The hashtag mediating role in Dilma Rousseff's impeachment process: Semiosis and transmedia] (Unpublished doctoral dissertation). Federal University of Minas Gerais, Belo Horizonte, Brazil.

Bergman, M. (2003). Peirce's derivation of the interpretant. *Semiotica, 1*(44), 1–17.

Bergman, M. (2007). The secret of rendering signs effective: The import of C. S. Peirce's semiotic rhetoric. *Public Journal of Semiotics, 1*(2), 2–11.

Bergman, M. (2009). *Peirce's philosophy of communication: The rhetorical underpinnings of the theory of signs*. London, England: Continuum.

Bergman, M. (2010). C. S. Peirce on interpretation and collateral experience. *Signs, 4*, 134–161.

Bertetti, P. (2014). Toward a typology of transmedia characters. *International Journal of Communication, 8*, 2344–2361.

Bruns, A., & Hanusch, F. (2017). Conflict imagery in a connective environment: Audiovisual content on Twitter following the 2015/2016 terror attacks in Paris and Brussels. *Media, Culture & Society, 39*(8), 1122–1141.

Colapietro, V. (1989). *Peirce's approach to the self: A semiotic perspective on human subjectivity.* New York: State University of New York Press.

Colapietro, V. (1995). Immediacy, opposition and mediation: Peirce on irreducible aspects of the communicative process. In L. Langsdorf & A. Smith (Eds.), *Recovering pragmatism's voice: The classical tradition, Rorty and the philosophy of communication* (pp. 23–48). Albany: State University of New York Press.

Colapietro, V. (2004). The routes of significance: Reflections on Peirce's theory of interpretants. *Cognitio, 5*(1), 11–27.

Dahlgren, P. (2013). *The political web: Media participation and alternative democracy.* Basingstoke, England: Palgrave Macmillan.

D'Andrea, C., Alzamora, G. C., & Ziller, J. (2015). Hashtags as intermedia agency resources before FIFA World Cup 2014 in Brazil. In N. Rambukkana (Ed.), *Hashtag publics: The power and politics of discursive networks* (pp. 115–126). New York, NY: Peter Lang.

Danesi, M. (2010). The history of philosophy as a semiotic process: A note on John Deely's monumental four ages of understanding. *Semiotica, 178*, 23–37.

Deledalle, G. (1997). Media between Balnibarbi and Plato's Cave. In W. Nöth (Ed.), *Semiotics of the media: State of the art, projects, and perspectives* (pp. 49–60). Berlin, Germany: Mouton de Gruyter.

Delwiche, A. (2017). Transmedia storytelling and the audience question. In B. W. L. D. Kurtz & M. Bourdaa (Eds.), *The rise of transtexts: Challenges and opportunities* (pp. 33–48). New York, NY: Routledge.

Deutsch, K. (1952). On communication models in the social sciences. *Public Opinion Quarterly, 16*, 356–380.

Elleström, L. (2010). The modalities of media: A model for understanding intermedial relations. In L. Elleström (Ed.), *Media borders, multimodality and intermediality* (pp. 11–50). New York, NY: Palgrave Macmillian.

Elleström, L. (2020). Transmediation: Some theoretical considerations. In N. Salmose & L. Elleström (Eds.), *Transmediations: Communication across media borders* (pp. 1–13). New York, NY: Routledge.

Evans, E. (2019). Transmedia television: Flow, glance, and the BBC. In M. Freeman & R. Gambarato (Eds.), *The Routledge companion to transmedia studies* (pp. 35–43). New York, NY: Routledge.

Evans, E. (2020). *Understanding engagement in transmedia culture.* London, England: Routledge.

Freeman, M., & Gambarato, R. R. (2019). *The Routledge companion to transmedia studies.* New York, NY: Routledge.

Gambarato, R. R., & Nanì, A. (2016). Blurring boundaries, transmedia storytelling and ethics of C. S. Peirce. In S. Maras (Ed.), *Ethics in screen writing: New perspectives* (pp. 147–175). Melbourne, Australia: Palgrave Macmillan.

Groshek, J., & Groshek, M. C. (2013). Agenda trending: Reciprocity and the predictive capacity of social network sites in intermedia agenda setting across issues over time. *Media and Communication, 1*(1), 15–27.

Herkman, J. (2012). Convergence or intermediality? Finnish political communication in the new media. *Convergence: The International Journal of Research into New Media Technologies, 18*(4), 369–384.

Hougaard, T. (2016). Hashtags: A new textual construct. *Rask, 44*, 57–73.

Husson, A. (2015, October 1). #Théoriedugenre, #gender: Deux hashtags à rôle argumentatif [#Theoryofgenre, #genre: Two hashtags with an argumentative role]. *(Dis)cursives*. Retrieved from https://cursives.hypotheses.org/170

Jenkins, H. (2006). *Convergence culture: Where old and new media collide*. New York: New York University Press.

Jenkins, H. (2009, December 12). Revenge of the origami unicorn: The remaining four principles of transmedia storytelling. *Confessions of an aca-fan*. Retrieved from http://henryjenkins.org/blog/2009/12/revenge_of_the_origami_unicorn.html

Jenkins, H. (2010, June 21). Transmedia education: The 7 principles revisited. *Confessions of an aca-fan*. Retrieved from http://henryjenkins.org/blog/2010/06/transmedia_education_the_7_pri.html

Jenkins, H. (2016). Youth voice, media, and political engagement: Introducing the core concepts. In H. Jenkins, S. Shresthova, L. Gamber-Thompson, N. Kligler-Vilenchic, & A. Zimmerman (Eds.), *Any media necessary: The new youth activism* (pp. 1–60). New York: New York University Press.

Jenkins, H. (2017). Transmedia logics and locations. In B. W. L. D. Kurtz & M. Bourdaa (Eds), *The rise of transtexts: Challenges and opportunities* (pp. 220–240). New York, NY: Routledge.

Johansen, J. (1993). Let sleeping signs lie: On signs, objects, and communication. *Semiotica, 97*(3/4), 271–295.

Kent, B. (1987). *Logic and the classification of the sciences*. Montreal, Canada: McGill-Queen's University Press.

Ketner, K. L., & Kloesel, C. (1986). *Peirce, semeiotic and pragmatism: Essays by Max H. Fisch*. Bloomington: Indiana University Press.

Kinder, M. (1991). *Playing with power in movies, television, and video games: From Muppet Babies to Teenage Mutant Ninja Turtles*. Berkeley: University of California Press.

Laucuka, A. (2018). Communicative functions of hashtags. *Sciendo: Economics and Culture, 15*(1), 56–62.

Malini, F., Goveia, F., Ciarelli P., Carreira, L., Herkenhoff, G., Regattieri, L., & Leite, M. V. (2014, August). *#vemprarua: Narrativas da revolta brasileira* [#cometothestreets: Narratives of the Brazilian revolt]. Paper presented at the XII Congresso da Associação Latino-Americana de Investigadores da Comunicação, Lima, Peru. Retrieved from http://labic.net/wp-content/uploads/VemPraRua-Narrativas-da-Revolta-brasileira.pdf

McQuail, D., & Windahl, S. (1993). *Communication models for the study of mass communication*. New York, NY: Routledge.

Mello, P. C. (2018, October 18). Empresários bancam campanha contra o PT pelo WhatsApp [Businesspeople pay for campaign against PT on WhatsApp]. *Folha de S. Paulo*. Retrieved from https://www1.folha.uol.com.br/poder/2018/10/empresarios-bancam-campanha-contra-o-pt-pelo-whatsapp.shtml

Mello, P. C. (2019, October 8). WhatsApp admite envio maciço ilegal de mensagens nas eleições de 2018 [WhatsApp admits illegal mass text messaging in the 2018 elections]. *Folha de S. Paulo*. Retrieved from https://www1.folha.uol.com.br/poder/2019/10/whatsapp-admite-envio-massivo-ilegal-de-mensagens-nas-eleicoes-de-2018.shtml

Nöth, W. (1995). *Handbook of semiotics*. Bloomington: Indiana University Press.

Nöth, W. (1997). Can pictures lie? In W. Nöth (Ed.), *Semiotics of the media: State of the art, projects, and perspectives* (pp. 133–146). Berlin, Germany: Mouton de Gruyter.

Nöth, W. (2011). Representation and reference according to Peirce. *International Journal of Signs and Semiotic Systems, 1*(2), 28–39.

Nöth, W. (2014). Human communication from the semiotic perspective. In F. Iberkwe-SanJuan & T. M. Dousa (Eds.), *Theories of information, communication and knowledge: A multidisciplinary approach* (pp. 97–119). New York, NY: Springer.

Parmentier, R. J. (1985). Sign's place in media res: Peirce's concept of semiotic mediation. In E. Mertz & R. J. Parmentier (Eds.), *Semiotic mediation: Sociocultural and psychological perspectives* (pp. 23–48). Orlando, FL: Academic Press.

Peirce, C. S. (1931–1958). *Collected papers of Charles Sanders Peirce* (C. Hartshorne, P. Weiss, & A. Burks, Eds.). 8 volumes. Cambridge, MA: Harvard University Press. (In-text references cite CP, followed by the volume number and paragraph number.)

Peirce, C. S. (1982–2000). *Unpublished manuscripts* (The Peirce Edition Project, Ed.). Bloomington: Indiana University Press. (In-text references cite MS, followed by the page number.)

Ponzio, A. (1990). *Man as a sign: Essays on the philosophy of language.* Berlin, Germany: Mouton de Gruyter.

Santaella, L. (1992). *A assinatura das coisas: Peirce e a literatura* [The signature of thing: Peirce and literature]. Rio de Janeiro, Brazil: Imago.

Santaella, L. (2003). Whats is a symbol? *S.E.E.D. Journal: Semiotics, Evolution, Energy, and Development, 2,* 54–60.

Santaella, L. (2004). Contribuições do pragmatismo de Peirce para o avanço do conhecimento [Contributions of Peirce's pragmatism to the advancement of knowledge]. *Revista de Filosofia, 16*(18), 75–86.

Santaella, L., & Nöth, W. (2004). *Comunicação e semiótica* [Communication and semiotics]. São Paulo, Brazil: Hacker.

Schaufeli, W. B. (2013). What is engagement? In C. Truss, K. Alfes, R. Delbridge, A. Shantz, & E. Soane (Eds.), *Employee engagement in theory and practice* (pp. 15–35). London, England: Routledge.

Severin, W. J., & Tankard, J. W. (1979). *Communication theories: Origins, methods, uses.* New York, NY: Hastings House.

Short, T. L. (2007). *Peirce's theory of signs.* Cambridge, England: Cambridge University Press.

Silveira, S. A. (2009). Game-ativismo e a nova esfera pública interconectada [Game-activism and the new interconnected public sphere]. *Líbero, 12,* 131–138.

Srivastava, L. (2009, March 4). Transmedia activism: Telling your story across media platforms to create effective social change. *Namac.* Retrieved from http://archive.li/8O1Rd

Taylor, M., & Kent, M. (2014). Dialogic engagement: Clarifying foundational concepts. *Journal of Public Relations Research, 26*(5), 384–398.

Vieira, V. (2013, May). *O papel da comunicação digital na primavera árabe: Apropriação e mobilização social* [The role of digital communication in the Arab Spring: Social appropriation and mobilization]. Paper presented at the V Congresso da

Compolítica, Curitiba, Brazil. Retrieved from http://www.compolitica.org/home/wp-content/uploads/2013/05/GT05-Comunicacao-e-sociedade-civil-Vivian PatriciaPeronVieira1.pdf

Yang, G. (2016). Narrative agency in hashtag activism: The case of #blacklivesmatter. *Media and Communication*, 4(4), 13–17.

Zappavigna, M. (2015). Searchable talk: The linguistic functions of hashtags. *Social Semiotics*, 25(3), 274–291.

2 The transmedia effect

Systemic complexity in transmedia storytelling

Signs, systems, and systemic complexity

Similar to Chapter 1, we address core concepts such as sign, system, and complexity (Gambarato, 2012; Weingartner & Dorn, 1990) to delve into the intricate streams of transmedia storytelling (Freeman, 2018; Freeman & Gambarato, 2019; Kerrigan & Velikovsky, 2016) and its essential world-building nature (Wolf, 2012, 2017). We refer to a qualitative conceptual study theoretically framed by the general theory of signs or Peircean semiotics and the general systems theory (Bertalanffy, 1993; Bunge, 1960, 1979) for the congruence they share: The sign is the liaison element that interweaves semiotics and systems. According to Peirce, a sign represents, to a certain extent, something to the mind. Moreover, "anything should be a sign" (CP 2.230), but nothing is a sign unless it is interpreted as one (CP 2.308) by continuous triadic relations in which each successive sign becomes an interpretant for the preceding one. Within the Peircean logic or semiotics, the sign is the domain of firstness that operates in the relation of substitution with the secondness, the sign's object, generating the thirdness, called the interpretant (Gambarato, 2012):

> A sign, or representamen, is something which stands to somebody for something in some respect or capacity. It addresses somebody, that is, creates in the mind of that person an equivalent sign, or perhaps a more developed sign. That sign which it creates I call the interpretant of the first sign. The sign stands for something, its object. It stands for that object, not in all respects, but in reference to a sort of idea, which I have sometimes called the ground of the representamen.
>
> (CP 2.228)

Building on the Peircean concept of sign is the grouped concept of system. The notion of system has become universal and is used extensively although there are diverse perspectives on the term. The definitions of system are based on conceptualizations from biology (Bertalanffy, 1993), psychology (McCulloch & Pitts, 1943), cybernetics (Wiener, 1948), and sociology

(Luhmann, 1995). Nevertheless, the notion of system generally refers to a cohesive assemblage of interrelated parts forming a unitary whole, and since Aristotle, the whole has been considered greater than the sum of its parts. The whole is not just the sum of its parts basically due to variable interactions that form the integrated whole. Changes in these interactions among the parts of the system would necessarily affect the whole:

> System thinking sees collections of interdependent components as a set of relationships and consequences that are at least as important as the individual components themselves. It emphasizes the emergent properties of the whole that neither arise directly, nor are predictable, from the properties of the parts.
>
> (Vassallo, 2017, para. 7)

We define system within the sphere of general systems theory—first developed by Ludwig von Bertalanffy in the 1950s—according to Mario Bunge's (1960, 1979) ontological approach. Bunge understands the notion of system as ontological in the sense that a system describes extremely general properties of things. According to Bunge (1979, p. 4), reality is systematic, and the universe is not composed by isolated (closed) systems but by open systems that exchange energy or matter with the environment. This idea is similar to the notion of intra- and extra-semiotic systems discussed in the previous chapter. The intra-systemic level corresponds to the mediation of the signs that compose the system, and the extra-systemic level is related to the mediation between the signs or components of the system and the other signs that form its environment.

A system therefore is a complex object, whose components are more interrelated than unrelated. The components are connected to each other and to their environment (*Umwelt*). A system (σ) is an ordered triple (Bunge, 1979, p. 5):

$$\sigma = \langle C, E, S \rangle$$

where
C = composition (set of components),
E = environment (milieu),
S = structure (set of relations on the union of C and E).

The composition (C) comprises the set of constitutive elements of the system, the environment (E) corresponds to the set of items to which the composition is connected, and the structure (S) refers to the relations among the components, and between them and the environment. The relations among the components configure the internal structure of the system while the relations between the composition and its environment are called the external structure. A system is considered closed when the external structure is empty, that is, when there are no interactions between the components of the system and the environment. Conversely, when there is an external structure, the system is called open (Weingartner & Dorn, 1990, p. 8). In addition, the properties of a system can change over time (t), and a system may be open in certain aspects and closed in others:

> Let P be a property of a system σ in an environment E (σ, t). The σ *is open with respect to P at t if P* is related, at t, to at least one property of things in E (σ, t)—otherwise σ is closed in the respect P.
>
> (Bunge, 1979, p. 10)

Bunge also emphasizes that parts of a system can also be systems, that is, subsystems. The surroundings of a system can be another system: the so-called supersystem (Weingartner & Dorn, 1990, p. 9). More importantly, the logic indicated by Bunge relates to "a system of nested systems" (1979, p. 11) rather than a hierarchical structure between subsystems, systems, and supersystems. "Considering this statement, a transmedia story could be seen as a supersystem composed of nested systems and subsystems like Russian dolls or Chinese boxes, for instance" (Gambarato, 2012, p. 73). Therefore, in the relation among the systems in a transmedia context, there is no hierarchy with one more relevant than the others; they are complementary.

Systems have essential parameters that generally characterize them. Parameters can be (1) basic (features that remain the same, independent of evolutionary processes) or (2) evolutionary (features that fluctuate over time). Basic parameters are (1) permanence, (2) the environment, and (3) autonomy. Evolutionary parameters comprise (1) composition, (2) connection, (3) structure, (4) integration, (5) functionality, (6) organization, and (7) complexity. In the scope of general systems theory, complexity—the focus of this chapter—can be better understood in correlation with connection and integration. Complexity, in the transmedia context, is a fundamental parameter for its relation not just with the intricate parts that compose a transmedia story but for all the implications in the interplay between these parts and the social environment where they are inserted. Connection refers to the system's relations and therefore can reveal complexity by the number and diversity of these relations. Integration is related to the emergence of subsystems, affecting the systemic complexity via the number of subsystems and their shared properties (Vieira, 2003).

Connection presupposes action, as it is an intense relation between parts of the system that impact the history of at least some of the elements involved. In this sense, elements are connected only if they act upon others, modifying somehow their behavior, trajectory, or history (Bunge, 1979). Connections are not mere relations, such as one element of the system is older than other; instead, one element exerts pressure upon another because the logic of a connection is that it makes some difference in its relata. This impact of one element upon another implies that two elements are connected only "in case at least one of them acts upon the other—where the action needed not consists in eventuating something but may consists in either cutting out or opening up certain possibilities" (Gambarato, 2012, p. 78). According to Bunge (1979), given the set of elements A and B, the Cartesian product $P = A \times B$ is defined as follows:

$$P = \left\{ \langle x, y \rangle / x \in A \,\&\, y \in B \right\}.$$

P constitutes arrangements between the elements of the set A and B, but it may involve some rule, law, or restriction that organizes the selection of these ordered pairs. The rule, law, or restriction will select a subset R (relation) as follows:

$$R = \left\{ \langle x, y \rangle \subset P \right\}.$$

Connections maintain the system over time, and although its intensity may vary, they are responsible for systemic stability and permanence, which is called cohesion (Vieira, 2003). In transmedia storytelling, connection is fundamental to develop relations (R), in which the environment (E) acts upon the set of components (C) and vice versa, such as in the case in which the audience (E) is offered by the transmedia project opportunities (C) to collaborate (for instance, by signing a petition in favor of a social cause), and this involvement of the audience has an impact (R) to promote the social cause in vogue and inspire social change. That is the basic structure of the notion of participation in transmedia stories, which we discuss further in this chapter.

A system subdivides itself into subsystems by integrating, a strategy that generates new shared properties. The level of integration is subordinated to the connections between the components of a system and its environment. "Systems whose components are tightly connected normally have a high degree of integration. Integration refers to the way subsystems are connected. The integration of subsystems communicates the content (information) to be interpreted" (Gambarato, 2012, p. 79). A transmedia experience has integration as an inherent parameter because the unfolding of a transmedia story naturally generates other systems and subsystems. The principle of worldbuilding—discussed later in this chapter—is intrinsically related to the notion of integration: A transmedia project is a storyworld capable of supporting multiple narratives across various media platforms and formats. Thus, complexity implies a higher degree of connection and integration. Nonetheless, systemic complexity is considered a free and difficult-to-define parameter that is, to a certain extent, always present. Complex systems tend to persist (the permanence parameter) over time and to adapt to the environment. In this sense, a transmedia project is more complex if it allows the audience to participate in it, leading to (1) unpredictable developments of the (super)system caused by the collaborative role of the audience, (2) the enhancement of the whole experience as the audience can find it more meaningful, and (3) the permanence of the story over time as it adapts itself to the environment and becomes integrated in the audience involvement.

Subsystems, systems, and supersystems within transmedia storytelling

Before delving into the correlations between transmedia storytelling and complex nested (super)systems, we must establish the differences between our approach and what in the early 1990s Marsha Kinder (1991) called the transmedia supersystem. Although Jenkins (2003) coined the term transmedia storytelling, Kinder used the word transmedia more than a decade earlier to designate the promotional practices involving merchandising, adaptation, and franchising embedded in a discourse of commercialism and commodification (Evans, 2011). In this context, Kinder (1991) postulates,

> A supersystem is a network of intertextuality constructed around a figure or group of figures from pop culture who are either fictional (like TMNT, the characters from *Star Wars*, the Super Mario Brothers, the Simpsons, the Muppets, Batman, and Dick Tracy) or "real" (like PeeWee Herman, Elvis Presley, Marilyn Monroe, Madonna, Michael Jackson, the Beatles, and, most recently, the New Kids on the Block). In order to be a supersystem, the network must cut across several modes of image production; must appeal to diverse generations, classes, and ethnic subcultures, who in turn are targeted with diverse strategies; must foster 'collectability' through a proliferation of related products; and must undergo a sudden increase in commodification, the success of which reflexively becomes a "media event" that dramatically accelerates the growth curve of the system's commercial success.
>
> (pp. 122–23)

Kinder's approach to transmedia supersystems as promotional strategies for fostering commercialism and commodification is discussed by Evans, who draws our attention to the fact that Kinder (1) "specifically use[s] the term [transmedia] to describe processes of cross-platform adaptation and marketing" (Evans, 2011, p. 21), and (2) establishes that the motivations behind transmedia supersystems are connected with the "economic system of Hollywood" (Evans, 2011, p. 21). Although not denying the commodification potential of transmediality emphasized by Kinder and other authors such as Kearney (2004)—who focuses on the notion of "transmedia exploitation" (p. 266) as invoking associations of commercialism over integrity, Evans clearly states that "there has been a shift in transmedia practice" (2011, p. 23), configuring a much more complex and enriching picture of transmediality.

The notion of transmediality embraces the broader practice of applying multiple media technologies to tell stories pertaining to a single storyworld, while the essence of transmedia storytelling—a subcategory of transmediality

(Freeman, 2018)—is more specifically related to expanding the stories within a single storyworld, using different text formats and media technologies to deliver storytelling to audiences in a potentially engaging and meaningful manner. In this sense, transmediality is a broader notion that embraces the particularities of transmedia storytelling (such as audience engagement). Corroborating Freeman's (2018) argument that transmedia storytelling is a subcategory of transmediality, (Evans, 2011, p. 19) states that "transmedia storytelling is the most well-known component of transmediality."

Dissecting the concept of transmediality, Konzack (2017) considers two ways of understanding mediality: (1) mediality as the reality created by the media and (2) mediality as media materiality. Within transmedia studies, both aspects can be considered: (1) transmedial worlds conveying a mediated world and (2) "the materiality of media productions and the effects upon the content of shifting modalities within different media representations" (p. 134). Furthermore, Konzack (2017) acknowledges that despite the economic potential intrinsically intertwined with transmedia dynamics, for audiences involved in transmedial worlds much more is at stake. They invest their time and often their heart in transmedia stories in a much more complex way that can possibly supersede mere commercialism.

Our approach to the relationship between transmedia storytelling and complex nested supersystems is grounded on this shift in transmedia practices discussed by Evans (2011) and is built upon multiple sign systems. "Transmedia signs do not require anchorage in definite objects; they form systems of cross-reference which may be open or closed" (Lemke, 2011, p. 585). Gambarato (2012) proposed comprehending transmedia storytelling as supersystems composed of systems (story, experience, platforms, business model, etc.) and each system of its respective subsystems. For instance, considering the story as a system, we would have as subsystems plot, characters, time, location, and so on. Gambarato (2012) applies Bunge's (1979) formula of a system $\sigma = \, < C, E, S >$ to the reality of transmedia storytelling TS = < (story, experience, platforms, business model, etc.), audience, audience engagement >:

> If Mario Bunge's system $\sigma = \, < C, E, S >$ is transposed to the realm of TS [transmedia storytelling], each (super)(sub)system has its set of constituent elements (C), its environment (E), and the relations between them (S). For instance:
>
> Supersystem
> TS = < (story, experience, platforms, business model, etc.), (community of people who share common interests related to the storyworld), (interaction, participation) >
>
> System
> Story = < (plot, characters, time, location, genre, settings, world, etc.), (community of people who share common interests related to the storyworld), (interaction, participation) >

Subsystem
Character = < (demographics, psychographics, role, hero's journey, location, etc.), (storyworld), (connection, integration) >.

(Gambarato, 2012, p. 73)

Beyond the main set of components (C) of transmedia projects (σ), such as the story and the media platforms involved, the relationship (S) between the components (C) and the environment (E) is fundamentally important within transmedia stories. Bourdaa (2013) extols the relevance of transmedia storytelling in creating spaces in between different parts of the story (or system), which is directly linked to the understanding of transmedia storytelling as interconnected supersystems.

The relationship between transmedia products and people interested in them corresponds to the relationship (S) between the set of components (C) of a system and its environment (E). This audience engagement, together with multiple media platforms and content expansion, is one of the pillars of transmedia storytelling. The active and/or dynamic (fluid) engagement of audiences (Nanì, 2019) is intrinsically associated with the notion of transmedia storytelling, and the main term directly related is participation. However, there are diverse approaches to conceptualize audience engagement in broader terms and participation more specifically. Corner (2011) considers different levels of intensity of personal contact with the media, starting with exposure, permeating engagement, and culminating in involvement. Corner (2011, p. 91) defines exposure as "casual 'glancing' contact" people have with media on a daily basis. Engagement is about selective attention dedicated to media, "a motivated selection from the range of possible connection with mediation" (p. 91), and involvement is a more intense form of engagement, "connecting with the mediation in a way that involves more sustained cognitive and affective work" (p. 91). Furthermore, Dahlgren (2009) considers being engaged as extending beyond an individual demonstrating cognitive interest and must involve an "affective investment" (p. 83), the same way Hill (2018) discusses the emotional range (positive/negative polarity) entangled in what she describes as the spectrum of engagement. Nevertheless, being engaged does not necessarily imply participation (Dahlgren, 2009). There are different degrees of audience engagement or different intensities. In this sense, if we consider engagement as an umbrella term or a necessary first step that could lead to more committed involvement of the audience with mediation, then participation, alongside interaction, would be variable instances of audience engagement within the transmedia realm, although we could be engaged without interacting or participating.

To define participation, and consequently interaction, Carpentier (2016) reminds us of the need to acknowledge the different perspectives on the concept given by two main approaches: political and sociological. Carpentier (2015), who differentiates access, interaction, and participation, focuses on the political approach to participatory theory, and we work within the sociological scope, as our goal is to understand participatory experiences in transmedia stories and how audiences can do it. Consequently, we focus on the sociological perspective of (media) participation and how it relates to systems theory. The political understanding of participation focuses on the power struggles in play in the context of participatory processes, which are power-driven and decision-making activities that could involve unbalanced power relations (Carpentier, 2015).

Drawing on the sociological viewpoint, Gambarato (2012, p. 74) states that although "an interactive project allows the audience to relate to it somehow, for instance, by pressing a button or control, deciding the path to experiencing it, but not being able to co-create and change the story," a participatory one "invites viewers/users/players to engage in a way that expresses their creativity in a unique, and surprising manner, allowing them to influence the final result." Co-creative media, as a key player in the notion of participation, is defined by Spurgeon et al. (2009, p. 275) as "a tool for describing the ways in which participatory media are facilitated by people and organisations, not just technology."

A transmedia supersystem that shares, at least to some extent, the power of decision with the audience and allows a participatory experience that impacts the transmedia outcome create an open system. "With an open system, the power of the many can outweigh the power of the few" (Maeda, 2006, p. 94). In this case, the relationship (S) between the composition (C) and the environment (E) deliberately exists and leads to a collaboration process that affects and transforms the systems involved to a larger or smaller degree. Open systems, even if they are open for a limited period in time (t) and/or are open in some aspects and not necessarily in all of them, allow for participation, implying an impact on the outcome. "Participation (S) occurs when the community of people who share common interests (E) can, with respect at least to a certain property (P), influence on the set (C) of components such as the story" (Gambarato, 2012, p. 75). In addition, in the case of participation, we have the connections (R) developed around the actions inflicted by the environment (E) on the composition (C).

Common ways of promoting participatory experiences within transmedia storytelling are co-creating content, voting, casting, taking part in live events, and so on. Closed systems, however, do not allow participation but embrace interaction: The audience can somehow interact with the transmedia project, although the opportunity to co-create or influence the outcome is not given to them. For instance, the audience can interact via social media, commenting on the story, proposing new insights for its development, suggesting plots and future growth, but without causing a concrete impact on the producers' power. The boundaries are set within the producers' decision power. Jenkins (2006, p. 133) discusses interaction as "the ways that new technologies have been designed to be more responsive to consumer feedback" and participation as something "open-ended, less under the control of media producers and more under the control of media consumers." Certainly, the degree and intensity of participatory experiences can vary. In closed systems, the external structure between (C) and (E) is empty. Carpentier (2015, p. 24) adds that "access to and interaction within a participatory process are necessary requirements for the participatory process to exist" but not the other way around: Interaction does not presuppose participation. For instance, audiences can interact on social media and reply to posts related to the transmedia story they enjoy. This is interaction, but this does not imply that they are participating in the development of the transmedia story. In contrast, when audiences can, for example, suggest plot progression via social media channels, and these suggestions are incorporated by the transmedia producers, interaction and participation are in place.

Although the power detention or the desire to retain control of intellectual property is still quite prominent in creative industries, media professionals are perfectly aware of the appeal that audience participation can have and of the relevance of concepts such as *produsage* and *prosumption* (Bruns, 2008). The logic behind developing open transmedia supersystems relies on the fact that the sense of belonging, the feeling of being part of a community likely motivates participants to share, defend, recommend, and promote the stories in which they are involved. "The trend towards transmedia storytelling is well positioned as it can offer richer, more immersive and meaningful experiences by marrying consumption with participation" (Rutledge, 2019, p. 350). Lance Weiler, filmmaker and transmedia producer, weighs in on the advantages of offering meaningful participatory experiences to audiences. He comments on the changes in the relationship between audiences and producers:

> Audience is dead. The reality is that what was once an audience is now what I consider to be collaborators. The relationship has totally changed. Democratization of tools turns audiences into their own media companies free to push button publish for the world to see. Authorship is shifting and as a result more people can be part of the storytelling. So in that sense participatory storytelling is an opportunity to take advantage of the connected world we currently live in. For me personally transmedia asks people to collaborate and to co-create stories that can be jumping off points to social connections and if I do that the stories will surely spread.
>
> (Giovagnoli, 2011, pp. 92–93)

A systemic approach to transmedia storytelling unveils the structural horizontal process behind open transmedia supersystems, although the degree of openness that this kind of project offers can vary greatly in intensity and in time. Wiehl (2018), studying the intricacies of the National Film Board of Canada's multifaceted project *Highrise* (a multiyear project that reveals the intimate digital lives of apartment building residents around the world), discusses six aspects of participation: (1) "co-creating and co-editing media material to reach a wider public," (2) "practices of co-creation when one moves from a hyperlocal to a global level," (3) "notions of authorship and issues of interface design," (4) "the role of software in co-creative participatory projects," (5) "productive tension between user-generated content and the 'authority' of archival material as well as interactive navigational user agency," and (6) "the interplay of interpretative participation, individual paths through material and the potential of self-reflexive interactive participatory documentary for re-examining one's own online and offline behavior" (p. 270). More importantly, Wiehl (2018) emphasizes the need to acknowledge that participation is not limited to user-generated content; participation is not reduced to uploading images, videos, and texts, for instance. Drawing on Gaudenzi's (2013) model of who, what, and when of participation, Wiehl (2018, p. 273) states that "participation can virtually affect every stage in the life cycle of (digital) artifacts." From casting to post-production, audiences can participate via voting, signing a petition, donating to a cause, crowdsourcing, crowdfunding, and so forth. A recent example is the creation of The Poussey Washington Fund (2019) after the seventh and final season of the hit Netflix series *Orange Is the New Black*. The producers of the series honored the character Poussey Washington, accidently killed by a prison officer who held her down on the floor and suffocated her in the fourth season, with a real-life fund to raise money for nonprofit organizations in the United States focused on criminal justice reform and immigrant rights, and support previously incarcerated women as they reintegrate into the community. Two months after the fund was launched in July 2019, more than US$317,000 had been raised (The Poussey Washington Fund, 2019). *Orange Is the New Black* promoted participation in other ways during the show's seven seasons. For instance, in 2015, a series of posters advertising the third season were "inspired by Tweets from fans" (Gilchrist, 2015, para. 1) worldwide.

Another example of ways to participate beyond user-generated content is *The Great British Property Scandal*, a transmedia project produced by Channel 4 and designed to inform and engage audiences and offer alternative solutions to the critical housing crisis in the United Kingdom. The participatory opportunities offered by *The Great British Property Scandal* were fundamental for the project's success. People could participate by (1) signing a petition to pressure the government to create a low-cost loan fund to help owners of empty properties refurbish their properties and put them back on the market, (2) reporting empty homes via the project's mobile application, and (3) volunteering to help with the renovations of empty properties to be put back into use. The project succeeded in the following ways: (1) More than 118,000 individuals signed the petition, (2) 10,000 empty homes were reported, (3) £17 million was allocated for the new low-cost loan fund in the United Kingdom, and (4) George Clarke, an architect and the host of *The Great British Property Scandal*, was appointed independent empty home advisor to the government (Gambarato, 2018).

The complexity of worldbuilding in transmedia storytelling

The complexity of transmedia supersystems, as pervasive narratives, can evoke a sense of disorder, disorientation, confusion, and even chaos. The transmedial worlds of *Star Wars* (Freeman, 2018; Guynes & Hassler-Forest, 2018) and *Doctor Who* (Hills, 2017) illustrate this sensation. Moreover, chaos and complexity are related, but although complexity can be chaotic, entropic, it can also be organized, ordered (Vieira, 2003). Jean-Pierre Dupuy, in an interview with Pessis-Pasternak (1992), discusses the essential difference between complexity and disorder that can be applied to understand transmedia supersystems:

> Why do we say that a system is complex, and not disordered? Both cases mean a deficit of understanding, an apparent lack of regularity. What is the difference between complexity and disorder? [...] The distinction that is established between a complex system and a disordered one is that, in the first case, there are functional properties: the system does something! One can then say that a complex system is a system apparently disordered, but behind it there is a hidden order.
>
> (Pessis-Pasternak, 1992, pp. 110–111, our translation)

A key aspect of complexity is difference: The complexity of a system relies on the heterogeneity of its set of components (C) among themselves and their differences in relation to the environment (E). Bunge (1979) emphasizes that there are various levels or degrees of complexity, implying that there are variations of intensities in the same properties of a given system. This feature is directly linked to the logic of transmedia storytelling, as it is inherently characterized by the expansion of content to the detriment of offering the same content in multiple media platforms and by audience engagement in the content. Thus, considering the multiple elements (C) of a transmedia system (story, experience, platforms, etc.) and the community (E) of people who share common interests related to it, the complexity of transmedia supersystems

> is not simply the multimodal complexity of the signs of the works included in the franchise. It also includes the complexity of the dispositions of users to interpret and identify with (or dis-identify from) semiotic elements (e.g. characters, themes, environments, events and outcomes) presented by the works.
>
> (Gambarato, 2012, p. 81)

Moreover, Lemke (2011) posits that the complexity of transmedia products extends further to the complexity of the media market and the social networks in which the public conducts its interactions with transmedial worlds. The complexity of transmedia supersystems embodies all its constitutive elements (C), (E), and (S), and it is not isolated from the complex social, cultural, economic, and political constructs in which we live.

Boni (2017, p. 18) emphasizes that "each media brick (official or fan-made) is a mini-world, a piece contributing to the constitution of a larger entity." This larger entity, or supersystem, forms a world: a storyworld, a transmedial world (Tosca & Klastrup, 2019). Storyworlds are defined by Andrew (1984) as intertextual structures that exist across multiple formats, allowing stories to unfold. Moreover, when discussing Charles Dickens, Andrew (1984) asserts that

> [t]he storyworld of Dickens is larger than the particular rendition of it which we call *Oliver Twist*... In fact, it is larger than the sum of the novels Dickens wrote, existing as a set of paradigms, a global source from which he could draw.
>
> (p. 55)

A storyworld, as a complex system, is larger than the sum of its parts. Boni (2017, p. 18), in the context of transmedia storytelling, adds that "[e]ventually, the sum of different uses and interpretations creates a result that exceeds the original work—in size, in shape, and in its intentions and directions—thereby creating a complex world." That is what happens with the world of *The Handmaid's Tale* (created by Margaret Atwood in 1985 and ever since immersed in an ongoing process of expansion), which will be analyzed in Chapter 3.

Jenkins (2006) first notes that transmedia storytelling "has become the art of world-building" (p. 114) or "the art of world-making" (p. 113) and later considers worldbuilding as one of the seven principles of transmedia storytelling—together with spreadability vs. drillability, continuity vs. multiplicity, immersion vs. extractability, seriality, subjectivity, and performance (Jenkins, 2009a, 2009b). McDowell (PlayableUCSC, 2013) ponders that "[w]orld building is an experiential, collaborative and creative process that integrates imagination and technology, creating story space from inception through iteration and prototyping, into manufacturing and delivery." The pioneering work of Klastrup and Tosca (2004, p. 409) establishes that "[t]ransmedial worlds are abstract content systems from which a repertoire of fictional stories and characters can be actualized or derived across a variety of media forms" and that they are "mental constructs shared by both the designers/creators of the world and the audience/participants" (2014, p. 297). We argue that it is not just about fiction. The same logic can apply to nonfictional transmedia storyworlds as well (see Gambarato & Alzamora, 2018; Kerrigan & Velikovsky, 2016). Jenkins agrees,

Most forms of transmedia are structured through a process of world-building. The concept of world-building emerged from fantasy and science fiction but has also been applied to documentary or historical fiction. Worlds are systems with many moving parts (in terms of characters, institutions, locations) that can generate multiple stories with multiple protagonists that are connected to each other through their underlying structures. Part of what drives transmedia consumption is the desire to dig deeper into these worlds, to trace their backstories and understand their underlying systems. Fictional texts imagine and design new worlds; documentaries investigate and map existing worlds.

(Jenkins, 2016, para. 12)

In addition, Wolf (2012, p. 68), in his seminal work on imaginary worlds, considers that building storyworlds is "transmedial in nature." Evans (2011, p. 27, original emphasis) states that "[t]ransmedia elements do not involve the telling of the same events on different platforms; they involve the telling of *new* events from the *same* storyworld." The question then, as posed by Freeman (2018), is what differentiates a basic storyworld naturally embedded in any story from the so-called worldbuilding process that distinguishes transmedial worlds? Freeman (2018) answers that the difference is how the spatiotemporality of storyworlds is expanded by additional media formats, exploring new elements of the transmedial world in ways that the audience recognizes the narrative as a complex and interconnected network, that is, a complex and interconnected supersystem. Bourdaa (2013, pp. 202–203) links the phenomenon of transmedia storytelling to the notion of complex narrative (and we would add the notion of complex supersystem) asserting that "the development of transmedia storytelling implies that a story is complex enough to create and expand a whole coherent universe around it."

Wolf (2017) extensively problematizes the process of designing worlds and focuses on four primordial aspects: (1) size, (2) scope, (3) shape, and (4) boundaries:

A world can be described according to its size, scope, shape, and boundaries. The size of the world depends on the number of world data describing it. [...] The scope of the world describes the extent of the space covered by the world itself; a world could be as large as a universe or as tiny as a small town. [...] The shape of the world, along with its boundaries, also determines much of the audience's experience. A story usually only takes the audience through part of the world, and even multiple stories may not exhaust all there is to see and visit.

(p. 68)

After these basic elements are set, cultures can be developed, which involve aspects such as particular worldviews and philosophies arising from people's experience of the world and its overall appearance in terms of distinctive costumes, architecture, and technologies. In the systemic structure, we can understand worldbuilding in the interplay between the components (C) of the system and how they relate to the environment (E). Anders (2013) discusses common flaws that should be avoided in the process of worldbuilding. He encourages, in the context of fictional or fictionalized worldbuilding, to (1) think about the basic infrastructure, such as how the society and economy operate; (2) explain why events are happening now, as opposed to 20 years ago or 20 years from now; (3) create fictional versions of real-life human ethnic groups, which are not only one dimensional (so include nuance); (4) avoid creating monolithic social, political, cultural, and religious groups (so include diverse perspectives); (5) avoid inventing a history that is completely logical, in the sense that it is important to have odd quirks and happenstances; (6) really give a strong sense of place, like what it smells like after it's been raining; and (7) avoid introducing some superpower, such as magic or advanced technology, without fully accounting for how it would change society.

Another feature that contributes to the complexity of worldbuilding in transmedia storytelling is the amalgamation of what could be considered the main text and paratext. Genette's concept of paratextuality within the literary realm is one of five types of transtextuality he proposed (together with intertextuality, metatextuality, hypertextuality, and architextuality). He defines paratext as all the material supplied by the author, editor, publisher, and so on that surrounds the main text. Genette and Maclean (1991, p. 264, original emphasis) present the formula *"paratext = peritext + epitex,"* differentiating peritext (titles and subtitles, pseudonyms, forewords, dedications, epigraphs, prefaces, intertitles, notes, epilogues, and afterwords) from epitex (interviews, author's comments, correspondence, diaries, and pretexts, for instance). Ferrándiz (2019, p. 429) argues that the relevance of the Genettian paratext to transmedia studies is built on the understanding of paratext "as a theoretical framework capable of explaining the diachronic genesis and synchronic functionality of transmedia textual proliferation." Ferrándiz (2019) also states,

> In any case, it is a complicated task to distinguish between those paratextual features which directly contribute to narrative progression (undoubtedly qualified for being components in TS [transmedia storytelling]) and those paratextual features that point to the work, but contribute nothing or very little to the narrative progression within it (although they contribute to the production of meaning in reception, for example, by anchoring generic expectations).
>
> (p. 432)

The "unstoppable transmedia text expansion in the era of telematic digital convergence" (Ferrándiz, 2019, p. 430) requires an update of Genette's theory to incorporate the transcendence of transmedia text across multiple media formats and platforms. Several authors (Dehry Kurtz & Bourdaa, 2017; Ferrándiz, 2019; Freeman, 2018; Mittell, 2013, 2014, 2015) in the transmedia realm discuss the content expansion by examining the role played by paratextual features in transmedia stories. The Internet brought a new light to paratextuality, facilitating access to and creation of paratexts. According to Mittell (2014, p. 254),

> [n]early every media property today offers some transmedia extensions, such as promotional websites, merchandise, or behind-the-scenes materials. These forms can be usefully categorized as *paratexts* in relation to the core text, whether a feature film, video game, or television series.

In addition to the multiplication of paratexts in the digital sphere, for instance, TV series, "even before their transmedia expansion," have "a great affinity with paratextuality" (Ferrándiz, 2019, p. 432) as the seriality and continuity aspects—both among Jenkins' (2009a, 2009b) seven core principles of transmedia storytelling—contribute to guarantee the unfolding of complex narrative systems and the long-term engagement with audiences. Although there are concrete implications revenue-wise, the affinity between transmedia storytelling and paratexts exceeds the mere monetary value, as this relationship is closely related to the systemic complexity of multiplatform products, retro-feeding audiences' interests within the transmedia supersystem. "For the industry, transmedia extensions might provide an additional revenue stream, but their primary function is to drive viewers back to the television series; for creators, transmedia storytelling must always support and strengthen the core television narrative experience" (Mittell, 2014, p. 255). Mittell (2013, 2014, 2015), acknowledging the flow of television text across multiple platforms, proposes the notion of paratextual orientation to reconcile the text and the paratext, "blurring the experiential borders between watching a programme and engaging with its paratexts" (2015, p. 7). In other words, orienting paratexts (such as wikis, guides, timelines, mapping chronologies, graphics, family trees, recaps, split-screen synchronizing, and reedited versions) unite transmedia paratexts (which contribute to the narrative expansion) and promotional paratexts (which promote and publicize stories):

> In the case of the TV series *Lost*, for instance, Lostpedia provides information about video games (*Lost: Via Domus*), ARG [Alternate Reality Game] (*The Lost Experience, Find 815*), mobisodes (*Lost: Missing Pieces*), novels (Gary Troup, *Bad Twin*), websites (Oceanic Airlines, Dharma Initiative, Janelle Granger Dairy ...), podcasts, among others. In addition, Lostpedia highlights the intertextual references of the series: the novels read by some of the characters (Dickens, Dostoyevsky, Joyce, Nabokov, Agatha Christie, and Stephen King, among

others); the biographies of the philosophers and scientists after whom some characters are named (Locke, Hume, Rousseau, Faraday) and their connection with the characters' personality and role; and the cultural matrixes referenced by the series: novels about shipwreck survivors in an apparently desert island (Defoe, Verne, H.G. Wells, Huxley, William Golding …); films and series about that same subject, whether original or adaptations, techno-scientific conspiracy theories, supernatural or mystical explanations of the events, etc.

(Ferrándiz, 2019, p. 433)

The current relevance of paratexts goes beyond the literary constrictions originally proposed by Genette and reflects the theoretical shift from the limitations of Genettian paratext to updated paratextuality across various formats and platforms expressed in the transmedia realm. The "paratext efficiently deploys its functions—promotional, guiding, and narrative—which should not be conceived as mutually exclusive, but as effects which are updated in all paratexts to varying degrees" (Ferrándiz, 2019, p. 435). Freeman (2018) considers that paratexts operate as text and as promotion—and we add, as guidelines. Paratexts represent the expansive form of intertextuality that transmediality encompasses. This intertextual expansiveness forms textual and paratextual connections within a transmedia supersystem, potentially folding paratext into text.

The transmedia effect

In 2019, several weeks after the release of the HBO documentary *The Inventor: Out for Blood in Silicon Valley*, the streaming service Hulu announced the development of the limited series *Theranos* (Matney, 2019). Theranos was a breakthrough technology company dedicated to revolutionizing the large blood-testing market. Elizabeth Holmes, a Stanford University dropout, founded the company in 2003 and became the wealthiest self-made female billionaire (Herper, 2016) by falsely claiming that their technology would require a minimum amount of blood to deliver cheaper, more convenient, and more accessible blood testing. In 2018, the company was liquidated, and Holmes was indicted on wire fraud and conspiracy charges. The story of the rise and fall of Theranos started with a report in the *Wall Street Journal* by investigative reporter John Carreyrou (2015) and unfolded across ABC Radio's podcast series *The Dropout*, the New York Times bestselling book *Bad Blood: Secrets and Lies in a Silicon Valley Startup*, the HBO documentary, and the upcoming movie *Bad Blood* and the Hulu limited series *Theranos*. Staffans (2013, para. 4) would call this the greenhouse effect: A greenhouse is "a structure built to house things that should be nurtured and grow," and it is "the structure that gives the ramifications, it is the roof and the walls that protect the other different elements from harsh conditions and even harsher weather" (para. 6). The analogy proposed by Staffans (2013) is that the greenhouse is the transmedia project or, more specifically, the storyworld upon which everything is based. The greenhouse expansion of the Theranos storyworld proved very fruitful in the fertile terrain of transmedia production. However, Theranos is not an isolated case in which a compelling story expands its branches across different media formats and platforms, forming a complex transmedia supersystem. There is a pattern, a trend, a drift. This is what we call the transmedia effect.

In the "age of plenty" (Ellis, 2000, p. 39) in which content is accessible through numerous technologies, we can see the growth of transmedia supersystems to the detriment of the repurposing of content across multiple media platforms observed in cross-media productions. Cross-media is a broader and more generic than transmedia (Gambarato, 2013) often referring "to releasing the same content [...] over multiple platforms" (Phillips, 2012, p. 19). We are historically used to the adaptation of books, comic books, and plays into films, for instance, but now we are progressively living in the time of expansion, of enlargement, of dilatation of content. The lines are becoming completely blurred: It is no longer about having a straightforward adaptation of content from one medium to another but about the continuation of extended storyworlds that are robust and exciting enough to function across multiple levels of interest from audiences to producers, to authors to financiers, forming what we defined previously as transmedia supersystems. Considering recent critically and publicly acclaimed cases such as *Big Little Lies*, *The Sinner*, and *The Handmaid's Tale*, we can foresee the impact of the transmedia effect.

The bestselling book *Big Little Lies* by Liane Moriarty (2014) was first adapted as an HBO limited series of the same name in 2017. The series starring Hollywood names such as Reese Witherspoon and Nicole Kidman became a hit, earning accolades from critics and the public alike—the first season of *Big Little Lies* won eight Emmy Awards and was nominated for 16 (Travers, 2017). Thus, it was not a surprise when HBO announced a second season, although that was not originally planned. In an interview with Travers (2017, para. 8), Kidman, who is one of the executive producers of the show, referred to the second season as, "This is inspired by the overwhelming response by audiences around the world, conceived once again by Liane Moriarty, realized by David Kelley and now in the hands of visionary filmmaker Andrea Arnold." Papandrea, another executive producer of the show, explained how *Big Little Lies* expanded its storyworld:

> Liane did have an idea, and we approached her about writing an outline, and what she delivered was really a novella, like a 170-page novella. And it was great. And then we took that and gave it to [showrunner] David E. Kelley.
>
> (Siegel, 2019, para. 7)

Although Kelley was responsible for writing the second season, Moriarty was directly involved, as it was her story. However, that is not always the case.

The Sinner was originally conceived as a closed-ended series produced by USA Network (also available on Netflix) in 2017 and was based on German author Petra Hammesfahr's book. The show, which tells the story of a young mother who stabs a random stranger without knowing why, became a surprising hit. Although all of the source material was used in the first season, the successful reach of the show prompted the development of a second season. Jessica Biel, the star of the first season and executive producer, commented that

> [i]nitially, the show was genuinely conceived as a limited series, so it was a surprise to us as well that, with the amazing viewership and the incredible journey that this show has taken, it was even a possibility to come back.
>
> (Flood, 2018, para. 5)

In addition, Derek Simonds, who is the showrunner responsible to create and manage the show, explained that "*The Sinner* is a standalone story, so for the series to return, the show would have to come up with a brand-new story from scratch" (Flood, 2018, para. 4, original italics). The solution was to transform the story into an anthology series. The second season aired in 2019 with the detective, Ambrose, played by Bill Pullman in the first season, as the protagonist. "The genesis of the new story was borne out of conversations Pullman had with creator Derek Simonds last year while filming season one" (Ng, 2018, para. 10), without the involvement of Hammesfahr.

Yet another way of expanding a storyworld is *The Handmaid's Tale* created by Margaret Atwood in her 1985 original book. The first season of the exceptional series produced by Hulu since 2017—which won numerous awards including Emmys and Golden Globes—was based on the book, but the subsequent seasons represented an entirely new endeavor. The showrunner Bruce Miller (2017) stated, "I do feel like so much of the first season was about building the world—that world building is just what we're continuing" (para. 15). He added that

> [i]t's very much a world built by Margaret, and we've been able to kind of take areas and little things that she's mentioned and bring them to life. And that has been energizing and also it just makes you realize how well constructed her stories are. That the world, as we expand it, holds up incredibly well. What is their penal system like, what is going on in the ex-pat community? All those things that she mentions in the book and we've expanded on are on such strong footing because Margaret thought them through so precisely.
>
> (Miller, 2017, para. 16)

Atwood has been involved in the Hulu series since the beginning as a consulting producer. She did not write the material for the show, but she gave her consent to the further development of her storyworld. Miller asks Atwood's opinion quite often and affirmed that "we are very lucky that she is involved and thoughtful and really appreciates the show and is excited by the new directions we're taking things in and very careful about reminding us of things" (Miller, 2017, para. 12). In September 2019, the future directions of *The Handmaid's Tale* storyworld experienced a fascinating complication with the publication of *The Testaments*, Atwood's official sequel to her original book. The book was launched after the third season aired and during the preparations for the fourth season to be released in 2020. The story takes place around 15 years after the end of the first book, and now the narrators of the story are the two daughters of the protagonist June and Aunt Lydia. How *The Testaments* will be intertwined with the *The Handmaid's Tale* series is still to be determined:

> Whether *The Testaments* will align with the TV show's universe remains to be seen. While Atwood is a producer on the series, and Miller has frequently referred to consulting with her while developing the show over the years, the book seems poised to stand alone. If they've coordinated their stories, it may enhance the TV version of Gilead, rather than contradicting it.
>
> (Miller, 2019, para. 12, original italics)

Possibly enhancing the TV series with synergy between the systemic elements of the sequel book opens up the possibility of making the transmedia supersystem created around Atwood's speculative fiction even more complex. The other media extensions in *The Handmaid's Tale* storyworld, such as an opera, a movie, and a graphic novel, are discussed and analyzed in Chapter 3.

Considering *Theranos*, *Big Little Lies*, *The Sinner*, and *The Handmaid's Tale* as examples of the complexity and pervasiveness of the transmedia effect, the point is, why are we seeing this effect increasingly frequently. Moreover, do we need all these transmedia stories? We could argue that transmedia practices are becoming so mainstream to the point of simply being the way stories are told in times of accessibility of multiple media technologies by diverse audiences. However, we could question the legitimacy of the business model and highlight the potential avoidance to risk investments in stories and storytellers that have not proven themselves worthwhile yet. Freeman and Gambarato (2019) conclude that

> [w]e return to our conceptualization of transmediality as the building of experiences across and between the borders where multiple media platforms coalesce, altogether refining our understanding of this phenomenon as specifically a mode of themed storytelling that, by blending

content and promotion, fiction and non-fiction, commerce and democratization, experience and participation, it affords immersive, emotional experiences that join up with the social world in dynamic ways. And in doing so, it becomes more than the sum of its parts—weaving through industry, art, practice, and culture.

(p. 11)

Nevertheless, "transmedia is not a remedy" (Piskov, 2019, p. 152) that will miraculously cure all the contagious diseases spread across the media industries. Transmedia storytelling is, instead, prophylactic: (1) Transmedia dynamics does not guarantee financial gain, although there is the potential to increase revenue; (2) does not necessarily attract a multitude of people, although its pervasiveness could reach diversified audiences; and (3) does not solve any of the media industry crises such as that seen in the global movie industry (which has seen constant decreases in box office revenue; Tam, 2018), although transmedia dynamics can concretely contribute to reignite the market. We are experiencing a still-evolving form of telling stories that the term transmedia storytelling ought to represent. We face an inevitable and unavoidable shift in the media industries (with the disruptive role of streaming services, the rise of technological developments such as virtual and augmented realities, participatory culture practices, media activism, etc.), and as posited by Evans (2011), in transmedia practices as well. In the midst of this transitional point in culture, transmedia storytelling functions as a prophylactic measure that plays the important role of converging technological and cultural improvements together with societal and behavioral changes to offer people a more meaningful and satisfying experience beyond the commercialism and commodification features of the recent media evolution past. The power of transmedia storytelling is highlighted by Phillips (2012):

> Any single-medium work can in theory make an audience laugh or cry. But make an audience feel directly involved in the events in a story? Whether we're talking about responsibility for sending a woman to her murder, or perhaps instead saving her life or introducing her to her partner, you just can't evoke that feeling with a book or a movie. This is the power of transmedia.
>
> (p. 5)

Freeman and Gambarato (2019) discuss the alleged prevalence of transmediality in the media and communication realms, pondering that it is not accurate to assume that transmedia practices exist in the same form, shape, and intensity across all creative industries. Nonetheless, the authors conceive transmedia practices as a mode of diversification across media industries, and that is the direction we are leaning toward.

"We live in a massively complex, intricately interconnected global system" (Vassallo, 2017, para. 6), and transmedia supersystems seem to be an inherent part of it.

References

Anders, C. J. (2013, August 2). 7 deadly sins of worldbuilding. *Gizmodo*. Retrieved from https://io9.gizmodo.com/7-deadly-sins-of-worldbuilding-998817537

Andrew, D. (1984). *Concepts in film theory*. Oxford, England: Oxford University Press.

Bertalanffy, L. (1993). *General system theory*. New York, NY: George Braziller.

Boni, M. (2017). Introduction: Worlds, today. In M. Boni (Ed.), *World building: Transmedia, fans, industries* (pp. 9–27). Amsterdam, the Netherlands: Amsterdam University Press.

Bourdaa, M. (2013). Following the pattern: The creation of an encyclopaedic universe with transmedia storytelling. *Adaptation, 6*(2), 202–214.

Bruns, A. (2008). *Blogs, Wikipedia, Second Life, and beyond: From production to produsage*. New York, NY: Peter Lang.

Bunge, M. (1960). Levels: A semantical preliminary. *The Review of Metaphysics,13*(3), 396–406.

Bunge, M. (1979). *Treatise on basic philosophy. Volume IV: Ontology: A world of systems*. Amsterdam, the Netherlands: Reidel.

Carpentier, N. (2015). Differentiating between access, interaction and participation. *Conjunctions: Transdisciplinary Journal of Cultural Participation, 2*(2), 7–28.

Carpentier, N. (2016). Beyond the ladder of participation: An analytical toolkit for the critical analysis of participatory media processes. *Javnost – The Public, 23*(1), 70–88,

Carreyrou, J. (2015, October 16). Hot startup Theranos has struggled with its blood-test technology. *The Wall Street Journal*. Retrieved from https://www.wsj.com/articles/theranos-has-struggled-with-blood-tests-1444881901

Corner, J. (2011). *Theorising media: Power, form and subjectivity*. Manchester, England: Manchester University Press.

Dahlgren, P. (2009). *Media and political engagement: Citizens, communication, and democracy*. New York, NY: Cambridge University Press.

Dehry Kurtz, B. W. L., & Bourdaa, M. (2017). *The rise of transtexts: Challenges and opportunities*. London, England: Routledge.

Ellis, J. (2000). *Seeing things: Television in an age of uncertainty*. London, England: Tauris.

Evans, E. (2011). *Transmedia television: Audiences, new media, and daily life*. New York, NY: Routledge.

Ferrándiz, R. R. (2019). A Genettian approach to transmedia (para)textuality. In M. Freeman & R. R. Gambarato (Eds.), *The Routledge companion to transmedia studies* (pp. 429–437). New York, NY: Routledge.

Flood, A. (2018, January 30). *The Sinner* season 2: Everything we know so far. *NME*. Retrieved from https://www.nme.com/blogs/tv-blogs/the-sinner-season-2-release-date-trailer-cast-news-plot-2169773

Freeman, M. (2018). New paths in transmediality as vast narratives: The state of the field. In P. Brembilla & I. De Pascalis (Eds.), *Reading contemporary serial television universes: A narrative ecosystem framework* (pp. 11–26). New York, NY: Routledge.

Freeman, M., & Gambarato, R. R. (2019). *The Routledge companion to transmedia studies*. New York, NY: Routledge.

Gambarato, R. R. (2012). Signs, systems and complexity of transmedia storytelling. *Communication Studies, 12*, 69–83.

Gambarato, R. R. (2013). Transmedia project design: Theoretical and analytical considerations. *Baltic Screen Media Review, 1*, 80–100.

Gambarato, R. R. (2018). Transmedia journalism and the city: Participation, information, and storytelling within the urban fabric. In R. R. Gambarato & G. Alzamora (Eds.), *Exploring transmedia journalism in the digital age* (pp. 147–161). Hershey, PA: IGI Global.

Gambarato, R. R., & Alzamora, G. (2018). *Exploring transmedia journalism in the digital age*. Hershey, PA: IGI Global.

Gaudenzi, S. (2013). *The living documentary: From representing reality to co-creating reality in digital interactive documentary* (Unpublished doctoral dissertation). University of London, London, England.

Genette, G., & Maclean, M. (1991). Introduction to the paratext. *New Literary History, 22*(2), 261–172.

Giovagnoli, M. (2011). *Transmedia storytelling: Imagery, shapes and techniques*. Pittsburgh, PA: ETC Press.

Gilchrist, T. (2015, April 28). *Orange Is the New Black* season 3 posters so good you'll want to paper your walls with them. *Pride*. Retrieved from https://www.pride.com/women/2015/4/28/orange-new-black-season-3-posters-so-good-youll-want-paper-your-walls-them

Guynes, S., & Hassler-Forest, D. (2018). *Star Wars and the history of transmedia storytelling*. Amsterdam, the Netherlands: Amsterdam University Press.

Herper, M. (2016, June 1). From $4.5 billion to nothing: Forbes revises estimated net worth of Theranos founder Elizabeth Holmes. *Forbes*. Retrieved from https://www.forbes.com/sites/matthewherper/2016/06/01/from-4-5-billion-to-nothing-forbes-revises-estimated-net-worth-of-theranos-founder-elizabeth-holmes/#7291d0d03633

Hill, A. (2018). *Media experiences: Engaging with drama and reality television*. London, England: Routledge.

Hills, M. (2017). Traversing the "Whoniverse": Doctor Who's hyperdiegesis and transmedia discontinuity/diachrony. In M. Boni (Ed.), *World building: Transmedia, fans, industries* (pp. 343–361). Amsterdam, the Netherlands: Amsterdam University Press.

Jenkins, H. (2003, January 15). Transmedia storytelling. *MIT Technology Review*. Retrieved from http://www.technologyreview.com/ biotech/13052/

Jenkins, H. (2006). *Convergence culture: Where old and new media collide*. New York: New York University Press.

Jenkins, H. (2009a, December 12). Revenge of the origami unicorn: The remaining four principles of transmedia storytelling. *Confessions of an aca-fan*. Retrieved from http://henryjenkins.org/blog/2009/12/revenge_of_the_origami_unicorn.html

Jenkins, H. (2009b, December 12). The revenge of the origami unicorn: Seven principles of transmedia storytelling (well, two actually. Five more on Friday). *Confessions of an aca-fan*. Retrieved from http://henryjenkins.org/blog/2009/12/the_revenge_of_the_origami_uni.html

Jenkins, H. (2016, November 15). Transmedia what? *Immerse*. Retrieved from https://immerse.news/transmedia-what-15edf6b61daa

Kearney, M. C. (2004). Recycling Jude and Corliss: Transmedia exploitation and the first teen-girl production trend. *Feminist Media Studies, 4*(3), 265–295.

Kerrigan, S., & Velikovsky, J. T. (2016). Examining documentary transmedia narratives through the living history of Fort Scratchley Project. *Convergence: The International Journal of Research into New Media Technologies, 22*(3), 250–268.

Kinder, M. (1991). *Playing with power in movies, television, and video games: From Muppet Babies to Teenage Mutant Ninja Turtles.* Berkeley: University of California Press.

Klastrup, L., & Tosca, S. (2004). Transmedial worlds—Rethinking cyberworld design. *Proceedings of the 2004 International Conference on Cyberworlds* (pp. 409–416). Tokyo, Japan. Retrieved from https://ieeexplore-ieee-org.proxy.library.ju.se/abstract/document/1366205

Klastrup, L., & Tosca, S. (2014). *Game of Thrones*: Transmedial worlds, fandom, and social gaming. In M. L. Ryan & J. N. Thon (Eds.), *Storyworlds across media* (pp. 295–314). Lincoln: University of Nebraska Press.

Konzack, L. (2017). Transmediality. In M. J. P. Wolf (Ed.), *The Routledge companion to imaginary worlds* (pp. 134–140). New York, NY: Routledge.

Lemke, J. (2011). Transmedia traversals: Marketing meaning and identity. In A. Baldry & E. Montagna (Eds.), *Interdisciplinary perspectives on multimodality: Theory and practice. Proceedings of the Third International Conference on Multimodality* (pp. 576–596). Campobasso, Italy: Palladino.

Luhmann, N. (1995). *Social systems.* Stanford, CA: Stanford University Press.

Maeda, J. (2006). *The laws of simplicity: Design, technology, business, life.* Cambridge, MA: MIT Press.

Matney, L. (2019, April 11). Hulu orders Theranos miniseries starring Kate McKinnon as Elizabeth Holmes. *Tech Crunch*. Retrieved from https://techcrunch.com/2019/04/10/hulu-orders-theranos-miniseries-starring-kate-mckinnon-as-elizabeth-holmes/

McCulloch, W., & Pitts, W. (1943). A logical calculus of ideas immanent in nervous activity. *Bulletin of Mathematical Biophysics, 5*, 115–133.

Miller, L. S. (2017, December 12). *The Handmaid's Tale* season 2 will tackle race issues as it tells new stories beyond the book. *Indie Wire*. Retrieved from https://www.indiewire.com/2017/12/handmaids-tale-season-2-race-golden-globes-1201906937/

Miller, L. S. (2019, July 15). Hulu's *Handmaid's Tale* is a model of long-form worldbuilding. *The Verge*. Retrieved from https://www.theverge.com/2019/7/15/20694746/hulu-handmaids-tale-season-3-margaret-atwood-worldbuilding-elisabeth-moss-ann-dowd

Mittell, J. (2013). Serial orientations: Paratexts and contemporary complex television. In J. Eckel, B. Leiendecker, D. Olek, & C. Pieporka (Eds.), *(Dis)orienting media and narrative mazes* (pp. 165–182). Bielefeld, Germany: Transcript.

Mittell, J. (2014). Strategies of storytelling on transmedia television. In M. L. Ryan & J. N. Thon (Eds.), *Storyworlds across media* (pp. 253–277). Lincoln: University of Nebraska Press.

Mittell, J. (2015). *Complex TV: The poetics of contemporary television storytelling.* New York: New York University Press.

Moriarty, L. (2014). *Big little lies*. London, England: Penguin.

Nanì, A. [bfmuniversity]. (2019, April 3). *The many folds of participation: Audiences and the media* [Video file]. Retrieved from https://vimeo.com/bfmuniversity/review/328402303/1708f97a62

Ng, P. (2018, June 14). How Bill Pullman channeled the inner torment of *The Sinner* (exclusive). *ET*. Retrieved from https://www.etonline.com/how-bill-pullman-channeled-the-inner-torment-of-the-sinner-exclusive-104045

Peirce, C. S. (1931–1958). *Collected papers of Charles Sanders Peirce*. C. Hartshorne, P. Weiss, & A. Burks (Eds.). 8 volumes. Cambridge, MA: Harvard University Press. (In-text references cite CP, followed by the volume number and paragraph number.)

Pessis-Pasternak, G. (1992). *Do caos à inteligência artificial* [From chaos to artificial intelligence]. São Paulo, Brazil: Unesp.

Phillips, A. (2012). *A creator's guide to transmedia storytelling: How to captivate and engage audiences across multiple platforms*. New York, NY: McGraw-Hill.

Piskov, A. (2019). *Challenges and opportunities of transmedia storytelling in the contemporary film industry* (Unpublished master's thesis). National Research University Higher School of Economics, Moscow, Russia.

PlayableUCSC. (2013, September 11). *Alex McDowell: World building (media systems #5)* [Video File]. Retrieved from https://www.youtube.com/watch?v=TH_C5Wgs_1A

Rutledge, P. (2019). Transmedia psychology: Creating compelling and immersive experiences. In M. Freeman & R. R. Gambarato (Eds.), *The Routledge companion to transmedia studies* (pp. 350–363). New York, NY: Routledge.

Siegel, T. (2019, May 30). *Big Little Lies* producer on season 2 and her "difficult" split from partner Reese Witherspoon. *The Hollywood Reporter*. Retrieved from https://www.hollywoodreporter.com/news/big-little-lies-producer-season-2-split-reese-witherspoon-1213673

Spurgeon, C., Burgess, J., Klaebe, H., McWilliam, K., Tacchi, J., & Tsai, M. (2009, July). *Co-creative media: Theorising digital storytelling as a platform for researching and developing participatory culture*. Paper presented at the Australia and New Zealand Communication Association Conference, Brisbane, Australia. Retrieved from https://eprints.qut.edu.au/25811/2/25811.pdf

Staffans, S. (2013, July 23). Transmedia: The greenhouse effect. *Simon Staffans Evolving Media*. Retrieved from https://simonstaffans.com/2013/07/23/transmedia-the-green-house-effect/

Tam, E. (2018, February 23). Global movie industry facing crisis. *Ejinsight*. Retrieved from http://www.ejinsight.com/20180223-global-movie-industry-facing-crisis/

The Poussey Washington Fund. (2019). *CrowdRise*. Retrieved from https://www.crowdrise.com/o/en/campaign/pwf

Tosca, S., & Klastrup, L. (2019). *Transmedial worlds in everyday life: Networked reception, social media, and fictional worlds*. London, England: Routledge.

Travers, B. (2017, December 8). *Big Little Lies* season 2 set at HBO: Reese Witherspoon and Nicole Kidman to star, Andrea Arnold to direct. *Indie Wire*. Retrieved from https://www.indiewire.com/2017/12/big-little-lies-season-2-renewed-hbo-andrea-arnold-reese-witherspoon-nicole-kidman-1201905443/

Vassallo, S. (2017, January 5). Design thinking needs to think bigger. *Fast Company*. Retrieved from https://www.fastcompany.com/90112320/design-thinking-needs-to-think-bigger?utm_source=facebook.com&utm_medium=social

Vieira, J. (2003, August). *Semiótica e complexidade* [Semiotics and complexity]. Paper presented at the I Jornada de Estudos em Semiótica e Complexidade: Sistemas e Cognição, São Paulo, Brazil.

Weingartner, P., & Dorn, G. (1990). *Studies on Mario Bunge's treatise.* Amsterdam, the Netherlands: Rodopi.

Wiehl, A. (2018). Participation that makes a difference and differences in participation: Highrise—An interactive documentary project for change. In A. S. Ross & D. J. Rivers (Eds.), *Discourses of (de)legitimization: Participatory culture in digital contexts* (pp. 269–286). New York, NY: Routledge.

Wiener, N. (1948). *Cybernetics or control and communication in the animal and the machine.* Cambridge, MA: MIT Press.

Wolf, M. J. P. (2012). *Building imaginary worlds: The theory and history of sub-creation.* New York, NY: Routledge.

Wolf, M. J. P. (2017). World design. In M. J. P. Wolf (Ed.), *The Routledge companion to imaginary worlds* (pp. 67–73). New York, NY: Routledge.

Part II

Methodological development

3 Methodological stance

Transmedia design analytical and operational model

Transmedia fundamentals

The representation of a storyworld through multiple media environments is not a new phenomenon (see Freeman, 2017) and has been labeled in various ways. The terms transmedia storytelling (Jenkins, 2003) and transmedial worlds (Klastrup & Tosca, 2004) "have proved to be the most influential" (Ryan & Thon, 2014, p. 14). The notion of the transmedia phenomenon can be traced to the theoretical elaboration of the *Gesamtkunstwerk* (total artwork) by the German composer Richard Wagner, who outlined the ideal of a single artwork. In this context, Wagner considered the contribution of different forms of art such as dance, music, and literature without the loss of autonomy among them. The idea of the *Gesamtkunstwerk* in the transmedia context is related to the systemic complexity of the sum of its parts forming a transmedia supersystem, as discussed in Chapter 2. Vukadin (2019) argues that for Wagner, the "experience of an artistic synthesis would help renew the feeling of togetherness and collective identity" (p. 35), but it "is essential to understand that in the case of transmedia the synthesis is achieved at the conceptual level and not at the level of expression or production" (p. 37).

The transmedia phenomenon can be conceived as (1) spontaneous clustering of texts or formats by different authors, both canonical and apocryphal, as in the case of the organic development of popular storyworlds such as *Harry Potter* and *Star Wars* (Dena, 2009; Ryan, 2014); (2) the deliberate distribution of narrative content across multiple media, as the so-called ideal form of transmedia storytelling conceptualized by Jenkins (2006) such as in the classic case of *The Matrix*; and (3) a hybrid form well characterized by the transmedia effect proposed in Chapter 2, in which the clustering of texts merges with the deliberate multiplatform distribution of content, such as in the case of *The Handmaid's Tale*.

To dissect the essence of transmedia stories, we start with the word transmedia itself, departing from the meaning of the prefix trans- and the conceptualization of media. The Latin prefix trans- means across, beyond, through, and transverse, conveying the idea of transcendence (Gambarato,

2013). Transmedia, as an adjective, would describe and qualify a noun. In the case of media, the prefix trans- can depict the idea of transcending various media, that is, extends beyond a single medium. Although the meaning of this commonly used prefix is quite clear, the meaning of media is not. In the first chapter, we discussed Peirce's notion that media can be understood as an expressive form that materializes sign mediation according to the sign's reference languages and the transformations related to the audience's repertoire and interests. However, Moloney (2019, p. 3545, original emphasis) acknowledges that *"[m]edia* is a problematic word. Contained within it are a number of conflated ideas that are often contextually misinterpreted." Ryan (2014), who defines media from a narratological viewpoint, considers that the polyvalent term medium involves semiotic substance and technological and cultural dimensions: (1) *"semiotic substance* encompasses categories such as image, sound, language, and movement" (p. 29, original emphasis); (2) *"technical dimension* includes not only media-defining technologies such as film, TV, photography, and so on but also any kind of mode of production and material support" (p. 29, original emphasis); and (3) *"cultural dimension* addresses the public recognition of media as forms of communication and the institutions, behaviors, and practices that support them" (p. 30, original emphasis). For Ryan (2014), the phenomena characterized as media include,

> (a) channels of mass communication, such as newspapers, television (TV), radio and the Internet; (b) technologies of communication, such as printing, the computer, film, TV photography, and the telephone; (c) specific applications of digital technology, such as computer games, hypertext, blogs, e-mail, Twitter, and Facebook; (d) ways of encoding signs to make them durable and ways of preserving life data, such as writing, books, sound recording, film, and photography; (e) semiotic forms of expression, such as language, image, sound, and movement; (f) forms of art, such as literature, music, painting, dance, sculpture, installations, architecture, drama, the opera, and comics; and (g) the material substance out of which messages are made or in which signs are presented, such as clay, stone, oil, paper, silicon, scrolls, codex books, and the human body.
>
> (p. 26)

Ryan (2014) stresses that the kind of medium chosen to tell which story (or parts of a storyworld) makes a difference in how stories can be told, which corresponds to Jenkins' (2003, para. 10) proposition that "each medium does what it does best." Ryan's categorization of media built on three pillars (semiotic, technical, and cultural) is influenced by Ong's (1982), Meyrowitz's (1993), and Wolf's (2002) postulates of literature, media, and narratology, respectively. Although Ryan's perspective on media is broadly accepted, Moloney (2019, p. 3548) criticizes that her three parallel approaches to media are designed as lenses of analysis rather than structures for practice, and her division of media into the 'semiotic substance' of language, image, music, and movement neglects the object and interaction and dismisses the potential of odor and flavor as media.

In the context of transmedia storytelling, Jenkins (2006) refers to historian Lisa Gitelman's (2006) model of media that is twofold: (1) A medium is a technology that enables communication, and (2) a medium is a set of integrated social and cultural practices that are developed around that technology. The different definitions have in common the understanding that a medium (plural media), such as radio, television, and the Internet, is a means of communication that reflects the sociocultural context in which the medium is inserted.

Moloney (2019) also discusses a nomenclature issue around the term media channel versus media platform—he prefers media channel. This topic is interesting because it is directly related to the transmedia design analytical and operational model we present later in this chapter. Both terms refer to "the place or environment in which a story is told" (Moloney, 2019, p. 3557), connecting the content to audiences, for instance, via television, radio, and print media. However, *channel* can be a problematic term because it is also used to describe a specific television data stream. *Platform*, according to Moloney (2019, p. 3558), is problematic because it "implies an elevated and purified pedestal for the information." Nevertheless, we use the term *media platform*, as it is vastly accepted and commonly used across different media industries.

More importantly, the term that is particularly of interest here is *transmedia extension*, as it plays a major role in the development of transmedia production and transmedia analysis of what has been produced. Jenkins (2011, para. 13) defines transmedia extension differentiating it from adaptation: "Basically, an adaptation takes the same story from one medium and retells it in another. An extension seeks to add something to the existing story as it moves from one medium to another." We do not focus on the nuances of the concept of adaptation and how it is related or not to transmedia storytelling (see Dena, 2009, 2019), as it is not the focal point of this book. We focus on understanding what a transmedia extension within a transmedia supersystem is and how it can be differentiated from the general term media platform in the context of transmedia production or analysis. Considering a book as an example of an extension within a transmedia project, the following scenario could exist: We could have a printed book, an e-book, an audiobook, or all of them. Electronic, audio, and printed books are different products that could have distinct business models, that could be launched at different points in time, that could be directed to diverse audiences, and so forth (Pratten, 2015). Therefore, it is important to consider them as separate transmedia extensions based on different media platforms: Print for the printed book and the Internet for the e-book and the audiobook (or compact disk). We could refer to a book as having distinct media formats (or forms). Moloney (2019, p. 3561) proposes a practical media taxonomy for complex media production and distinguishes the transmedia phenomenon as involving "many stories, many media forms, many media channels." He explains,

> Transmedia storytelling, as defined by Henry Jenkins (2003, 2006), implements the many media forms of multimedia and delivers them on the many media channels of crossmedia. In addition, it tells many stories rather than one and does so expansively rather than redundantly. Entertainment media companies design a franchise to be delivered across multiple media forms and media channels in ways that inspire viewers to actively engage in the story.
>
> (Moloney, 2019, p. 3561)

As media forms, Moloney (2019, p. 3560) includes "from text to audio, motion pictures, photographs, or graphic data visualizations, among others," and as media channels (or platforms, as we call them), he mentions television, print, and radio, for instance.

Another fundamental aspect to discuss before we delve into the structure of our analytical and operational model is the alleged fiction and nonfiction divide. Some cultures and languages, such as Bosnian, Croatian, and Serbian, do not necessarily distinguish between fiction and nonfiction: These languages refer to them all as stories (Lea, 2016). For instance, in Bosnian "there are no words for fiction and nonfiction, or the distinction thereof" (Lea, 2016, para 1), as "a literary text is not defined by its relation to truth or imagination" (Lea, 2016, para 2). The fiction and nonfiction divide (or lack of) is a current topic of discussion drawing on the classic definitions in the literature realm that fiction is aligned to imagination and nonfiction to belief (Currie, 1990; Walton, 1990) and recent research that defies these assumptions (Friend, 2012; Matravers, 2014). Film studies also have a long tradition of discussing the clean cut between fiction and nonfiction in the context of documentaries (Barnouw, 1974; Nichol, 1992; Winston, 2013). Nevertheless, in the transmedia realm, it seems quite clear that the true/false dichotomy of the fiction/nonfiction divide does not necessarily serve the purposes of the complexity of stories to which we are exposed:

> The conception of storyworld that I have just outlined goes against the popular (and inaccurate) belief that nonfictional stories are true while fictional stories are false. On the contrary, nonfictional stories can be either true or false with respect to their reference world, but fictional ones are automatically true in the world about which they are told.
>
> (Ryan, 2014, pp. 33–34)

In addition, Zipfel (2014, p. 105) stresses that "not everything in a fictional world is invented. Fictional worlds are, as Umberto Eco puts it, 'parasitic' upon real world." Kerrigan and Velikovsky (2016) advocate for the relevance of transmedia dimensions in nonfiction arguing that "[n]on-fiction transmedia draws on the same definitions as fiction transmedia" (p. 233), and "[n]on-fiction transmedia is an extant and ever increasing phenomenon" (p. 237). Although transmedia storytelling emerged from fictional entertainment (Kinder, 1991; Jenkins, 2003, 2006), several studies already connect transmediality to nonfiction and blur the lines between fiction and nonfiction, such as in the case of journalism, activism, education, politics, and so on (see Freeman & Gambarato, 2019; Gambarato, 2016, 2018; Gambarato & Alzamora, 2018; Gambarato & Medvedev, 2015; Gambarato & Nanì, 2016; Gambarato & Tárcia, 2017; Scolari, 2018). In the midst of the defiance of the fiction and nonfiction divide, we present the transmedia design analytical and operational model that is applicable to fictional and nonfictional stories—and those in between.

Transmedia design analytical and operational model

In 2013, Gambarato proposed the transmedia project design analytical model because transmedia studies, as a new academic subject, lacked its own specific methods and methodologies that would consider a transmedia project as a complex systemic unit (Gambarato, 2012) involving multiple dimensions, such as narrative, marketing, business model, and audience. At the time, the usual approach presupposed methodologically separate analytical perspectives related to some of these dimensions, drawing on methods derived from narratology, semiotics, and business administration, for instance. In 2011, Von Stackelberg (2011, p. 115) offered "an ontology for transmedia narrative design" that represented a more comprehensive view of transmedia projects, but his extremely detailed framework of the intricacies of creating transmedia stories and designing audience engagement proved to be impractical for implementation. Therefore, Gambarato's (2013, 2014) model differentiated itself by considering transmedia projects as supersystems and presenting a model that could be effectively implemented. The model was developed to address the essential features behind the projects understood as a whole, contributing to support the analytic needs of transmedia designers and producers and applied research for media industries. Since then, other relevant methodological tools directly aimed at facilitating the analysis and/or operationalization of transmedia projects have emerged, such as Srivastava's (2013) narrative design canvas; Ciancia's (2015) transmedia design framework; Ciancia, Piredda, and Venditti's (2018) storyworld canvas; Moloney's (2018) decision flow model for transmedia journalism; and Lovato's (2018) nonfiction transmedia script. For a thorough overview of different transmedia design models, see

Gambarato (2019), and for transmedia journalism models, see Gambarato and Alzamora (2018).

The qualitative nature of Gambarato's (2013) model contributes to the understanding of the design process of multiplatform projects. Originally, the model presented 10 specific topics—(1) premise and purpose, (2) narrative, (3) worldbuilding, (4) characters, (5) extensions, (6) media platforms and genres, (7) audience and market, (8) engagement, (9) structure, and (10) aesthetics—that were guided by a series of practicable questions. Over the years, the model was applied in the classroom to teach undergraduate and graduate students in media and communication in countries such as Estonia, Russia, Brazil, and Sweden. The applicability of the model was tested in undergraduate and graduate theses and in applied research within fictional and nonfictional transmedia projects (see Alzamora & Tárcia, 2014; Ciancia, 2018; Gambarato, 2018; Gambarato & Medvedev, 2015), as well as in workshops with media professionals and students. Although the model proved to be useful and efficient, the applications revealed that aspects could be improved, such as reorganizing some topics that could be grouped together, simplifying the application process and avoiding the occurrence of potential repetitive aspects. Thus, we propose a revised version of Gambarato's (2013) model that we call the *transmedia design analytical and operational model*. The revised model is more dynamic: it is reduced in size but not in scope to highlight that the model analyzes existing projects, and guides the operational practice of new transmedia projects. Five main topics—(1) story, (2) premise, (3) extensions, (4) audience, and (5) structure—emerged from the reorganization and reallocation of the previous 10 topics. (1) Story represents the convergence of worldbuilding, narrative, and character; (2) premise remains as before; (3) extensions is now united with media platforms and genres, and aesthetics; (4) audience is an amalgamation of audience and market, and engagement; and (5) structure remains a single topic. In the process of reorganizing and reallocating the topics, we also restructured the series of practicable questions that accompany each topic to reduce the number of topics and avoid potential repetitions.

Lemke (2011) argues that larger transmedia complexes have already grown beyond the capacity of individuals to cogently analyze them, which means that communities may be needed to investigate transmedia phenomena. In this sense, the model's structure is not deceptively intended to address the transmedia phenomenon in all its possible scope but to focus on the design of transmedia projects to help scholars and practitioners better organize their approach to complex transmedia supersystems. The model is objective, but it is certainly not restrictive, as its analytical and operational perspectives are not limited to the questions and prepositions presented below. Other questions and layers of understanding can be added. Although the methodological stance we propose is qualitative, quantitative methods could also be combined with the model if appropriate. We introduce the five constitutive topics of the transmedia design analytical and operational model below.

Story

The world the story inhabits determines the narrative but, moreover, the possibility to expand the transmedia supersystem. The storyworld should be robust enough to support expansions, as this is a *sine qua non* condition for transmedia storytelling. The world of a transmedia supersystem could eventually function as a primary character of the story because of the major role the system could play—think of Pandora, the world of the transmedia franchise *Avatar*. Long (2007) reiterates the shift from the traditional character-building approach toward a worldbuilding one as inherent to transmedia stories, and Saldre and Torop (2012) emphasize worldmaking as an essential feature of transmedia stories with the broader scope of its applicability.

A narrative creates "a world and populate[s] it with characters and objects" (Ryan, 2004, p. 8). In this sense, Phillips (2012, p. 149) suggests to "make your audience a character, too." In the same way the world can play a major role in transmedia supersystems and be considered a character of its own, the involvement of the audience, as the main specificity of transmedia storytelling, can offer the opportunity for the audience to play a determinant role as well.

> To create characters for transmedia stories is more than to describe who they are, what they like or dislike, and how they look. The features of the characters and the way they appear across all the platforms should be in unison
>
> (Gambarato, 2013, p. 91)

As a strategy for (1) intertwining storyworlds, specific narratives, and characters; (2) expanding the narrative; and (3) motivating audiences to migrate from one medium to another within a given transmedia supersystem, negative capability and migratory cues can be used. In the context of storytelling, negative capability indicates the ability to build strategic gaps into a narrative to provoke a sense of uncertainty and mystery in the audience (see Long, 2007, pp. 53–59). Associated with negative capability are migratory cues that represent these gaps' functions as directional pointers for intertextual connections within the storyworld (see Long, 2007, pp. 139–166). The following practicable questions should be considered:

1 What is the central world in which the project is set?
2 How is the world presented geographically?
3 What would be the summary of the storyline?

4   What is the timeframe of the story?
5   What are the strategies for expanding the narrative? For instance, are negative capability and migratory cues included?
6   Who are the primary and secondary characters of the story?
7   Could the storyworld be considered a primary character?
8   Could the audience be considered a character?

Premise

Bernardo (2011) advises that a transmedia story must be based on a premise and must state clearly what it is about. "The purpose, the reason for which a transmedia project exists, is key to define not just how, where, and to whom the project is oriented, but above all to determine for what it serves" (Gambarato, 2013, p. 90). A clearly defined premise and purpose are fundamental not only because without them people likely would not be interested in engaging in the project but also because they serve as a basis for understanding why the project was structured in one way instead of another. For instance, if the purpose of a project is not to make a profit, this can guide the choice of the media extensions in different ways—depending on what it is available to (and affordable by) the producers—than in projects that are meant to make a profit. Relevant questions that may be considered:

1   What is the project about?
2   Is it a fictional, nonfictional, or mixed project?
3   What is its fundamental purpose? Is it to entertain, to teach, to inform, or to market a product?

Extensions

A transmedia project necessarily involves more than one medium and can embrace more than one genre (science fiction, action, comedy, etc.). The strategy for expanding transmedia supersystems presupposes the types of media extensions and what they serve, considering variables such as the purpose, the target audience, and the timeline for the release of the extensions.

> Selecting the platforms that will be part of a transmedia project is the art of matching the right content to the right audience throughout the most appropriate way, which includes platforms and devices that are suitable to the challenge. Each medium has its own distinctive characteristics and should contribute to the whole transmedia experience. The platform timing, or roll-out, is equally important for the project design, i.e. when the platforms will be released according to the project objectives, business model and resources.
>
> (Gambarato, 2013, p. 92)

Furthermore, Harvey (2014) emphasizes that "central to transmedia story-telling is consistency—perhaps of scenario, of plot, of character—expressed through narrative and iconography" (p. 279). Within the storyworld, consistency and continuity, or the logic of the story, should be maintained throughout the extensions. In addition, the aesthetic components of a transmedia project, such as visuals, color palettes, graphics, fonts, shapes, textures, and audio, are powerful tools for attracting and maintaining audience engagement. "The design elements do not function as mere illustration of the content. Actually, they are part of the story themselves" (Gambarato, 2013, p. 95). Therefore, the following questions should be pondered:

1 What media extensions (film, book, video game, comic book, mobile app, etc.) are involved in the project?
2 Does each media extension enrich the story?
3 What devices (computer, game console, tablet, mobile phone, etc.) are required by the project?
4 What is the roll-out strategy for releasing the media extensions?
5 Which genres (action, adventure, detective, science fiction, fantasy, etc.) are present in the project?
6 What types of visuals (animation, video, graphics, a mix) are used in the project?
7 Is it possible to identify specific design styles in the project?

Audience

Scoping the audience is crucial to more appropriately deliver a transmedia experience. The rules of digital engagement proposed by Mike Dicks (see Nikolic, 2016; Pratten, 2015) describe quantitatively that 75% of the audience are passive spectators (traditional content), 20% are players (interactive content), and 5% are producers (deep content). Although these numbers can vary greatly across contexts, it is undeniable that in the transmedia realm audiences take multiple roles as more active and/or dynamic (fluid) audiences, as discussed in Chapter 2. In this context, transmedia projects can function as cultural attractors and/or cultural activators. Jenkins (2006), borrowing from Pierre Lèvy's (1997) understanding of collective intelligence, defines cultural attractors as projects that attract people of similar interests (consequently, individuals begin to pool their knowledge together) and cultural activators as projects that give audiences something to do, some meaningful form of participation. Highlighting audience engagement in transmedia stories, Scolari states that "transmedia narratives can be represented as a centrifugal process: From an initial text a narrative big bang is produced, in which new texts will be generated to reach user-generated content" (Mungioli, 2011, p. 130). User-generated content (UCG) is a key participatory element in transmedia supersystems, as emphasized in Chapter 2.

In terms of the market, the financial issues around transmedia projects are not restricted to the traditional production model of films, for instance, in which it is commonly necessary to raise money in advance and mainly throughout investors. Transmedia projects can range from multimillion-dollar Hollywood productions to low-cost, crowdfunded, and grassroots productions. Different business models, such as free, premium (costumers have to pay to have access), freemium (a combination of free and premium), and crowdfunding (funding a project by raising small amounts of money from a large number of people), can be part of transmedia productions. Pertinent questions to reflect on are the following:

1 Who is the target audience of the project?
2 What is the project's business model?
3 What are the mechanisms of interaction in this project?
4 Is participation also involved in the project?
5 Does the project work as a cultural attractor or activator?
6 Is user-generated content (fan fiction, parodies, recaps, mashups, etc.) part of the project?

Structure

The organization of a transmedia project, the arrangement and integration of its elements, and how they interrelate to each other within a transmedia supersystem can offer concrete elements for analysis. Gambarato (2013, p. 94) suggested that a "visual map or chart of its elements in space and time can facilitate the visualization of the project," and Hayes (2011, p. 13) adds that "one or two very detailed charts will show how platforms, and the channels within them, are interconnected and how content and data flows around this technical ecosystem." Another important structural aspect of a transmedia project is when the transmedia process began, that is, when the starting process of developing a transmedia storyworld occurs. Davidson (2010) uses the terms proactive and retroactive to refer to stories that are designed to be transmedia from the beginning and to stories that became transmedial *a posteriori*, respectively. Proactive transmedia projects are considered transmedial from the beginning, full of tie-ins planned from the very beginning. In contrast,

> retroactive transmedia stories are the ones that start to be planned after the fact normally based on a successful preexistent project. This is the case when a book, for example, is already created and it is subsequently expanded to become a transmedia experience
>
> (Gambarato, 2013, p. 87)

as we discussed in relation to the transmedia effect presented in Chapter 2.

As there is no one-model-fits-all type of transmedia project, there are different terms (see Dena, 2009; Mittell, 2014; Phillips, 2012, Pratten 2015) to describe different types of transmedia stories. For their overarching reach, and because they embrace more explicitly the inherent complexity of transmedia supersystems, we prefer Pratten's (2015) terminology: (1) transmedia franchise, (2) transmedia portmanteau, and (3) complex transmedia experience.

> [A] [t]ransmedia franchise, according to Pratten, is a series of individual media outlets, such as a comic book, a TV show, a film, etc. Each media platform involved is independent except that they cover different narrative spaces, such as prequels and sequels. The 'classical' example of this model is *The Matrix* (1999) by the Wachowski brothers. In between each feature film, additional content (including graphic novels, animations, video games and memorabilia, for instance) were released to give the audience a richer understanding of the storyworld and to help keep fans engaged. Other examples could be TV series *24*, *Mad Men*, and *Heroes*, for instance.
>
> (Gambarato, 2013, p. 85)

Portmanteau transmedia refers to multiple platforms contributing to a single experience. The core aspect is that the content is distributed simultaneously throughout different media platforms, and each part is necessary for the audience to understand and enjoy the story. The main examples proposed by Pratten (2015) of this type of transmedia story are alternate reality games (ARGs): An ARG "covers a single narrative across multiple platforms—each alone insufficient to carry the complete narrative but like puzzle pieces they must be assembled to complete the story" (Gambarato, 2013, p. 86). An ARG is an interactive narrative that blends real-life treasure hunting, interactive storytelling, and an online community, conflating a series of complicated puzzles normally involving online and offline experiences. Well-known examples of ARGs are *The Beast* (2001), connected to Steven Spielberg's film *A.I.: Artificial Intelligence*; *I Love Bees* (2004), linked to the video game *Halo 2*; *Why So Serious?* (2007), associated with Christopher Nolan's film *The Dark Knight*; and *The Maester's Path* (2011), related to the HBO series *Game of Thrones*.

Pratten (2015) calls complex transmedia experience the third type of transmedia story, which combines franchise and portmanteau, offering the audience a broader experience. Thus, this type of transmedia project is a hybrid produced by the integration of the previous two types. A well-known example is the TV series *Lost*:

> A prominent example of a complex transmedia experience is the TV series *Lost* (ABC, 2004–2010), which incorporates traces of franchise (TV series, mobisodes, books, and more) and an ARG called the *Lost*

Experience, produced in 2006. The ARG contributed to the storyworld expansion, revealing the background story of the Hanso Foundation and the DHARMA (Department of Heuristics and Research on Material Applications) Initiative, which were at the heart of *Lost*. *Lost Experience* played a key role luring audiences to the *Lost* universe.

(Gambarato & Nanì, 2016, p. 151)

Regarding the structure, the following questions can be contemplated:

1   When did the transmediation begin? Is it a proactive or retroactive project?
2   Is this project closer to a transmedia franchise, a portmanteau transmedia story, or a complex transmedia experience?
3   What are the possible endpoints of the project?
4   How is the project structured?

To facilitate the application of the revised model, it is briefly described and summarized in the following table (see Table 3.1) and schematically visualized in the radial diagram (see Figure 3.1). A radial diagram flows from the inside out or the outside in.

Analysis can lead to synthesis (to praxis) and therefore the analysis of an intricate transmedia project such as *The Handmaid's Tale*, which represents the idea of the transmedia effect, can simultaneously illustrate the applicability of the revised model and contribute to advance transmedia practices. Freeman (2016) reassures that "our role as media industry studies scholars is perhaps to be brainstormers and analysts to help theoretically advance cutting-edge media industry workings" (p. 205).

Case study: transmedia design analysis of *The Handmaid's Tale*

We chose *The Handmaid's Tale* as a case study based on the following rationale: (1) the need for a fictional case to start with, as our goal is to develop the analytical model further, which serves fictional and nonfictional transmedia stories; (2) although it is important for the logic of the chapter and the methods section to include a fictional case, we wanted to choose a compelling example that would not be far from the core of the book, which is the connection between transmedia dynamics and real stories; (3) the recognition that *The Handmaid's Tale* presents an admirable and fascinating case of how a fictional story from the 1980s became so relevant and sparked a wave of user-generated content, audience engagement, and diversified activism especially related to Trump administration issues; and (4) the relevance of *The Handmaid's Tale* as an example of longform worldbuilding that goes above and beyond the adaptation and dramatization realms to become a truly complex transmedia supersystem.

Table 3.1 Concise description of the transmedia design analytical and operational model

Nr.	Topic	Practicable questions
1	**Story** The building of a storyworld with its narratives and characters that is robust enough to support expansions.	What is the central world in which the project is set? How is the world presented geographically? What would be the summary of the storyline? What is the timeframe of the story? What are the strategies for expanding the narrative? For instance, are negative capability and migratory cues included? Who are the primary and secondary characters of the story? Could the storyworld be considered a primary character? Could the audience be considered a character?
2	**Premise** What the project is about and why it exists.	What is the project about? Is it a fictional, nonfictional, or mixed project? What is its fundamental purpose? Is it to entertain, to teach, to inform, or to market a product?
3	**Extensions** Transmedia storytelling involves multiple media in which the storyworld will be unfolded and experienced.	What media extensions (film, book, video game, comic book, mobile app, etc.) are involved in the project? Does each extension enrich the story? What devices (computer, game console, tablet, mobile phone, etc.) are required by the project? What is the roll-out strategy for releasing the media extensions? Which genres (action, adventure, detective, science fiction, fantasy, etc.) are present in the project? What types of visuals (animation, video, graphics, a mix) are used in the project? Is it possible to identify specific design styles in the project?
4	**Audience** Scoping the audience is fundamental to more appropriately deliver the transmedia experience. Transmedia storytelling involves some level of audience engagement.	Who is the target audience of the project? What is the project's business model? What are the mechanisms of interaction in this project? Is participation also involved in the project? Does the project work as a cultural attractor or activator? Is user-generated content (fan fiction, parodies, recaps, mashups, etc.) part of the project?
5	**Structure** The organization of a transmedia project, the arrangement of its constituent elements, and how they interrelate to each other offer concrete elements for understanding the project.	When did the transmediation begin? Is it a proactive or retroactive project? Is this project closer to a transmedia franchise, a portmanteau transmedia story, or a complex transmedia experience? What are the possible endpoints of the project? How is the project structured?

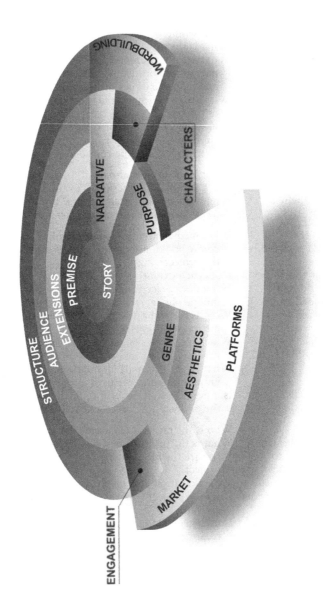

Figure 3.1 Transmedia design analytical and operational model.

Story

"Sometimes, discovering a new fictional world is like forming a crush on a relative stranger" (Miller, 2019, para. 1). Despite all the excitement of discovering a new storyworld, it often does not hold up the more you learn about it, and disappointment and disinterest can occur. Fortunately, that is not always the case, and it seems clear by now that disenchantment did not happen as *The Handmaid's Tale* storyworld evolved in recent years. The well-known Canadian writer Margaret Atwood published *The Handmaid's Tale* in 1985. The book tells the story of Offred, a handmaid in the Republic of Gilead, a totalitarian and theocratic state that replaced part of the United States. Gilead—plagued by environmental issues, toxic wastelands, and pollution—has dangerously low reproduction rates, and consequently, the handmaids (the fertile caste in this dystopian society) are assigned to bear children for those elite families who cannot conceive. The freedom of all women in Gilead is completely restricted, and they are constantly monitored by the state and inside their households. Gilead's reality is brutal and cruel, and women suffer excruciating moral and physical abuse and oppression, such as systematic rapes, disfigurements, mutilations, and prohibitions on access to money and reading materials. "The religious theme lies in the background of the plot and is used to justify several of the perpetrated evil-doings in the story" (Mascio, 2019, p. 2). The storyworld built around Gilead represents such a powerful and eloquent picture of what it is like to live there, and the design of this fictional autocratic state with its caste-based system determines the destiny of the story to an extent, that Gilead itself could be considered a protagonist in *The Handmaid's Tale*. "The TV series clearly depicts the construction of a society ruled according to a strict caste-based system, easily recognizable by viewers because in many instances they are expressed through visual, linguistic and behavioral codes" (Mascio, 2019, p. 5). Atwood created not only the world of Gilead but also worked on its evolution first in conjunction with Bruce Miller, the showrunner of the Hulu series *The Handmaid's Tale* launched in 2017 (and currently in production for the fourth season), and in 2019 with the launch of the original's book sequel *The Testaments*. Atwood's storyworld has the potential to continue even further:

> In terms of worldbuilding, Atwood gave Miller a road map that could theoretically stretch centuries into the future. And Miller and his creative team have been skilled at inventing new ways to illustrate how the country of Gilead—a separatist state in a splintered America—operates politically and personally.
>
> (Miller, 2019, para. 4)

One strategy for expanding *The Handmaid's Tale* storyworld is exploring the past and the future of the main characters. For instance, in the TV series, Bruce Miller's team of writers expanded the character backstories and flashbacks to explain the changes and circumstances that led to the rise of Gilead (Miller, 2019). In *The Testaments*, Atwood examines the future of Gilead around 15 years after the events described in the final scene of the original book with the two daughters of the protagonist Offred/June among the narrators with Aunt Lydia, a notorious villain in the handmaid's story-world (Feldman, 2019b). The dichotomy hidden behind the two names of the protagonist Offred/June is relevant: "The double/dual is in effect one of the main themes of the novel. The same narrative structure develops through the highlighting of on-going oppositions: before and after, freedom and imprisonment, fertility and sterility, [and] secularism and religion" (Mascio, 2019, p. 2). Interestingly, in the book, Offred's real name is omitted:

> While many readers believe the book contains a deliberate hint as to what it is, Atwood's choice to keep Offred nameless was quite deliberate at the time. [...] The show, meanwhile, doesn't just choose to name Offred. It makes the reveal—'my name is June'—the bold final note of the premiere. It's just one of the ways the show has sought to bring this world to life, while also building a foundation that could last for years on the small screen.
>
> (Miller, 2017a, para. 10)

In a detailed explanation, Atwood stated that "[s]ome have deduced that Offred's real name is June, since, of all the names whispered among the Handmaids in the gymnasium/dormitory, 'June' is the only one that never appears again. That was not my original thought, but it fits" (Cummins, 2019, para. 2). Moreover, the development of primary characters such as Commander Fred Waterford and his wife Serena Joy (whom Offred serves) beyond the framework provided by the book and the first season of the TV series demonstrates how the transmedia supersystem around Gilead evolved and unfolded in front of an eager global audience. Joseph Fiennes, the actor who portrays Commander Waterford, commented on the development of his character:

> what I think about is those young folks dressing up as handmaids in Alabama, silently protesting [against their new, very restrictive abortion legislation]; you feel as if you're in something very important and very pertinent to people. So, it's great. At least I've done my bit for society, I've illustrated the patheticness of misogyny. Fred is very thinly illustrated in the book, so I didn't know how it would open up. It's luck, I think. I just got lucky, lucky, lucky.
>
> (Williams, 2019, para. 19)

The eloquence of the story took contemporary audiences by storm as handmaid June (portrayed by actress Elisabeth Moss in the TV show) fights within the autocratic regime to try to destroy it when the world's political climate shows astonishing parallels with the speculative fiction of Gilead. The launch of the TV series in early 2017, right after the election of Donald Trump as the president of the United States, received critical and public accolades, and the series rapidly became a social phenomenon: "a symbol of the new resistance, with the handmaids' uniform co-opted by protesters at US courthouses, on marches, and in Hollywood itself" (Mulkerrins, 2018, para. 2). The audience became a character as well.

The resurgent *The Handmaid's Tale* was discussed by Žižek (2019) in the context of what Jameson (1991) called "nostalgia for the present":

> it is permeated by the sentimental admiration for our liberal-permissive present ruined by the new Christian-fundamentalist rule, and it never even approaches the question of what is wrong in this present so that it gave birth to the nightmarish Republic of Gilead.
>
> (para. 9)

Joseph Fiennes, commenting on the timing of the show's launch, stated, "We got lucky with the zeitgeist" (Williams, 2019, para. 6). Nobody could predict the overwhelming impact of the show based on a well-known story, as the first season had been filmed before the election: "They woke up the next morning and said, 'We're a different show.' Nothing about the show changed, but the frame changed," stated Atwood (Setoodeh, 2018, para. 17)—except nostalgia for the present arose:

> During another year, this show might have had less of an impact, but in 2017, watching 'The Handmaid's Tale' ended up feeling like a primal scream; one which echoed back in a way to make us feel heard. And it also just so happened to be beautifully acted, written, and directed, every step of the way.
>
> (Travers, Miller, Nguyen, & Greene, 2017, para. 15)

Premise

Atwood's process of creating the original dystopian world of Gilead is entirely based on real facts that happened at some point in history in some part of the world. She explained,

> I had been thinking about this book for a while. I had been collecting newspaper clippings, which one did in those days. There was no internet. So, my rule for it was, nothing goes in that didn't have a precedent in real life—somewhere, sometime.
>
> (Setoodeh, 2018, para. 4)

Bacci (2017, p. 155) argues that "[d]ystopic scenarios are commonly used to criticize current trends, societal norms, or political systems." *The*

Handmaid's Tale did it back in the 1980s and does it now in the late 2010s. Moreover, Atwood blurs the line between fiction and nonfiction to a dramatic extent that amazes audiences and incorporates a sort of prophetic tone in her prose. According to Goethe, few people have the imagination for the truth of reality (Moorhead, 1930), implying that our imagination can easily fall short in comparison to the real world. For instance, the main feature of Gilead's society is its theocratic stance and the caste system in which the dominant class monopolizes everything that is valuable, including the manipulation of fertile women as handmaids. Society aggregates the handmaids and divides them among the sterile elite families. Atwood (2017) posited that there is a biblical precedent: the story of Jacob and his two wives Rachel and Leah, and their two female servants. One man, four women, and a dozen descendants whom the servants could not claim because they belonged to the wives.

> The Handmaids are trained for their new roles at Gilead's The Rachel and Leah Center (aka The Red Center). The center is a direct reference to the Old Testament story of Rachel and her sister Leah, both of whom married Jacob. While Leah had no trouble conceiving children, Rachel was unable to get pregnant. Frustrated, Rachel offered up her handmaid, Bilhah, to Jacob as a 'vessel' through which she could have children. Bilhah gave birth to two sons, both of whom were named by Rachel. The story serves as an inspiration not only for the role of the Handmaids as 'breeders,' but for the entire founding of Gilead. The group that overthrew the United States government and established Gilead in Atwood's dystopian novel is named Sons of Jacob.
>
> (Regalado, 2019, para. 5–7)

Mascio (2019) states that the biblical precept of the Genesis where Jacob laid with a servant at his wife Rachel's request to conceive a child depicts the handmaid as a tool in the service of God's will. *The Handmaid's Tale*, according to Atwood (2017), was based on several different facets of reality: group executions, sexist laws, book burnings, the Lebensborn program (a state-supported registered association in Nazi Germany with the aim of increasing the birth rate of Aryan children), the theft of children in Argentina by generals, witchcraft cases, the 17th-century Puritan theocracy in the United States, the history of slavery, the history of polygamy in the United States, and so on (see Regalado, 2019). The list is long and includes the story's fashion: The demure clothes in Gilead come from Western religious iconography, with wives wearing the blue of purity of the Virgin Mary and the handmaids dressing in vivid red related to the blood of childbirth and menstruation but also connected to Mary Magdalene. In addition, red is easier to see if they try to escape.

"Despite its dystopian future setting, Hulu's *The Handmaid's Tale* often feels all too real—and it's not by accident" (Wigler, 2019, para. 1).

The chilling level of reality of the TV show is increased by the involvement of the consultant Andi Gitow, a United Nations (UN) executive media producer. The goal is to authentically represent real conflicts and struggles, such as those seen in the series in relation to the immigration of traumatized people from Gilead to Canada and their journey toward rehabilitation (Wigler, 2019). The first two seasons have "undeniably made countless implicit references to sociopolitical conditions around the world," and the trailer for the third season goes one step further to allegedly make "its most explicit references to U.S. politics yet" (Park, 2019, para 1) as a clear allusion to Ronald Reagan's 1984 *Morning in America* reelection campaign ad:

> 'It's morning again in America, and under the leadership of President Reagan, our country is prouder and stronger and better. Why would we ever want to return to where we were less than four short years ago?' the narrator concluded, in a line that seems like something straight from Atwood's pen.
>
> (Park, 2019, para. 4)

Discussing transmedia television, Evans (2011, p. 25) indicates that "the potential pleasure offered in such moments is precisely the ambiguous merging of reality and fiction as the audience immerses themselves in that 'paranoid mist', allowing their engagement with the story world to spread away from the television."

Although *The Handmaid's Tale* is a commercial transmedia supersystem with clear financial interests, the purpose of the project—expanded through the transmedia effect—arguably exceeds the mere commercialization and commodification instances of the storyworld. Atwood affirmed that *The Handmaid's Tale* is no longer her own (Cummins, 2019):

> 'It's been an example of a work escaping from its name—its box—and coming alive through the imaginations of its readers. I can't even say that it is 'my' 'Handmaid's Tale.' It seems to have taken a life of its own that is not under the control of its first creator (me) and its other creators (the makers of the show),' the author says in the book 'The Art and Making of The Handmaid's Tale.'
>
> (Salvi, 2019, para. 10)

Gilead bears uncanny parallels to the world we live in, and even the criticisms of the TV show (see Brown, 2018; Hill, 2019; Miller, 2018), because of the dark evolution of its storyworld, especially regarding women's oppression, seem to denote how impactful and socially relevant the debates raised by the series are. Žižek (2019) argues that Atwood's Gilead illustrates our fascination with other people's pain in the sense that "the sight of the other's suffering is the obscure cause of desire which sustains our own happiness (bliss in heaven)—if we take it away, our bliss appears in all its sterile stupidity" (para. 7). Žižek (2019) ponders that

> The novel and the television series allow us to dwell in the weird pleasure in fantasising a world of brutal patriarchal domination. Of course, nobody would openly admit the desire to live in such nightmarish world, but this assurance that we really don't want it makes fantasising about it, imagining all the details of this world, all the more pleasurable. Yes, we feel pain while experiencing this pleasure, but psychoanalyst Jacques Lacan's name for this pleasure-in-pain is *jouissance*.
>
> (para. 8)

The parallels in terms of the militarization of the United States and Gilead are undeniable. The book portrays this militarization as the new normal, and the TV series reinforces it via Aunt Lydia's affirmation that this will be normal one day. Moss, who stars and produces the series, has no tolerance for people who do not want to watch the show because it is too frightening, too gruesome. She stated, "I hate hearing that someone couldn't watch it because it was too scary," and this is "[n]ot because I care about whether or not they watch my TV show; I don't give a shit. But I'm like, 'Really? You don't have the balls to watch a TV show?'" "This is happening in your real life. Wake up, people. Wake up" (Mulkerrins, 2018, para. 21). The mix of reality and speculative fiction in this case contributes to the meaningfulness of this transmedia supersystem. Evans (2011) concludes that "transmedia texts have become less about promoting a central television programme or film, and more about creating a coherent, deliberately cross-platform narrative experience" (p. 20) and that is the case of *The Handmaid's Tale*, a commercial project with much deeper aspirations than exclusively making a profit.

Extensions

> The TMW [transmedial world] is not defined by the material entity of any particular instantiation (the media platform) but by the shared idea of the world, a sort of platonic approach that situates the ontological status of the TMW in a disembodied plane. We call this mental image 'worldness,' and a number of distinguishing and recognizable features of the TMW originate from the first version, or *instantiation*, of the world but can be elaborated and changed over time.
>
> (Klastrup & Tosca, 2014, p. 297)

The Handmaid's Tale storyworld—originated in the first book—has evolved and unfolded across different media platforms, generating a variety of media extensions. However, although not all these extensions represent an expansion of content, all are part of the *worldness* mentioned by Klastrup and Tosca and contribute to form *The Handmaid's Tale* transmedia supersystem. The media extensions in this case are (1) the original book (Atwood, 1985) written by Atwood in Berlin, Germany, and available in multiple formats; (2) the 1990 feature film (starring Natasha Richardson and Faye Dunaway, with a screenplay by Harold Pinter); (3) the BBC radio drama in 2000; (4) the 2000 opera *The Handmaid's Aria* written by distinguished Danish composer Poul Ruders; (5) multiple stage play versions and ballets; (6) the ongoing TV series launched in 2017; (7) accounts on major social media networks, such as Facebook, Twitter, and Instagram; (8) numerous merchandise items such as t-shirts, posters, mugs, and costumes; (9) the 2019 graphic novel with illustrations by Canadian artist Renée Nault; and (10) the sequel book *The Testaments* (Atwood, 2019) available in multiple formats. In September 2019, Hulu and MGM announced that they would develop *The Testaments* for the screen: "It's unclear at this stage what form The Testaments will take—whether it will be folded into the existing Hulu series or developed as a separate work" (Feldman, 2019a, para. 1).

Especially after the success of the TV series, the amount of *The Handmaid's Tale* merchandise available increased considerably. Items such as t-shirts with iconic phrases from the story—"blessed be fruit," "praise be," "under his yes"—and the handmaids' red robes and white bonnets acquired a symbolic value: "In fact, in a very short time *The Handmaid's Tale* has become a sort of cultural symbol, being recognized and shared globally" (Mascio, 2019, p. 1). Merchandise can function as a paratext, and "whereas they may serve a promotional purpose they are integrated into the text" (Evans, 2011, p. 27). Notwithstanding, there are branding and marketing ideas that can go terribly wrong. The producers of the TV series suffered a "thunderous social media backlash" (Jerde, 2019, para. 1) after launching a line of wines named after the main female characters on the show: Offred, Ofglen, and Serena Joy. "The wines faced criticism for being a tone-deaf marketing ploy, as the show is about a dystopian America where women have little freedom and rights" (Clark, 2018, para. 2). The products were immediately canceled.

To spread expanded content—paratexts—such as behind-the-scenes imagery and stories, UGC such as fan art and fan fiction, and promote the TV show with trailers, GIFs, and awards, for instance, Hulu producers incorporate various accounts on online social media networks. However, the transmedia extensions that most effectively represent the expansion of *The Handmaid's Tale* storyworld are the TV series and the sequel book. It is not by chance that Mittell (2014, p. 253) argues that "[f]ew storytelling forms can match serial television for narrative breadth and vastness." Although the first season of the series is regarded as a direct adaptation of the original book, Elisabeth Moss pointed out that the first season was not a simple facsimile of the book, either: timelines were altered, some details were changed, while partial sentences were extrapolated from the text to create entire scenes and stories. 'We were faithful to the idea and the tone and the messages of the book,' she says, 'but we kept characters alive that died, and we did things that were never in the book, so we're not afraid of that.'

(Mulkerrins, 2018, para. 9)

From Season Two onward, the series evolved and further developed the story but always in close collaboration with Atwood. Showrunner Bruce Miller "confirmed that Atwood has been just as involved this [second] season as she was last time, even though much of the original novel's plot was covered by those first ten episodes" (Miller, 2017b, para. 12). Eventually, other details of the original book recur in later seasons. Fiennes, in a recent Instagram post, mentioned his excitement at seeing a line from the book appear in Season Three:

I've been waiting for this line from the book 2 seasons, and finally they put it in episode. In the book at the end of chapter 10, well before he has asked her to go in secret to his office, Offred said: 'I ought to feel hatred for this man. I know I ought to feel it, but it isn't what I do feel. What I feel is more complicated than that. I don't know what to call it. It isn't love.' This shows her feelings towards the Commander are complex in terms of what her feelings are not. They are not 'love', they are 'more complicated' than that. I see it like twisted sympathy or Stockholm syndrome.

(Fiennes, 2019)

The concept of *The Testaments* is based on Atwood's interaction with audiences since the first book was published and her observations of the real world. She posited, "Dear Readers: Everything you've ever asked me about Gilead and its inner workings is the inspiration for this book. Well, almost everything! The other inspiration is the world we've been living in" (Penguin, 2018, para. 6). The relationship between the book sequel and the subsequent seasons of the TV series is still to be determined. Nevertheless, the closeness maintained between Atwood and Miller's creative team seems strong enough to sustain the growth of *The Handmaid's Tale* world without discrepancies and discontinuity.

Regarding the devices needed to access this transmedia supersystem, audiences must have a TV set or a computer, tablet, or mobile phone screen, and in relation to genre, *The Handmaid's Tale* is considered dystopian speculative fiction, exploring social and political structures.

The visuality and iconography of *The Handmaid's Tale* world are among its powerful features. Although there were several visual representations *of The Handmaid's Tale* world before the TV series premiered in 2017, the

Hulu production exceled at presenting extremely well-crafted cinematography, set design, costume design, and so on. The expansion of the story-world with the subsequent seasons also involved the further development of the series iconography. For instance, the second season presented the Colonies, "nightmarish bucolic" (Grobar, 2018, para. 1) areas that have been contaminated by pollution and radioactive waste. Referring to the colors of the Colonies, production designer Elisabeth Williams stated that "it was also important that we have these golds and amber colors, and light blues. It's very reminiscent of Dutch paintings, and yet you have these dying women working the soil and basically killing themselves to better Gilead" (Grobar, 2018, para. 5). The characters' wardrobe is one of the main visual elements explored in the book and in all the visual representations for the functionality of clothing in defining the caste-based society. Atwood, for example, described the blue of the elite wives as a virginal blue, a sky blue, in reference to the Virgin Mary. However, the TV show took some creative license to expand the color palette. Ane Crabtree, the show's costume designer, explained,

> I am a huge rabid fan of Margaret Atwood, and of course followed the novel for much of what we did. When we first got started with Season One, the design went into a very dark emotional version of the red and the blue in the book, which is one reason we didn't do sky blue. Our red became blood red, and the idea for the teal blue followed thereafter. We play with color in the camera work and the use of filters in our show, and we wanted something that was hauntingly beautiful, and hauntingly disrupted. I'm a fan of the original film, and Margaret Atwood is a producer on our show so I could write to her and ask questions at any time. I followed Margaret's story for many of the costume ideas, but I did change out the striped dresses for the Econo-wives; instead I did grey.
>
> (Aloi, 2018, para. 12)

The visuality of the show in general and the costume design in particular were re-signified by the appropriation audiences made of it. We discuss this point next.

Audience

The Handmaid's Tale is a premium project in terms of the business model, as audiences must pay to access its major media extensions, such as the books, the film, and the streaming service TV series. As the original book is Atwood's seminal work praised worldwide, this storyworld has been of interest to global audiences for several decades. The renewed interest in the story marked by the launch of Hulu's series in 2017 (concomitantly with Donald Trump's election as the U.S. president), and its audience reach is evidenced by the appropriations of the story made by the public. In 2017, before the series premiere, women dressed as handmaids appeared on the streets of New York City and Los Angeles as a marketing stunt to promote the show. Suddenly, however, they were no longer viral marketing: They became political protests (Miller, 2017a). In March 2017, they appeared in front of the Austin, Texas, state capital building to protest in favor of abortion rights. A political action group, NARAL Texas, was inspired by the promotional stunt for Hulu's show and organized the first handmaid-themed protest. About this episode, Atwood commented,

> They were in the Texas Legislature surrounded by men with guns. It could have been a still right out of [the show]. It was uncanny … They're now an immediately recognizable symbol—they have been for a while, but I can't control them now. They're out of control.
>
> (Miller, 2017a, para. 8)

This topic is relevant not only in the United States. In reference to abortion legislation, in July 2018, a group of women marched in front of the Argentinian Congress in Buenos Aires to protest in favor of abortion rights (Abdala, 2018). In 2019, the same topic resurged with the latest abortion ban in Alabama, and handmaids were there to protest (Salvi, 2019). The political action group Handmaid Coalition publishes online on their website handmaidcoalition.org guidelines for making red robes and white bonnets and organizing a handmaids' protest.

In January 2018, during the Golden Globe Awards ceremony, handmaids were found outside the ceremony's venue: The women were the self-proclaimed Hollywood Handmaids group demanding "an end to sexual assaults and inequalities in the industry" (Mulkerrins, 2018, para. 3). Mascio (2019, p. 7) argues that the handmaids' uniforms "become therefore the symbol of protest also partially comprising the #Metoo movement." The #MeToo movement has fought against sexual harassment and sexual assault since 2006, but it regained traction in 2017 in the midst of the widespread sexual abuse allegations against Hollywood film producer Harvey Weinstein. In addition, women dressed as handmaids have protested in Ireland and in England:

> 'The Handmaid's Tale' dressed pro-choice protesters in 2018 during Ireland's successful referendum to revoke the eighth amendment of its constitution—by inserting a subsection recognizing the equal right to life of the pregnant woman and the unborn. The costume was also worn by abortion rights campaigners in Buenos Aires. In London, protestors sported the red-and-white suit to protest US President Donald Trump's administration and his policies during his visit.
>
> (Salvi, 2019, para. 3–4)

Women's reproductive rights became an issue directly connected to *The Handmaid's Tale* storyworld, and recently, the cast of the Hulu show participated in the campaign "Abortion care is healthcare" promoted by *Harper's Bazaar* and Planned Parenthood (*Harper's Bazaar*, 2019). Another form of activism linked to *The Handmaid's Tale* takes place online with memes, selfies, and especially hashtags, such as #nolitetebastardescarborundorum (don't let the bastards grind you down), #Ofputin (in reference to Trump as a handmaid of Russian President Vladimir Putin), and #underhiseye as symbolic political resistance. Mascio (2019) highlights that the use of hashtags by audiences represents "not only a shared knowledge, namely the fact that the viewers of the tv series recognize themselves" but also "manifests itself as part of a language of women's resistance; a verbal tool acquiring value thanks to its sharing and viral dissemination" (p. 6).

For the premiere of the show's third season in 2019, Hulu promoted *The Handmaid's Tale* with 140 sculptures of women in New York to balance the ratio of statues of men to women in the city: "Of the 150 statues of humans around New York City, 145 are attributed to men, including 10 of generals, five of Christopher Columbus, and another five of George Washington" (Swant, 2019, para. 1). Hulu, commenting on the fact that there are just five statues honoring women in New York, stressed that it is "a shockingly small number, especially when compared to the 145 statues that honor men. Or the 23 statues featuring animals" (The Handmaid's Tale, 2019, para. 3). Hulu's statues representing women's roles in history were made of mirrors, and up close, they gave people the opportunity to interact as they could see themselves reflected in each statue. Furthermore, the TV show offered audiences the opportunity to participate in an authorized fan fiction promotion on Wattpad—"a popular publishing platform for original fiction as well as officially approved tie-in properties" (Miller, 2017a, para. 21)—and to be part of a fan art challenge on Instagram (The Handmaid's Tale [@handmaidsonhulu], 2019) with their own user-generated content. Deuze (2017) addresses the audience collaborative role in transmedia stories:

> Transmedia storytelling is particularly inspiring in its inclusion of the media ensemble, and in its use of the audience in all aspects of the creative process: From generating story ideas to gathering information, from contributing parts of the narrative and research to assisting in its funding and distribution, and from marketing the content to following it up with comments and additional story lines.
>
> (p. 32)

Mittell (2014) proposes the so-called what if transmedia approach in reference to cases in which "transmedia poses hypothetical possibilities rather than canonical certainties, inviting viewers to imagine alternative stories and approaches to storytelling that are distinctly not to be treated as potential canon" (p. 273). More importantly, the examples above show that *The Handmaid's Tale* conflates opportunities for audience interaction and participation that are offered by the producers and by the audiences themselves. In this sense, *The Handmaid's Tale* transmedia supersystem functions as a cultural attractor, uniting people around a common interest, and a cultural activator, giving them the chance to act on and influence the story outcomes, as proposed by Jenkins (2006). Mascio (2019) concludes that "[t]hese are not only fandom's actions as forms of tribute, praise or appropriation of a text; but rather symbols of a kind of sensitivity—propensity—for cultural and political issues" (p. 6). This phenomenon is not exclusive to *The Handmaid's Tale*. For instance, following the worldwide frisson around the film *Joker* (2019) with actor Joaquin Phoenix as the protagonist, "protestors in Chile, Lebanon, Hong Kong, and Iraq have been wearing the 'Joker' clown makeup at public demonstrations protesting government corruption and elitism" (Sharf, 2019, para. 1).

Structure

The Handmaid's Tale is a retroactive project that was not planned to become transmediatic from the beginning. On the contrary, this is a typical case of what we called the transmedia effect in Chapter 2, in which adaptations of the original book across different media platforms gave place to the expansion of its storyworld due to renewed public interest and artistic and political relevance of its core premise. *The Handmaid's Tale* presents itself as a transmedia franchise with independent media extensions inserted in the same storyworld. As Fiennes posits, "[t]here are fans of the book, and there are people who discovered the book through the show" (Williams, 2019, para. 19). Audiences can therefore have different entry points to the story, and there is no endpoint to *The Handmaid's Tale* storyworld as far as can be seen by the launch of the sequel book more than three decades after the first book and the diverse activism appropriations of *The Handmaid's Tale* story in the social-political sphere inspired by the TV series.

Epilogue

Deuze (2017, p. 20) uses the term Martini media, "meaning media that's available when and where you want it with content moving freely between different devices and platforms" to characterize our current media life. As we analyzed in the case of *The Handmaid's Tale*, the multiple media extensions in this transmedia supersystem represent the freedom audiences experience in times of Martini media. Moreover, Deuze (2017) emphasizes the necessity to "stay mindful about the affective engagement of publics with their communities, and of media workers with their field," because "it is that emotional connection that most intensely determines the way these constituencies experience and give meaning to their roles as citizens, consumers, and co-creators of reality" (p. 33). In the context of the TV series, Bourdaa (2013) describes transmedia storytelling as the latest way to imagine and create it:

> now the story has to be complex with a compelling seriality and mythology, engaging for fans to dive emotionally and intellectually into, innovative in its narration and in the way it makes fans interact. It has to have a community of practices and a solid fan base, and finally it has to spread its story and narration across various media platforms. It also has to support fans' collective intelligence in the form of participative sites, like FringePedia, where fans can collect and share information in order to collate the whole dispersed universe of the show.
>
> (p. 213)

With the most recent developments of Atwood's storyworld, *The Handmaid's Tale* seems to have acquired all these features, contributing not only to expansion of the work's transmedia supersystem but also to relevance of disseminating the work's core political criticism, amplification of audience reach and penetration, and the empowerment in favor of collective change amid social relationships and the institutions and discourses of inequality. Evans (2011) states that a "fictional world is an imaginative space that the viewers can lose themselves in" and added that viewers "can lose themselves in a range of different contexts and in which a variety of values and conflicts concerning the relationship between text, viewer and technology come into play" (p. 39). *The Handmaid's Tale* is more than a fictional world. It is a form of storytelling that draws a blurred line in its relation to reality and allows audiences to lose themselves in the world to an extent that surpasses the imaginative and speculative space to affect and motivate them to promote concrete social change.

References

Abdala, V. (2018, July 10). Por el aborto, marchan vestidas com "El cuento de la criada" [For abortion, they march dressed up as "The Handmaid's Tale"]. *Clarín*. Retrieved from https://www.clarin.com/cultura/aborto-marchan-vestidas-cuento-criada_0_HkYiR2GQX.html

Aloi, P. (2018, May 1). "The Handmaid's Tale" costume designer wants to fuel the fire with visuals. *Medium*. Retrieved from https://medium.com/the-establishment/the-handmaids-tale-costume-designer-wants-to-fuel-the-fire-with-visuals-62d08305bc16

Alzamora, G., & Tárcia, L. (2014). Proposed methodology for transmedia news story analysis: A comparative study of The Float Project and The Great British Property Scandal: Every empty counts (2012) in the UK. In: *Proceedings of the 2014 Interactive Narratives, New Media & Social Engagement Conference* (pp. 19–27). Toronto, Canada.

Atwood, M. (1985). *The handmaid's tale*. Toronto, Canada: McClelland & Stewart.

Atwood, M. (2017, May 15). Margaret Atwood: Maldita profecia [Margaret Atwood: Unsacred prophecy]. *El País Semanal*. Retrieved from https://brasil.elpais.com/brasil/2017/05/12/eps/1494603374_701338.html?id_externo_rsoc=FB_BR_CM

Atwood, M. (2019). *The testaments*. New York, NY: Talese/Doubleday.

Bacci, F. (2017). The originality of *The Handmaid's Tale* & *The Children of Men*: Religion, justice, and feminism in dystopian fiction. *Metacritic Journal for Comparative Studies and Theory, 3*(2), 154–172.

Barnouw, E. (1974). *Documentary: A history of the non-fiction film*. Oxford, England: Oxford University Press.

Bernardo, N. (2011). *The producers guide to transmedia: How to develop, fund, produce and distribute compelling stories across multiple platforms*. London, England: CR Entertainment.

Bourdaa, M. (2013). Following the pattern: The creation of an encyclopaedic universe with transmedia storytelling. *Adaptation, 6*(2), 202–214.

Brown, M. (2018, May 28). *The Handmaid's Tale*: Margaret Atwood tells fans to chill out. *The Guardian*. Retrieved from https://www.theguardian.com/tv-and-radio/2018/may/28/the-handmaids-tale-margaret-atwood-tells-fans-to-chill-out-about-tv-divergences?CMP=Share_iOSApp_Other

Ciancia, M. (2015). Transmedia design framework: Design-oriented approach to transmedia research. *International Journal of Transmedia Literacy, 1*(1), 131–145.

Ciancia, M. (2018). *Transmedia design framework: Design-oriented approach to transmedia practice*. Milan, Italy: Franco Angeli.

Ciancia, M., Piredda, F., & Venditti, S. (2018). The design of imaginary worlds. Harnessing narrative potential of transmedia worlds: The case of Watchmen of the Nine. *Facta Ficta Journal of Narrative, Theory & Media, 2*(2), 113–134.

Clark, T. (2018, July 11). A line of wines inspired by Hulu's *The Handmaid's Tale* was killed within hours of its launch after online backlash. *Business Insider*. Retrieved from https://www.businessinsider.com/the-handmaids-tale-inspired-wine-canceled-after-backlash-2018-7?utm_content=buffer40615&utm_medium=social&utm_source=facebook.com&utm_campaign=buffer-dessert&r=US&IR=T&IR=T

Cummins, F. (2019, April 16). What's in a name? Authors on choosing names for their characters. *The Guardian*. Retrieved from https://www.theguardian.com/books/2019/apr/16/whats-in-a-name-authors-on-choosing-names-for-their-characters

Currie, G. (1990). *The nature of fiction*. Cambridge, England: Cambridge University Press.

Davidson, D. (Ed.). (2010). *Cross-media communications: An introduction to the art of creating integrated media experiences*. Pittsburgh, PA: ETC Press.

Dena, C. (2009). *Transmedia practice: Theorising the practice of expressing a fictional world across distinct media and environments* (Unpublished doctoral dissertation). University of Sydney, Sidney, Australia.

Dena, C. (2019). Transmedia adaptation: Revisiting the no-adaptation rule. In M. Freeman & R. R. Gambarato (Eds.), *The Routledge companion to transmedia studies* (pp. 195–206). New York, NY: Routledge.

Deuze, M. J. P. (2017). Media life and media work. In P. Serra & S. Sá (Eds.), *Televisão e novos meios* [Television and new media] (pp. 17–37). Covilhã, Portugal: Labcom.IFP.

Evans, E. (2011). *Transmedia television: Audiences, new media, and daily life.* New York, NY: Routledge.

Feldman, L. (2019a, September 4). Exclusive: Hulu and MGM are developing Margaret Atwood's *The Testaments* for the screen. *Time.* Retrieved from https://time.com/5668056/the-testaments-hulu-margaret-atwood/?utm_medium=social&xid=time_socialflow_facebook&utm_campaign=socialflow&utm_source=facebook

Feldman, L. (2019b, September 10). Let's break down the most mysterious parts of *The Testaments*, with a little help from Margaret Atwood. *Time.* Retrieved from https://time.com/5673535/the-testaments-plot-questions-margaret-atwood/

Fiennes, J. [@justjosephfiennes]. (2019, June 12). *I've been waiting for this line from the book 2 seasons* [Post]. Instagram. Retrieved from https://www.instagram.com/p/BynSiSDAdBV/?igshid=lyrn1zj1gm1a

Freeman, M. (2016). *Industrial approaches to media: A methodological gateway to industry studies.* London, England: Palgrave Macmillan.

Freeman, M. (2017). *Historicising transmedia storytelling: Early twentieth-century transmedia story worlds.* New York, NY: Routledge.

Freeman, M., & Gambarato, R. R. (2019). *The Routledge companion to transmedia studies.* New York, NY: Routledge.

Friend, S. (2012). Fiction as a genre. *Proceedings of the Aristotelian Society, 112,* 179–209.

Gambarato, R. R. (2012). Signs, systems and complexity of transmedia storytelling. *Communication Studies, 12,* 69–83.

Gambarato, R. R. (2013). Transmedia project design: Theoretical and analytical considerations. *Baltic Screen Media Review, 1,* 80–100.

Gambarato, R. R. (2014). Transmedia storytelling in analysis: The case of Final Punishment. *Journal of Print and Media Technology Research, 3*(2), 95–106.

Gambarato, R. R. (2016). The Sochi Project: Slow journalism within transmedia space. *Digital Journalism, 4*(4), 445–461.

Gambarato, R. R. (2018). Russia: Interactive documentary, slow journalism and the transmediality of Grozny: Nine cities. In M. Freeman & W. Proctor (Eds.), *Global convergence cultures: Transmedia earth* (pp. 206–226). New York, NY: Routledge.

Gambarato, R. R. (2019). A design approach to transmedia projects. In M. Freeman & R. R. Gambarato (Eds.), *The Routledge companion to transmedia studies* (pp. 401–409). New York, NY: Routledge.

Gambarato, R. R., & Alzamora, G. (2018). *Exploring transmedia journalism in the digital age.* Hershey, PA: IGI Global.

Gambarato, R. R., & Medvedev, S. (2015). Grassroots political campaign in Russia: Alexei Navalny and transmedia strategies for democratic development. In J. Svensson & V. Kumar (Eds.), *Promoting social change and democracy through information technology* (pp. 165–192). Hershey, PA: IGI Global.

Gambarato, R. R., & Nanì, A. (2016). Blurring boundaries, transmedia storytelling and the ethics of C.S. Peirce. In M. Steven (Ed.), *Ethics in screenwriting: New perspectives* (pp. 147–175). Melbourne, Australia: Palgrave Macmillan.

Gambarato, R. R., & Tárcia, L. (2017). Transmedia strategies in journalism: An analytical model for the coverage of planned events. *Journalism Studies, 18*(11), 1381–1399.

Gitelman, L. (2006). *Always already new: Media, history and the data of culture.* Cambridge, MA: MIT Press.

Grobar, M. (2018, June 11). "The Handmaid's Tale" production designer Elisabeth Williams expands series' world, introducing the colonies. *Deadline*. Retrieved from https://deadline.com/2018/06/the-handmaids-tale-elisabeth-williams-production-design-interview-news-1202361094/

Harper's Bazaar. (2019, June 12). The cast of "The Handmaid's Tale" has a message for America: "Abortion care is healthcare." Retrieved from https://www.harpersbazaar.com/culture/film-tv/a27917483/handmaids-tale-planned-parenthood-abortion-psa/

Harvey, C. B. (2014). A taxonomy of transmedia storytelling. In M. L. Ryan & J. N. Thon (Eds.), *Storyworlds across media* (pp. 278–294). Lincoln: University of Nebraska Press.

Hayes, G. (2011). *How to write a transmedia production bible*. Sydney, Australia: Screen Australia.

Hill, L. (2019, July 11). With their white feminist bias, TV's prestige dramas continue to fail. *Indie Wire*. Retrieved from https://www.indiewire.com/2019/07/white-feminist-bias-handmaids-tale-big-little-lies-game-of-thrones-1202157104/

Jameson, F. (1991). *Postmodernism, or, the cultural logic of late capitalism*. Durham, NC: Duke University Press.

Jenkins, H. (2003, January 15). Transmedia storytelling. *MIT Technology Review*. Retrieved from http://www.technologyreview.com/biotech/13052/

Jenkins, H. (2006). *Convergence culture: Where old and new media collide*. New York: New York University Press.

Jenkins, H. (2011, July 31). Transmedia 202: Further reflections. *Confessions of an aca-fan*. Retrieved from http://henryjenkins.org/blog/2011/08/defining_transmedia_further_re.html

Jerde, S. (2019, July 11). Wine line inspired by The Handmaid's Tale goes as poorly as you might expect. *Adweek*. Retrieved from https://www.adweek.com/tv-video/wine-line-inspired-by-the-handmaids-tale-goes-as-poorly-as-you-might-expect/

Klastrup, L., & Tosca, S. (2004). Transmedial worlds—Rethinking cyberworld design. *Proceedings of the 2004 International Conference on Cyberworlds* (pp. 409–416). Tokyo, Japan. Retrieved from https://ieeexplore-ieee-org.proxy.library.ju.se/abstract/document/1366205

Klastrup, L., & Tosca, S. (2014). *Game of Thrones*: Transmedial worlds, fandom, and social gaming. In M. L. Ryan & J. N. Thon (Eds.), *Storyworlds across media* (pp. 295–314). Lincoln: University of Nebraska Press.

Kerrigan, S., & Velikovsky, J T. (2016). Examining documentary transmedia narratives through the living history of Fort Scratchley project. *Convergence: The International Journal of Research into New Media Technologies, 22*(3), 233–249.

Kinder, M. (1991). *Playing with power in movies, television, and video games: From Muppet Babies to Teenage Mutant Ninja Turtles*. Berkeley: University of California Press.

Lea, R. (2016, March 24). Fiction v nonfiction: English literature's made-up divide. *The Guardian*. Retrieved from https://www.theguardian.com/books/2016/mar/24/fiction-nonfiction-english-literature-culture-writers-other-languages-stories

Lemke, J. (2011). Transmedia traversals: Marketing meaning and identity. In A. Baldry & E. Montagna (Eds.), *Interdisciplinary perspectives on multimodality: Theory and practice. Proceedings of the Third International Conference on Multimodality* (pp. 576–596). Campobasso, Italy: Palladino.

Lèvy, P. (1997). *Collective intelligence: Mankind's emerging world in cyberspace.* New York, NY: Plenum Trade.

Long, G. (2007). *Transmedia storytelling: Business, aesthetics and production at the Jim Henson Company* (Unpublished master's thesis). Massachusetts Institute of Technology, Cambridge, MA.

Lovato, A. (2018). The transmedia script for nonfictional narratives. In R. R. Gambarato & G. Alzamora (Eds.), *Exploring transmedia journalism in the digital age* (pp. 235–254). Hershey, PA: IGI Global.

Mascio, A. (2019, March). *TV series between entertainment and politics: The Handmaid's Tale.* Paper presented at the International Symposium Media Mixing, Lund, Sweden.

Matravers, D. (2014). *Fiction and narrative.* Oxford, England: Oxford University Press.

Meyrowitz, J. (1993). Images of media: Hidden ferment—and harmony—in the field. *Journal of Communication, 43*(3), 55–66.

Miller, L. S. (2017a, June 1). For shows like "The Handmaid's Tale" and "American Gods," literary adaptations are the new fan fiction. *Indie Wire.* Retrieved from https://www.indiewire.com/2017/06/handmaids-tale-american-gods-fan-fiction-1201834371/

Miller, L. S. (2017b, December 12). "The Handmaid's Tale" season 2 will tackle race issues as it tells new stories beyond the book. *Indie Wire.* Retrieved from https://www.indiewire.com/2017/12/handmaids-tale-season-2-race-golden-globes-1201906937/

Miller, L. (2018, May 2). The relentless torture of "The Handmaid's Tale." *The Cut.* Retrieved from https://www.thecut.com/2018/05/the-handmaids-tale-season-2-review.html

Miller, L. S. (2019, July 15). Hulu's "Handmaid's Tale" is a model of long-form worldbuilding. *The Verge.* Retrieved from https://www.theverge.com/2019/7/15/20694746/hulu-handmaids-tale-season-3-margaret-atwood-world-building-elisabeth-moss-ann-dowd

Mittell, J. (2014). Strategies of storytelling on transmedia television. In M. L. Ryan & J. N. Thon (Eds.), *Storyworlds across media* (pp. 253–277). Lincoln: University of Nebraska Press.

Moloney, K. (2018). Designing transmedia journalism projects. In R. R. Gambarato & G. Alzamora (Eds.), *Exploring transmedia journalism in the digital age* (pp. 83–103). Hershey, PA: IGI Global.

Moloney, K. (2019). Proposing a practical media taxonomy for complex media production. *International Journal of Communication, 13,* 3545–3568.

Moorhead, J. K. (Ed.). (1930). *Conversations of Goethe with Eckermann.* New York, NY: Dutton. (Original work published 1825.)

Mulkerrins, J. (2018, May 5). Elisabeth Moss on "The Handsmaid's Tale": "This is happening in real life. Wake up, people." *The Guardian.* Retrieved from https://www.theguardian.com/tv-and-radio/2018/may/05/elisabeth-moss-handmaids-tale-this-is-happening-in-real-life-wake-up-people?CMP=Share_iOSApp_Other

Mungioli, M. C. (2011). Narratives, languages and media in the context of interactive digital technologies: Interview with Carlos A. Scolari. *MATRIZes:Revista do Programa de Pós-Graduação em Ciênciasda Comunicação da Universidade de São Paulo, 4*(2), 127–136.

Nichol, B. (1992). *Representing reality: Issues and concepts in documentary.* Bloomington: Indiana University Press.

Nikolic, V. (2016). *Independent filmmaking and digital convergence: Transmedia and beyond.* Waltham, MA: Focal Press.

Ong, W. J. (1982). *Orality and literacy.* New York, NY: Methuen.

Park, A. (2019, February 4). *The Handmaid's Tale* Season 3 trailer spoofs Ronald Reagan's 1984 campaign ad. *W Magazine.* Retrieved from https://www.wmagazine.com/story/the-handmaids-tale-season-3-trailer

Penguin. (2018, November 28). Margaret Atwood's sequel to *The Handmaid's Tale: The Testaments.* Retrieved from https://www.penguin.co.uk/articles/2018/nov/margaret-atwood-announces-sequel-handmaids-tale-the-testaments.html?fbclid=IwAR1WDyg7DteklqODBI-bwJfBHsWUZ2XZFIQROz1dB2nv0wjreMyiJzbUw3I

Phillips, A. (2012). *A creator's guide to transmedia storytelling: How to captivate and engage audiences across multiple platforms.* New York, NY: McGraw-Hill.

Pratten, R. (2015). *Getting started with transmedia storytelling: A practical guide for beginners.* London, England: Creative Space.

Regalado, M. (2019, August 26). 9 nightmarish things in *The Handmaid's Tale* inspired by history. *Insider.* Retrieved from https://www.insider.com/handmaids-tale-based-on-real-world-origins-history-events-2019-8?utm_content=bufferf9687&utm_medium=social&utm_source=facebook.com&utm_campaign=buffer-ti

Ryan, M. L. (2004). *Narrative across media: The language of storytelling.* Lincoln: University of Nebraska Press.

Ryan, M. L. (2014). Story/worlds/media: Turning the instruments of a media-conscious narratology. In M. L. Ryan & J. N. Thon (Eds.), *Storyworlds across media* (pp. 25–49). Lincoln: University of Nebraska Press.

Ryan, M. L., & Thon, J. N. (2014). *Storyworlds across media.* Lincoln: University of Nebraska Press.

Saldre, M., & Torop, P. (2012). Transmedia space. In I. Ibrus & C. A. Scolari (Eds.), *Crossmedia innovations: Texts, markets, institutions* (pp. 25–44). Frankfurt, Germany: Peter Lang.

Salvi, P. (2019, May 29). Margaret Atwood says *The Handmaid's Tale* is no longer her own, has taken a "life of its own." *Meaww.* Retrieved from https://meaww.com/the-handmaids-tale-author-margaret-atwood-dystopia-american-reality-womanhood-life-own

Scolari, C. A. (2018). *Teens, media and collaborative cultures: Exploiting teens' transmedia skills in the classroom.* Barcelona, Spain: Universitat Pompeu Fabra.

Setoodeh, R. (2018, April 10). Margaret Atwood on how Trump helped *The Handmaid's Tale. Variety.* Retrieved from https://variety.com/2018/tv/news/margaret-atwood-handmaids-tale-trump-feminism-1202748535/

Sharf, Z. (2019, October 28). The face of Joaquin Phoenix's Joker is turning up at government protests around the world. *Indie Wire.* Retrieved from https://www.indiewire.com/2019/10/joker-government-protests-lebanon-hong-kong-1202185602/

Srivastava, L. (2013, November 12). The narrative design canvas. *Transmedia Activism.* Retrieved from https://transmediaactivism.wordpress.com/

Swant, M. (2019, June 6). Hulu is promoting *The Handmaid's Tale* with 140 sculptures of women in New York. *Adweek.* Retrieved from https://www.adweek.com/brand-marketing/hulu-is-promoting-the-handmaids-tale-with-140-sculptures-of-women-in-new-york/

The Handmaid's Tale. (2019). A monumental omission. *CNN*. Retrieved from https://edition.cnn.com/interactive/Hulu/ShapeOfHistory/

The Handmaid's Tale [@handmaidsonhulu]. (2019, July 5). Fan art challenge [Instagram photo]. Retrieved from https://www.instagram.com/p/BzjFyZOApNG/?igshid=1jaxkf11jfiis

Travers, B., Miller, L. S., Nguyen, H., & Greene, S. (2017, December 5). The top 10 TV shows of 2017. *Indie Wire*. Retrieved from https://www.indiewire.com/2017/12/best-tv-shows-series-2017-1201903817/

Von Stackelberg, P. (2011). *Creating transmedia narratives: The structure and design of stories told across multiple media* (Unpublished master's thesis). State University of New York Institute of Technology, Utica, NY.

Vukadin, A. (2019). *Metadata for transmedia resources.* Cambridge, MA: Chandos.

Walton, K. L. (1990). *Mimesis as make-believe: On the foundations of the representational arts.* Cambridge, MA: Harvard University Press.

Wigler, J. (2019, June 18). Blessed be the truth: Inside *The Handmaid's Tale* and the United Nations' Creative Alliance. *The Hollywood Reporter*. Retrieved from https://www.hollywoodreporter.com/live-feed/handmaids-tale-season-three-creator-bruce-miller-breaks-down-united-nations-involvement-1218770

Williams, Z. (2019, August 12). Joseph Fiennes: "I've done my bit for society – I've illustrated the patheticness of misogyny." *The Guardian*. Retrieved from https://www.theguardian.com/tv-and-radio/2019/aug/12/joseph-fiennes-ive-done-my-bit-for-society-ive-illustrated-the-patheticness-of-misogyny

Winston, B. (2013). *The documentary film book.* London, England: British Film Institute.

Wolf, W. (2002). Das Problem der Narrativität in Literatur, bildender Kunst und Musik: Ein Beitrag zu einer intermedialen Erzähltheorie [The problem of narrativity in literature, visual arts and music: A contribution to an intermedial narrative theory]. In V. Nünning & A. Nünning (Eds.), *Erzähltheorie transgenerisch, intermedial, interdisziplinär* [Narrative theory transgenic, intermedial, interdisciplinary] (pp. 23–104). Trier, Germany: Wissenschaflicher Verlag Trier.

Zipfel, F. (2014). Fiction across media: Towards a transmedial concept of fictionality. In M. L. Ryan & J. N. Thon (Eds.), *Storyworlds across media* (pp. 103–125). Lincoln: University of Nebraska Press.

Žižek, S. (2019, September 14). Margaret Atwood's work illustrates our need to enjoy other people's pain. *Independent*. Retrieved from https://www.independent.co.uk/voices/margaret-atwood-handmaids-tale-testaments-human-rights-slavoj-zizek-a9105151.html

4 Application of the transmedia design analytical and operational model to journalism

Transmedia journalism fundamentals

According to Gambarato and Alzamora (2018) and Canavilhas (2018), the advent of digitization has increased conceptual confusion in the realm of media and journalism. Multimedia, crossmedia, intermedia, and transmedia storytelling are terms frequently used in covering news in liquid, fluid, and participative environments (Bauman, 2000). Transmedia storytelling is one of the newest terms, and how it applies to journalism has prompted several discussions due to difficulties in adapting the concept to (1) the periodicity of the publications, (2) the short production cycles, and (3) the coverage of daily reality:

> As expected, in the early years, authors sought to label what defines transmedia journalism, focusing initially on two essential fields: 1) Narrative, namely the relation between content and media (Moloney, 2011; Renó & Flores, 2012; Alzamora & Tárcia, 2012), and 2) the user's participation in the contents (Davis, 2013). In addition to these fields, other authors have dealt with some particularities of transmedia journalism, such as the possible formats (Canavilhas, 2013), the factors that affect production (Hayes, 2011), and the design (Serrano Telleria, 2016).
>
> (Canavilhas, 2018, p. 4)

Dominguez (2012) warns against the risk of putting new labels on old practices, and Scolari (2013) argues that journalism itself was born transmediatic. Since the advent of mass media, facts have been reported through mixed media—radio (before the Internet), then television, and finally, next-day newspapers and weekly magazines. Engagement, at that time, occurred through telephone calls to the newsroom or letters. Although various types of media are used to present and to cover events in journalism, not every news production is transmediatic; most content dispersed across different media platforms is simply being repurposed. According to Tavares and Mascarenhas (2013), "it is not rare that a news story extends across multiple platforms with mass and post-mass functions. However, this is not enough to call an article as a transmedia narrative" (p. 200). Jeff Gomez (2010), a pioneering transmedia storyteller, emphasizes that the essence of transmedia journalism "is to allow a closer dialogue between the viewer, the journalist and the media company. When there is dialogue it is easier to make changes" (para. 4). Transmedia storytelling is about expanding, not repeating, content.

In 2009, Jenkins (2009a, 2009b) issued the seven core principles of transmedia storytelling, which were discussed in previous chapters. Moloney (2011) later proposed applying Jenkins's core principles to journalism: (1) spreadability, the viral spread of a story through user sharing; (2) drillability, the search for more details, or official content expansion (including social networks); (3) continuity and seriality, maintaining consistency and exploiting the characteristics of each medium while keeping the audience's attention for a significant amount of time; (4) diversity, adding other viewpoints, including the public's, to the information; (5) immersion, generating alternative forms of storytelling so the public digs deeper; (6) extractability, applying the journalist's work in everyday life to the public's commitment; (7) real world, showing all shades of news without focusing on simplification; and (8) inspiration to action, pursuing public intervention in real actions to find solutions to problems. The topic inspiration to action can cause controversy, as it could be questioned whether journalism's role is to lead the public to take meaningful action, but digital journalism is moving toward user-generated content and action (Gambarato & Alzamora, 2018).

Looney (2013) presents five additional suggestions for building transmedia news features: (1) Keep the content unique. Instead of repeating information on different media platforms, use different parts of the story that match the strength of each medium and maximize the user experience. (2) Provide seamless points of entry. Ensure that the media platforms make all interactions simple and direct. (3) Partner up. Transmedia news is often complex, requiring the involvement of other companies, producers, and businessmen. (4) Keep it cost-effective. There are costly projects, but it is possible to produce transmedia news cheaply, for example, using social media to expand the story. (5) The story is number one. Many creative tools may do more harm than help; therefore, always put the story first. These direct, simple features, though difficult to achieve, can contribute concretely to understanding transmedia journalism and guiding its potential production.

Spreading the story through complementary platforms is the goal of many news companies. For instance, by using television, radio, mobile media, and the Internet, the BBC reached 90% of the British population during the 2012 London Summer Olympics; 47.4 million accessed online BBC coverage throughout the Summer Games (BBC, 2013). The challenge is more evident when building an interactive and engaging environment or turning journalism into a conversation (Anderson, Dardenne, & Killenberg, 1994).

Although the 2012 Summer Games were called "the Social Olympics" by the media, collective narrative-building attempts were still modest. Spreading the news through different screens (the one-ten-four strategy) and giving the user control only multiplied the same content on different devices, creating a video hub instead of an engaging atmosphere (Tárcia, 2015). The one-ten-four strategy was proposed by BBC for the London Olympics, meaning one service, ten products, and four screens (see Rivera, 2011).

How news and information are gathered, produced, and disseminated has been profoundly altered, challenging the transmissive tradition of mass media. The "increasing number of producers and disseminators of news as well as the instantaneity of global news flow indicate that journalistic practice is changing" (Heinrich, 2011, p. 2). This new paradigm means that one must rethink not only multiple media, cross-production, and different platforms but also copyright, remixability (Lessig, 2008), crowdsourcing, crowdfunding, and diverse funding modes. The issue of limited time and staff must also be considered to make sense of the disparate parts of multiple stories from different sources (Craig, 2011; Pase, Goss, & Tietzmann, 2018).

Another important aspect of the changing journalism environment is consumers' increasing tendency to quickly change information-gathering habits. When journalism goes mobile, alternative news production and consumption methods change people's relationships with the news they access (Herreros & Vivar, 2011; Jones & Salter, 2012). Mobile phones change the relationships of journalists, news, and what we used to call the audience. Mobile technology includes other modes of communication and enriches traditional journalism (Herreros & Vivar, 2011). Bauman's (2000) liquid society is characterized by mobility and individualization in media consumption.

Corporations are still learning to listen, filter, and engage with social news and use social networks like Twitter, Facebook, YouTube, TikTok, and Instagram. Citizens are also learning "how to harness the power of social news flows, very often to create news reports that challenge those of the mainstream" (Jones & Salter, 2012, p. 126). Technological forces are often close to political and cultural changes. The increase in mobile phone penetration can significantly disrupt the political process, forcing alternative ways of framing news, such as with the Madrid bombings (2004) and the Iranian elections (2009). Social news and information flow are now characterized by unpredictability, classlessness, and a lack of hierarchy, with spin-offs that journalism must address.

Although every newsworthy event could be transmediatic, transmedia journalism is optimized when it becomes a proactive planned process with journalists assuming responsibility for building a story world where the prosumers (Toffler, 1980), consumers who are also media producers, are engaged. Moloney (2011, p. 12) emphasizes that "daily journalism, with its time-constrained brevity, is not a viable option. Transmedia must be designed carefully and developed with a lengthy lead time to be effective." Transmedia-breaking news journalism is still possible, but a transmedia mindset is necessary in the newsroom to use transmedia strategies properly, as Janet Kolodzy (2012) proposed. According to Kolodzy, telling stories across media platforms requires journalists to be audience-centric, story-driven, tool neutral, and very professional. Canavilhas (2014) suggests that journalism styles truly adapted to transmedia storytelling are the native styles of online journalism, like reportage, newsgames, and interactive infographics, due to the content's digital nature and the possibility of producing deeper news. According to Jenkins (2009b), the opportunity to offer deeper and contextualized content is a core principle of transmedia storytelling and transmedia journalism. This aspect alone can make a difference in a superficially saturated online news scenario.

We consider transmedia journalism and other applications of transmedia storytelling in fictional and nonfictional realms to be characterized by the involvement of (1) multiple media platforms, (2) content expansion, and (3) audience engagement. Transmedia journalism can take advantage of different media platforms like television, radio, print media, and, above all, the Internet and mobile media to tell deeper stories. Rather than repeating the same message on multiple platforms, expanding the content is the essence of transmedia storytelling and therefore should be the focal point of transmedia journalism. The narrative is enriched by extended content. Audience engagement involves mechanisms of interactivity, like selecting the explored elements, reading the text as an option, watching a video, enlarging photos, accessing maps, clicking hyperlinks, and sharing information through social networks. Audience engagement deals with participation via, for instance, remixing content and creating original user-generated content (Gambarato & Tárcia, 2017). For Dahlgren and Carpentier (2013), "participation captures a specific set of social practices that deal with the decision-making practices of actors" (p. 45). Participation is intertwined with other concepts, especially empowerment and involvement—as discussed in Chapter 2—enhancing the journalistic experience. These three basic characteristics of transmedia journalism (multiple media platforms, content expansion, and audience engagement) are contemplated in the analytical model we propose and support the analysis of transmedia strategies in news coverage of planned events.

Planned mega events

We understand planned mega events as

> a dispositive constituted as a high visibility, periodic and planned global production, subject to its own regulations, with significant economic and political connotations, of journalistic importance, stressed by local and transnational interests and a hybrid communication flow,

characteristic of the process of media convergence, composed of diverse, participatory, questioning audiences, although also contradictory and complacent.

(Tárcia, 2015, p. 117)

Getz (2012) proposed a typology of planned events and stressed that any event can have multiple functions, experiences, and meanings. He suggested six groups: (1) cultural celebrations (festivals, heritage commemorations, carnivals, religious rites, pilgrimages, parades); (2) business and trade (meetings, conventions, fairs, exhibitions, markets, corporate events, educational/scientific congresses); (3) arts and entertainment (scheduled concerts, shows, theater, art exhibits, installations and temporary art shows, award ceremonies); (4) political and state (summits, royal spectacles, VIP visits, military and political congresses); (5) private functions (rites of passage, parties, reunions, weddings); and (6) sport and recreation (league play, championships, one-off meets, tours, fun events, sport festivals). Differently, Bowdin, McDonnell, Allen, and O'Toole (2012) proposed categorizing events by size: (1) major events (events attracting significant visitor numbers, media coverage, and economic benefits); (2) hallmark events (events identified with the "spirit or ethos" of a town); and (3) mega events (events affecting entire economies and reverberating in global media).

In the context of media studies, Dayan and Katz (1992) discuss a media event as a real-time televised transmission of an extraordinary and preplanned public event that does not occur inside broadcasting studios. Dayan and Katz distinguish three basic scripts for media events: (1) contests, (2) conquests, and (3) coronations. Contests, such as the Olympic Games and the *Fédération Internationale de Football Association* (FIFA) World Cup, embody "rule-governed battles of champions"; conquests are found in "the live broadcasting of 'giant leaps for mankind,'" while coronations are ceremonies seen during royal weddings and funerals (Dayan & Katz, 1992, p. 26). The meanings of the media events are framed by the organizers. The media work as a bridge for viewers, joined in front of the television and other screens through today's multicentered power structure (Hepp & Couldry, 2010). In this context, it is also important to emphasize that some events, particularly mega events (Roche, 2000), are mediated phenomena, planned to be broadcast positively, which means that journalism strategies must cope with promoter restrictions and public relations (PR) strategies. Scholars such as Moragas, Rivenburg, and Larson (1995) and Panagiotopoulou (2010) discuss how the Olympic Games became the most watched global television program and how each city and country hosting them pay much attention to producing and broadcasting the best possible television program. Commercial and institutional interests contribute to event complexity, sometimes sponsored by global organizations controlling broadcasted images. Usually, journalists must be accredited and are not free to walk around and interview central figures like the athletes. With organization and big media centers comes news standardization, a restriction on transmedia coverage. "At many major sporting events, the journalists themselves are not actually watching the sport live; they are simply watching television feeds of the action and basing their copy, in part, on this" (Boyle, 2006, p. 80). Engaging in social media with athletes and the public can be a good strategy for avoiding the sameness and surpass the control promoters have over the public media image of the event. However, in elite sports, even an athlete's Twitter account might be mostly managed by PR personnel. Having a well-planned infrastructure and professional PR help can be useful and facilitate coordinating transmedia coverage.

Analytical and operational model for transmedia news coverage of planned events

Our analytical and operational model for planned events addresses fundamental features in transmedia strategies of journalistic coverage to contribute to the analytic needs of scholars and journalists. Analysis can lead to synthesis (Liestøl, 2003), the third stage of argument in the Hegelian dialectic—which comprises thesis, anthesis, and synthesis. Analyzing transmedia strategies can improve transmedia journalism practices. Therefore, this model helps scholars analyze transmedia strategies of planned events and helps journalists develop transmedia strategies. The analytical and operational model examines the strategies behind journalistic coverage in the transmedia space but is not restrictive. To facilitate understanding and application of the model, the description of each topic is accompanied by a series of related questions (see Table 4.1), following the pattern we presented in Chapter 3. Other questions and layers could be added. Qualitative and quantitative methods, such as interviews, documentary research, and data mining, could be applied depending on the nature of the question and the availability of data. This revised version of the model shows the reorganization and reallocation of the previous 10 topics originally developed by Gambarato and Tárcia (2017). This process of revising the model also restructures the series of practical questions accompanying each topic to avoid potential repetitions. The following model applied to journalism reproduces the same overall structure of the transmedia design analytical and operational model presented in Chapter 3 as fictional and nonfictional transmedia stories share the same core principles. Thus, the method draws on the transmedia project design analytical model developed by Gambarato (2013) and revised in Chapter 3. This model establishes five main topics—(1) story, (2) premise, (3) extensions, (4) audience, and (5) structure—and practical questions regarding news storytelling, media platforms, and audience engagement (see Table 4.1).

Story

When thinking about transmedia production in journalism, the team of researchers at the National University of Rosario, Argentina, "is convinced that the core of transmedia storytelling resides in the story world (or the

Table 4.1 Concise description of the analytical and operational model regarding transmedia news coverage of planned events

Nr.	Topic	Practicable questions
1	**Story** The building of a storyworld with its narratives and sources that is robust enough to support expansions. The news coverage of the event involves primary and parallel stories.	Is the event big enough to support expansions throughout multiplatform coverage? What elements of the news story (who, what, where, when, why, and how) of the event are involved in the coverage? What are the timeframe and territory of the news story? Who are the primary and secondary sources of information regarding the event and its parallel stories? What is the approach of these sources? Are the sources official, nonofficial, or both? Can the audience be considered a source?
2	**Premise** What the news project is about and the reason why it exists.	What is the planned event agenda? What is its core theme? What is the fundamental purpose of the event? What is the magnitude of the event? Is it local, regional, or global? What type of content is involved in the coverage (sports, culture, politics, economics, etc.)?
3	**Extensions** News stories meant to spread throughout multiple media platforms should not simply transpose or repurpose the content from one medium to another but expand the news, taking advantage of the media platforms available.	Which media extensions (television program, documentary, book, newsgame, social media networks, mobile application, etc.) are involved in the transmedia coverage? Does each media extension enrich the story? Which devices (computer, game console, tablet, mobile phone, etc.) are required by the project? What is the roll-out strategy for releasing the media extensions? Which journalistic genres (informative, opinion, interpretation, diversional, and utilitarian) and formats (news, report, interview, article, column, letter, chronicle, review, etc.) are present in the coverage? What types of visuals are used (animation, video, graphics, holography, augmented reality, etc.) in the transmedia coverage? Is it possible to identify specific design styles in the project?

Nr.	Topic	Practicable questions
4	**Audience** Scoping the audience is fundamental to more appropriately deliver the transmedia experience. Transmedia storytelling involves some level of audience engagement.	Who is the target audience of the transmedia coverage? What mechanisms of interaction are included in this coverage? Is participation also involved in the coverage? Is there user-generated content related to the news story (upload of images, videos, etc.)? Are there any policies restricting the disclosure of user-generated content? What is the transmedia coverage's business model? Does it involve open platforms, open television channels, cable TV, satellite, pay-per-view, a monopoly, and so on?
5	**Structure** The organization of a transmedia project, the arrangement of its constituent elements, and how they interrelate to each other offer concrete elements to understand the project.	When did the transmediation begin? Is the transmedia coverage planned in advance? How is the coverage structured? What costs are involved? Is the event coverage successful revenuewise? Where will the journalists work, and how will they access the sources and venues? What regulations and policies are related to the journalistic coverage?

narrative universe)" (Lovato, 2018, p. 239). According to Lovato (2018, p. 240), "the elements of the story and their implications are the first steps that must be solved by a transmedia producer" and must be executed long before thinking, imagining, and designing the platforms and technologies involved. Gambarato and Tárcia (2017) ponder that:

> Transmedia strategies necessarily comprehend the unfolding of a story world across various media platforms. The story world goes beyond a single story and characterizes the potential of the content to be expanded. News stories inserted in the transmedia space are not different: the story world in which the news stories are placed should be robust enough to support multiplatform expansions. In terms of news stories, it is possible to understand the story world as it is presented geographically (location) and metaphorically (set of news stories).
>
> (p. 1392)

Furthermore, Moloney (2018) states that "defining a real-world story world is an act of delimitation rather than expansion. As any subject taken from the real-world interconnects infinitely with every other, more than a broad subject identification is required" (p. 89).

For large-scale journalistic coverage, planning begins months (or years) before, with production surveys, relevant information from previous events, and information about each agent involved. This document is widely circulated in the newsroom, including the reporters' schedule and the responsibilities of each department and medium involved. The planning document also indicates details such as coverage rules, available structure, limitations imposed by producers, image transmission agreements, and social network use. For instance, according to Tárcia (2015, 2016), six people took three years to plan BBC's 2012 Olympics coverage. A total of 765 professionals were accredited to work at the Olympic Games. Official coverage began in 2010 with reports of various events promoted by the International Olympic Committee (IOC). Usually, the official broadcaster of the Olympics has a biased view of the event, compromising in promoting it in a positive way (Tárcia, 2015, 2016). Horne (2012) suggests that changes in resistance and media contestation reflect different phases of the buildup to the Olympic Games or other sports mega events. The different media forms and technologies add more layers to the narratives (Tárcia, 2015, 2016).

According to Wenner and Billings (2017), a mega event, and its coverage content can be framed, in three editorial perspectives: (1) belief in the economic and social benefit of the event; (2) an ambivalent or negotiated position, a belief that people see some aspects as positive while others are negative; and (3) a critical view of the mega event, a belief it benefits only the upper class and rejecting the ideological rhetoric suggesting these events are good for everyone.

The framing editorial view has implications for transmediatic coverage considering all the characters involved: (1) the journalists and professionals reporting the event; (2) news story characters; (3) information sources; (4) the audience members as collaborators and prosumers; and (5) the news location. If we consider primary and parallel news stories, we must consider primary and parallel characters, too. According to mega-event producers, we practically see a more complex and layered list of characters. Most have very restrictive media rules, and normal accredited media and broadcasters' rights holders are separate from the official broadcasters. The practical questions considered for this topic are as follows:

1   Is the event big enough to support expansions throughout multiplatform coverage?
2   What elements of the news story (who, what, where, when, why, and how) of the event are involved in the coverage?
3   What are the time frame and territory of the news story?
4   Who are the primary and secondary sources of information regarding the event and its parallel stories? What is the approach of these sources? Are the sources official, nonofficial, or both?
5   Can the audience be considered a source?

Premise

As proposed by Gambarato and Tárcia (2017),

> The nature of the planned event, its magnitude and comprehensiveness, and its premise and purpose can directly influence and potentially frame the journalistic coverage. The involvement of different news sections and multiple media platforms in the coverage is connected to the event itself. For instance, a global sporting event naturally involves other sections in addition to Sports, considering the event's massive international penetration and interests beyond the sports competition.
>
> (p. 1388)

The constraints and limitations imposed by the promoters and commercial exploitation agreements influence the transmedia plan. Journalists should understand what the political limits of the coverage, in case there are any significant narrative changes, such as complaints, accidents, or any other negative circumstance (Tárcia, 2015). The following questions are proposed about the premises needed to plan and analyze mega-event coverage:

1 What is the planned event agenda? What is its core theme?
2 What is the fundamental purpose of the event?
3 What is the magnitude of the event? Is it local, regional, or global?
4 What type of content is involved in the coverage (sports, culture, politics, economics, etc.)?

Extensions

Transmedia strategies are based on pervasive stories attracting audience engagement. "It is not about offering the same content in different media platforms, but it is the worldbuilding experience, unfolding content and generating the possibilities for the story to evolve with new and pertinent content" (Gambarato, 2013, p. 82). News stories meant to be spread throughout multiple media platforms should not be transposed or merely repurposed from one medium to another but expand the news, taking advantage of the media platforms available. "Spreadability of media, if not at first embraced, is now an element of nearly every journalism production" (Moloney, 2011, p. 64). Moloney (2018) also considers that the scope of the planned stories should be examined to determine "which story for each separate media channel will quickly engage the target public while also alluding to what more will come through subsequent stories the series" (p. 89). The challenge of writing a transmedia news story and designing a narrative universe for multiple platforms must be considered since the beginning to achieve the desirable objective of offering a more meaningful experience to the audience:

> Far from the protection of monomediatic thinking, transmedia narratives demand the design of a complex and coherent narrative universe where each piece can contribute to the totality of the story, generating connections and deepening the narrative lines without forgetting the specific format characteristics of each chosen medium.
>
> (Lovato, 2018, p. 240)

When planning or analyzing media mega-event coverage, one must identify what media channels will reach the public while best using the information gathered. Defining the media formats that best tell each part of the stories is also important. Video is a powerful tool for telling strong stories, but audio, photos, infographics, virtual reality, and newsgames can be used to reach or conquer distinct audiences. One challenge for the Olympics is young people's and women's lack of interest in sports. Planning different extensions and formats can be part of the strategy for corporate media coverage (Tárcia, 2015). Therefore, the following questions should be pondered:

1   Which media extensions (television program, documentary, book, newsgame, social media networks, mobile application, etc.) are involved in the transmedia coverage?
2   Does each media extension enrich the story?
3   Which devices (computer, game console, tablet, mobile phone, etc.) are required by the project?
4   What is the roll-out strategy for releasing the media extensions?
5   Which journalistic genres (informative, opinion, interpretation, diversional and utilitarian) and formats (news, report, interview, article, column, letter, chronicle, review, etc.) are present in the coverage?
6   What types of visuals are used (animation, video, graphics, holography, augmented reality, etc.) in the transmedia coverage?

Audience

The relationship between the story and the people interested in it is an essential aspect of transmedia strategies connected to entertainment, journalism, branding, and education. Interaction and participation, as discussed in the previous chapters, are basic strategic mechanisms for engaging people in the news. Interactivity allows the audience to relate by pressing a button, deciding the path to experience the news, and inserting comments, without necessarily influencing or changing the news. Participation invites audience members to engage by expressing their thoughts and configuring co-creation, allowing the audience to influence the final result of the news coverage by sending questions or having requests incorporated in the coverage, expressing their thoughts by wearing costumes, carrying posters or messages, or producing their own photos or videos (user-generated content). As discussed in Chapter 2, transmedia productions that allow participation are characterized as open systems, where audience members can influence the result and change the news. Closed systems are transmedia initiatives that allow interaction without participation (Gambarato, 2012). The audience can act, react, or interact without interfering with the news.

Lewis (2012) proposed a hybrid logic of adaptability and openness as the norm for digital journalism. The convergence of mass and social media is centered on editorial planning, which deals with audience or citizen participation in producing and circulating information. The journalistic narrative in transmedia dynamics is ideally participatory, globally exchangeable, and continuously expandable.

Moloney (2018) writes about "key publics," "best channel to reach those publics," and "how to turn stories into conversations" (p. 90). It means keeping in mind to whom the event was targeted or what kind of public it aims to reach. By all means, it is necessary to connect the public to the platforms and narratives used in the transmedia coverage. "A successful production will enable social commenting, sharing, remixing and amateur production of the work produced" (Moloney, 2018, pp. 90–91). Pertinent questions to consider are the following:

1   Who is the target audience of the transmedia coverage?
2   What mechanisms of interaction are included in this coverage?
3   Is participation also involved in the coverage?
4   Is there user-generated content related to the news story (upload of images, videos, etc.)?
5   Are there any policies restricting the disclosure of user-generated content?
6   What is the transmedia coverage's business model? Does it involve open platforms, open television channels, cable TV, satellite, pay-per-view, a monopoly, and so on?

Structure

This analytical and operational model focuses on the transmedia strategies in the news coverage of planned events. Therefore, one or more media enterprises behind the coverage are analyzed. The organization of transmedia journalistic coverage, the professionals involved, and the infrastructure available indicate how the operations were planned and executed. Visual solutions, like maps, charts, and infographics, can help visualize the entire process. Referring to transmedia production, Hayes (2011) states that "one or two very detailed charts will show how platforms, and the channels within them, are interconnected and how content and data flows around his technical ecosystem" (p. 13). Regarding the structure, the following questions can be contemplated:

1   When did the transmediation begin? Is the transmedia coverage planned in advance?
2   How is the coverage structured?

3   What costs are involved? Is the event coverage successful revenuewise?
4   Where will the journalists work, and how will they access the sources and venues?
5   What regulations and policies are related to the journalistic coverage?

Case study: mega sporting events (2014 Sochi Winter Olympics, 2014 FIFA World Cup, 2016 Rio Summer Olympics, 2018 FIFA World Cup)

Between 2014 and 2018, Alzamora, Gambarato, and Tárcia applied this methodology to study the coverage of mega sporting events that occurred in Brazil and Russia: (1) 2014 Sochi Winter Olympic Games (Russia), (2) 2014 FIFA World Cup (Brazil), (3) 2016 Rio Summer Olympics (Brazil), and (4) 2018 FIFA World Cup (Russia). We synthesize previous studies but mostly use the Rio Olympic Games and Globo Network coverage as an example because we consider it a mature experience of journalistic transmedia coverage of a planned mega event even with the limitations imposed by the event organizers.

According to Wüthrich (2016), for most sports organizations, the sale of broadcasting and media rights is the biggest source of revenue. The IOC awarded Globo, Brazil's largest media group, the broadcast rights for free TV on a non-exclusive basis and for subscription TV, Internet, and mobile platforms on an exclusive basis until 2032 (IOC News, 2015). In 2009, Globo and two other Brazilian media companies—Bandeirantes and Rede Record—secured the rights for 2016 Rio Olympics in a deal that included the 2014 Sochi Winter Olympics. In Russia, ANO Sports Broadcasting was created as the local official broadcaster for the 2014 Sochi Olympics. The broadcasting pool encompassed Channel One, Russia1, and the satellite broadcaster NTV+. The channels shared broadcasting time.

The FIFA World Cup is followed by hundreds of millions of people across the globe thanks to television and other media platforms. FIFA's TV Division manages and maintains a close relationship with many media rights licensees. Broadcast rights to all FIFA events, including the FIFA World Cup and the FIFA Women's World Cup, are handled through FIFA TV in Zurich, Switzerland. In 2012, the Federation announced it had extended its broadcast rights agreement with Brazilian broadcaster Globo to the 2018 FIFA World Cup in Russia and the 2022 FIFA World Cup in Qatar. The agreement with Globo covers cable, satellite, terrestrial, mobile, and broadband Internet transmission across the country. Globo, a FIFA broadcast partner since 1970, committed to unprecedented presence and coverage levels during the 2014 FIFA World Cup Brazil, including free TV coverage as agreed on by the two parties and FIFA distribution policies (FIFA, 2012).

Story

The Olympic Games and FIFA World Cups always provide intriguing and controversial storylines. According to Wenner and Billings (2017), the Olympics cycle itself has become an ever-present media story. In the year the Games are hosted, there is coverage of political and economic decisions related to the Olympic Games. Different newsworthy issues emerge at different stages before, during, and after the Games themselves.

The planning for mega sporting events usually starts two years before the event. Programming schedules provide content about the event in sport shows, journalism, and entertainment. The initial media coverage is often focused on two central areas: budget and facilities. Once the Olympic Games commence, the focus turns to the venues (Horne & Whannel, 2012; Tárcia, 2015; Wenner & Billings, 2017).

Although the fundamental purposes of the coverage are the games, the athletes, and their performances, the media are also aware of surrounding issues like political demonstrations; political, health, and economic crises; doping scandals; social issues and more (Gambarato, Alzamora, & Tárcia, 2016, 2018; Gambarato, Alzamora, Tárcia, & Jurno, 2017). For example, the 2014 Winter Olympics took place in the region surrounding Sochi, Russia. Sochi is located on the Black Sea coast and is known as a summer holiday mecca. The mountain venues for the Games were located 50 kilometers away in the North Caucasus, historically known for conflicts and battles for independence. Sochi was a peculiar choice for the Olympic Games, and this became a central theme of the news coverage. Holding the Olympics in this problem area represented a triumph for President Vladimir Putin—a demonstration of power (Gambarato et al., 2016). Bidding to host the Olympics occurred right after Putin's victory in the so-called Second Chechnyan War. As Putin announced in January 2014, there is a nationalistic aspect to hosting the Olympics as it "strengthens the morale of the nation" (Caryl, 2014, para. 8).

Another example of issues reported in connection to mega sporting events occurred in 2015, when American prosecutors indicted about 40 individuals and entities associated with FIFA on a broad range of corruption charges, including racketeering, wire fraud, and conspiracy to launder money. Possibly worried that associating with FIFA exposed them to reputational and financial jeopardy, big companies such as Emirates, Continental, Johnson & Johnson, and Sony refused to renew their sponsorship contracts. The scandal had wide repercussions in the media worldwide (BBC, 2016; Globo TV, 2015; McLaughlin & Botelho, 2015; Rosenberg & Ingram, 2015).

The 2016 Rio Olympic Games faced numerous unfavorable situations, including an ongoing outbreak of the mosquito-borne Zika virus in Brazil; the pollution of Guanabara Bay, which was the venue for the sailing and windsurfing competitions; political instability; economic crisis; the city's crime problems; and the Russian doping scandal and participation restrictions (Carney & Phelps, 2016; DW, 2016; Gomez, 2016; *The Guardian*, 2015; Sun, 2016).

As with the 2014 Winter Olympics, the choice of Russia as host of the 2018 FIFA World Cup was challenged. Controversial issues included the high level of racism in Russian football and discrimination against lesbian, gay, bisexual, transgender, queer (LGBTQ) individuals in Russian society. Russia's involvement in the ongoing conflict in Ukraine also led to calls for the tournament to be moved, particularly following Russia's annexation of Crimea in 2014 and support of separatists in Donbass. Then FIFA President Sepp Blatter rejected requests to move the tournament.

The 2015 allegations and criminal investigations of corruption, including a Swiss inquiry into the bidding process for the 2018 World Cup, intensified public discussion of the appropriateness of Russia as World Cup host. In late May 2015, President Putin said he viewed the corruption investigations as an American attempt to oust Sepp Blatter as punishment for supporting Russia as the host of the 2018 World Cup.

Regarding the organizational aspects of mega sporting events, usually this kind of event occurs in different cities or places in a city and the journalists work in a media center. For example, the Rio 2016 Olympic Games were held in four clusters in Rio de Janeiro: Maracanã, Barra da Tijuca, Copacabana, and Deodoro. FIFA World Cup in Brazil took place in five cities: Belo Horizonte, Brasília, Manaus, Salvador, and São Paulo. In Sochi, 11 new venues were built for the 2014 Games in two groupings: the coastal cluster and the mountain cluster. The mountain cluster venues were situated in Krasnaya Polyana, connected to the coastal cluster by a new railway (IOC, 2014).

In terms of rules and regulations, the Olympic Games and FIFA World Cups have strict guidelines for the use of official marks. The news media are welcome to use the official marks for legitimate editorial and information purposes, provided the journalists do not create any undue association between the tournament and any entities other than FIFA's commercial affiliates (FIFA, 2014a). The public cannot use FIFA's official logos, symbols, and other graphic trademarks on any social media platform. FIFA's Protected Terms (e.g., the event titles) cannot be used to imply that a page is officially related to the FIFA World Cup (FIFA, 2014a).

Media companies have officially compromised with these two mega events, as these companies have struggled publishing negative news about the Olympic Games and their major figures, because of the commercial relations in the contracts as broadcasting partners (Tárcia, 2015). But the storyworld has always been full of stories, building a fascinating universe for transmedia coverage.

Premise

The modern Olympic Games or Olympics is a leading international sporting event. Thousands of athletes from around the world participate in a variety of competitions. More than 200 nations come together every two years, with the Summer and Winter Games occurring individually every four years but two years apart—this staggered system has been followed only since 1992. Inspired by the ancient Olympic Games held in Olympia, Greece, from eighth century BC to fourth century AD, Olympics is considered a rich narrative universe of facts and controversies.

The XXII Olympic Winter Games took place February 7–23, 2014. The fundamental purposes of the coverage were the Games, the athletes, and their performances. In Sochi, a record number of more than 2,800 athletes participated (more than 40% female), and 12 sports were added to the program, including biathlon mixed relay, snowboard parallel slalom, and women's ski jumping (IOC, 2014). The XXXI Olympic Summer Games took place August 5–21, 2016, in Rio de Janeiro, Brazil. More than 11,000 athletes represented 205 national Olympic committees, including first-time entrants Kosovo, South Sudan, and the Refugee Olympic Team. Three hundred six events spanning 42 sport disciplines took place in 32 venues in just 16 days (Long, 2016).

The FIFA World Cup is a football competition contested by national team members of FIFA. The championship has been awarded every four years since the inaugural tournament in 1930. The FIFA World Cup is considered the most prestigious world association football tournament, and it is the most widely followed sporting event, exceeding even the Olympics (Pumerantz, 2012).

The 20th FIFA World Cup took place in Brazil from June 12 to July 13, 2014, after the country was awarded hosting rights in 2007. Thirty-one national teams advanced through qualification competitions to join the host nation in the final tournament. Sixty-four matches were played in 12 cities across Brazil. The FIFA World Cup was considered as one of the most political tournaments with an "unprecedented level of outrage and debate over poverty, Fifa, commercialism and occasionally football" (Kaiser, 2014, para. 2).

The 2018 FIFA World Cup was the 21st tournament and took place in Russia from June 14 to July 15, 2018. The finals involved 32 teams. Sixty-four matches were played in 12 venues across 11 cities. It was the first World Cup to use the video assistant referee (VAR) system. It was also the most expensive World Cup, costing about $14.2 billion (ESPN, 2018). The event was marked by its branding. The logo was unveiled by cosmonauts at the International Space Station and projected onto Moscow's Bolshoi Theatre during an evening television program. The official mascot (a wolf) was selected through a university design competition. A public vote was used to select from three finalists—a cat, a tiger, and a wolf.

Extensions

Over the years, despite imposed restrictions by event right holders, media companies have found creative ways of expanding the stories using different media platforms and inventive formats. This was before 2016, when Globo Network became a planned transmedia supersystem and started integrating coverage and professionals in a complex, planned narrative universe using its structure, journalists, analysts, and commentators.

For the Sochi 2014 Games, Channel One's Olympic coverage embraced TV broadcasting, online live streaming, a special website (olymp.1tv.ru), social media networks (Facebook, Twitter, VKontakte, and Odnoklassniki), and mobile applications. The tent pole of the coverage was television. All extensions were canonical and maintained news storytelling continuity. They helped keep the audience interested and informed over the two-week mega event. The social media opportunities made available by Channel One spread the content, while mobile application initiatives offered in-depth content. Channel One's efforts to make the second-screen experience available during the Olympics were aligned with international media tendencies regarding second-screen, especially after the London 2012 Games. However, Channel One still did not advance toward a full-fledged transmedial experience because the broadcasters tended to repurpose content, rather than offer new content (Gambarato et al., 2016).

For the 2014 FIFA World Cup, the coverage's tent pole was also television and marked by second-screen engagement. According to Facebook, Twitter, Instagram, and Google reports, the coverage broke all social media records at the time (Massiah, 2014). The most commented match of the "World Cup was not the final but Brazil's 7–1 defeat by Germany in the semi-finals. On Twitter it attracted 35.6m tweets during the game. The figure was a Twitter record for the most-discussed single sports game eve" (Massiah, 2014, para. 2). As the fifth largest Internet population in the world (71 million unique visitors/month), Brazil demonstrated its deep interest in the event through its citizens' online behavior (Vieira, 2014).

The extensions showed different sides of news storytelling. They helped keep the audience interested and informed throughout the two-week event. Social media opportunities made available by Globo spread the content, while mobile application initiatives offered a certain amount of in-depth information. However, Globo Network did not advance toward a full-fledged transmedial experience, as the broadcasters repurposed content instead of offering new content, following the restrictions imposed by FIFA (Gambarato et al., 2017).

For the Rio 2016 Games, Globo Network planned the "biggest coverage in the broadcaster's history after the inauguration of its Olympic Studio" (Rede Globo, 2016b, para. 1). The extended coverage involved all Globo Group media platforms: TV, print, Internet, and radio. For instance, Globo Group's cable sports channel SporTV broadcasted 100% of the competitions live, using 56 signals across TV and the Internet. Subscribers could choose from among 56 broadcasting options available in computer, tablet, and smartphone applications. The video-on-demand platform SporTV Play offered special programs and an interactive video player that displayed pause and rewind options, allowing users to choose events by date and sport (Rede Globo, 2016c). Likewise, the SporTV Rio 2016 mobile application granted users exclusive access to the channel's schedule and medals table. This application, using augmented reality technology, allowed users to receive notifications about the events schedule, information about their favorite athletes, and access to a services guide to Rio de Janeiro showing tourist attractions, means of transportation, bike rentals, police stations, hospitals, and health centers in three languages: Portuguese, Spanish, and English (Rede Globo, 2016a).

This distinctive coverage, although still prioritizing mass media transmission logic, included several multiplatform extensions created in the Olympic Studio. The content aired in the multiscreen environment enabled various possibilities for exploring journalistic content and interacting via social media networks. During the broadcasts, public participation in online social media, mediated by the hashtag *#SomosTodosOlímpicos* [#WeAreAllOlympians], was exhibited live on a large screen at the Olympic Studio. The aim was to update the content on different media platforms used during the news coverage while promoting audience engagement through social media interactions. Although feed updates on networks like Twitter, Facebook, and Instagram were prioritized, a genuine expansion was observed on Snapchat. In an unprecedented partnership (Rede Globo, 2016c), the profile "Snapredeglobo" offered specific content on Snapchat's "Live Stories" feature, including photos and videos behind the scenes of the event recorded by journalists, commentators, and fans, thus establishing a news coverage strategy based on multiplatform broadcasting where specific content was given to certain media extensions to foster engagement.

The multiplatform perspective of Globo Network's Olympic news coverage involved numerous journalistic styles (news stories, articles, interviews, and opinion pieces). Television broadcasts prevailed among the journalistic strategies adopted by the broadcaster, particularly for national news programs and sports programs on public access channels like Globo Esporte. Public access broadcasts favored first, the most popular sports in the country (football, volleyball, and gymnastics) and second, the competitions in which Brazilian athletes participated. Cable channels favored specific sports such as fencing and archery. In both cases, there was a strong online correlation through websites, mobile applications, and social media profiles.

The website globoesporte.com broadcasted 100% of the Olympic Games events on two live streaming channels. Scores were updated in real time on this website. The video-on-demand platform Globo Play offered free content, complementing the public access channel on a 24-hour basis. Users could access competitions that had already happened in an on-demand catalogue organized by athletes, sports, and participating nations. Globoesporte.com also produced exclusive content, including a series of special narratives containing infographics, videos, and specific interactive spaces. Among them were the (1) *Mapa das Medalhas* [Medals Map], where users could filter results by athlete, sport, and chronology since the beginning of the competitions; (2) *Biotipo dos Atletas* [Athletes' Biotype], where 60 athletes, at least one from each sport, were photographed to display the body shape befitting each sport; (3) *Baía de Guanabara* [Guanabara Bay] featured profiles of residents and workers of the region, seeking to depict the area's safety and urban features; (4) *Medalhões Olímpicos* [Olympic "Big Medals"], athletes' profiles in comics and animations; (5) *Time de Ouro* [Golden Team], a series of videos profiling 11 Globo Network commentators who were former acclaimed Olympic athletes; (6) *Meu Pódio Olímpico* [My Olympic Podium], an application showcasing caricatures where users could choose their favorite athletes and share the experience on Facebook; and (7) *Mapa da Tocha* [Torch Map], the Olympic Torch relay with data on dates, people, and places (Esporte e Mídia, 2016).

Although the multiplatform coverage of the event focused mainly on TV, the Internet, radio, and print media were included. Globo Group—including Globo Network (TV), Globosat (cable TV), Infoglobo (print media), and Globo Radio System (radio)—temporarily launched the CBN Globo Radio Station, aggregating Olympic content in a 24-hour schedule produced by Globo Radio and CBN Radio. The radio station was also available online and on mobile applications. The printed newspapers *O Globo* and *Extra* jointly launched the digital platform Infoglobo Rio 2016, providing exclusive behind-the-scenes services and highlights of the Games in real time. The editorial content prepared for Infoglobo included supplementary inserts in printed newspapers, such as (1) *Rio Olímpico, uma nova cidade* [Olympic Rio, a new city], regarding the transformations in the city for the Games; (2) *Guia dos Jogos Olímpicos Rio 2016* [Guide to the 2016 Rio Olympic Games], a complete guide to the Games; (3) *Cadernos de esporte especiais–Jogos Olímpicos Rio 2016* [Special sports supplement–2016 Rio Olympic Games], comprising daily special coverage; and (4) *Cadernos especiais gratuitos* [Free special supplements], a free bilingual publication distributed at and around the Olympic Park (Propmark, 2016).

The content produced by Globo Network in the scope of the broadcaster's multiplatform coverage of the Olympic Games complemented each other but eventually became redundant, favoring users' choices based on their mediatic consumption habits. It was possible to identify the valorization of second-screen applications and geolocation, and the interaction on online social media networks, stemming from journalistic content offered by the broadcaster.

Globo Network's coverage of the Olympic Games excelled in journalistic accuracy, combined with technological innovation. No language innovations were observed in relation to, for instance, initiatives of incorporating virtual reality narratives or newsgames in content expansion. However, editorial planning produced sophisticated broadcasting and information access strategies, made available by the broadcaster throughout multiple media platforms. The use of augmented reality in mobile applications, such as Globo Rio 2016, allowed the audience to, for example, receive real-time information about what was happening at specific locations. *Globolinha*, the coverage's mascot, could be visualized by users when they accessed data about ongoing matches based on geolocation, in similar aesthetics as Pokémon Go. Thus, augmented reality added to the Games transmissions in real time and enriched the audience experience.

Technological advancements were highlighted by holographic projections and the partnership between Globo Network and the Japanese broadcasting organization NHK for live transmissions in the ultrahigh-definition (UHD) 8K format during the Opening and Closing Ceremonies of the Games. The 8K technology defines a cutting-edge standard in image quality, offering a resolution 16 times better than current high definition (HD) used in digital television (Lobo, 2016). However, this noteworthy broadcasting did not result in direct transmedia expansion in journalism. The series of special narratives produced by globoesporte.com, extensively employing infographics, comics, and animations, is another example of the preoccupation with creating a refined aesthetics, grounded in the production of autonomous and complementary narratives in Globo Network's digital news coverage. However, Globo Network's coverage presented some possibilities for audience participation, a crucial aspect in developing transmedia narratives (Gambarato et al., 2018).

Audience

As emphasized in previous chapters, user-generated content is a key element of transmedia supersystems as a participatory form of engagement. However, participation may be subject to copyright in mega sporting events, which compromises the broad participation of audiences.

During the 2014 Sochi Winter Games, audiences interacted by posting comments on social networks and voting in online polls organized by Channel One. The audience could follow the hyperlinks on the channel's website, social media communities, and mobile applications, characterizing interaction but not participation. However, mega events such as the Olympics stimulate user-generated content, and Sochi was no exception, generating Internet memes, parodies, illustrations, games, and more. Due to IOC rules, user-generated content was not used in Channel One coverage (Gambarato et al., 2016).

During the 2014 FIFA World Cup, an impressive television audience (FIFA, 2014b) and the prominent second-screen experience (IBM, 2016) denote the emergence of a new scenario for journalism, in which "the integration of diverse media environments favors hybridity between the logic of transmission, which is typical of mass media, and the logic of sharing, which is typical of social media" (Gambarato et al., 2016, p. 1449).

Despite limitations, Globo Network managed to promote audience engagement by using distinct strategies in the 2016 Rio Olympic Games. The multiplatform audience during the coverage registered an unparalleled growth rate. The cable channel SporTV, Globo's main coverage channel, reached 38 million people during 2,400 hours of broadcasting in 17 days. This is 27% more than all the spectators of the broadcaster's three direct competitors (ESPN, Fox, and BandSports) and 29% more than all the spectators reached by SporTV during the coverage of the London 2012 Games. During the Rio 2016 Games, SporTV and SporTV 2 led prime-time cable television (Stycer, 2016).

The event made a significant impact on different media platforms in the network's news coverage strategy. TV broadcasting registered an increase of 40% of people reached compared to the London 2012 Games. Between August 3 and 21, 2016, the free-to-air Globo Network channel reached 177 million people, 53.5 million more than the London 2012 Games, a 43% increase. The group's digital platforms registered 6.5 million users, with peaks at the Opening and Closing Ceremonies. The broadcast of the Closing Ceremony drew a 27 audience rating, the highest since the 1996 Atlanta Olympics. Globoesporte.com reached a daily average of 15 million accesses during the Games, with a historical record set during the women's football semi-final between Brazil and Sweden: 20.1 million views (Mermelstein, 2016). These numbers show that the multiplatform coverage strategy was successful: Globo Network beat audience records and became the leader of that segment, reaching a varied public with a robust, diversified editorial project. However, this does not mean that audience participation widely permeated editorial planning, even if participation was discernible in specific contexts, such as social media (Gambarato et al., 2018).

According to a study by the marketing company SocialBrain (Soutelo, 2016), Globo Network received more engagement than any other brand through social media during the 2016 Rio Olympic Games. Throughout the Games, Globo Network's profile on Twitter posted 1,800 tweets, generating around 180,000 shares. The hashtag #*SomosTodosOlímpicos* [#WeAreAllOlympics], created by the broadcaster, was mentioned 234,000 times on Twitter between August 3 and 21, 2016, 10 times more than the hashtag #NBCOlympics of the American TV network NBC, which registered 22,000 mentions on Twitter during the same period. Globo Network's coverage became a trending topic on Brazilian Twitter 509 times and globally 165 times. Facebook registered around 830 posts with the hashtag #*SomosTodosOlímpicos* [#WeAreAllOlympics], generating around 6 million accesses. On Instagram, this hashtag was deployed for around 630 posts, with nearly 5.8 million likes. On Snapchat, the broadcaster's profile registered about 730,000 daily visits (Soutelo, 2016). The engagement generated on social media networks, especially when the Globo Network hashtag was used, indicates that the hashtag acted as a symbolic articulation of the broadcaster's posts on social media. This mechanism of interaction stimulates social involvement in news dissemination based on contemporary habits of information consumption. Therefore, social engagement around this hashtag boosted Globo Network's presence on social media. This element is extremely important for the editorial strategy adopted by the company in its multiplatform coverage of the event because it emphasizes the relevance of online social media networks in diffusing journalistic information (Gambarato et al., 2018).

In this sense, the Olympic Games became the most talked-about event ever on Instagram, with 916 million interactions between 131 million Instagram users (G1, 2016). Twitter Brazil organized the challenge #*Tweet-Campeão* [#ChampionTweet], which designated whoever achieved the highest number of views on their profile and mentions on social media the winner. Ana Paula Renault, a participant in the Globo Network Big Brother Brazil reality show, won the contest with a tweet that yielded 3.4 million views and 35,000 mentions. As a reward, her tweet was projected on *Arcos da Lapa*, one of many tourist attractions in Rio de Janeiro. She celebrated her victory on Twitter by using, among others, the hashtag #*SomosTodosOlímpicos* (Joven Pan, 2016). This action demonstrates the social pervasiveness of the hashtag created by Globo Network for the Olympic Games, in the social interactions on Twitter during that period and in the online and offline connections.

Overall, the broadcaster's audience engagement strategy privileged interaction to the detriment of participation. In this scenario, the IOC rules and regulations decreased the opportunities to foster participation during the Games (Gambarato et al., 2018).

Globo Network had a clear communication strategy for the event. Sergio Valente, the Globo Network communication coordinator for the 2014 FIFA World Cup, highlighted that their communication project had three vectors: (1) The World Cup is broader than the broadcaster, (2) the role of TV broadcasting is to create an agenda for the population during the World Cup, and (3) the communication should create value for World Cup sponsors such as Ambev, Coca-Cola, Itaú, Johnson & Johnson, Hyundai, Magazine Luiza, Nestlé, and Oi, whose investments totaled R$1.438 billion, or US$700 million (Penteado, 2014). Valente explained that the whole strategy was drawn from the event's vignette, whose motto was *Agora somos todos um* [Now we all are one]. The goal was to show that on game day, all of Brazil was moved by the same thing: the FIFA World Cup. To communicate this goal, for example, Globo Network used the hashtags #*SomosUmSó* [#WeAllAreOne] and #*GloboNaCopa* [#GloboInTheCup] on online social networks. Globo Network broadcast all 64 World Cup matches (56 condensed in a one-hour transmission), with tactical analysis by commentators and the use of technology to engage the audience, such as second-screen experience, graphics, holograms, and interactive experiences with virtual players. All Globo Network TV shows, including variety and sports shows, produced special World Cup content. Coverage was also provided separately by Globo Network subsidiaries, such as Sport TV, Globo TV, and CBN radio. In total, six channels (two free-to-air and four pay-TV) broadcast the games.

According to audience numbers for official 2018 FIFA World Cup broadcast data, a combined 3.572 billion viewers, more than half the global population aged above four years, tuned in to football's ultimate competition (FIFA, 2018). The global in-home TV audience watching at least one minute of coverage totaled 3.262 billion, while a further estimated 309.7 million people had no coverage in home but caught the action on digital platforms, in public viewing areas, or in bars and restaurants, boosting the total audience by 9.5% (FIFA, 2018). On average, viewers watching on TV at home engaged with the coverage for longer than during previous FIFA World Cups: 3.04 billion viewers caught at least three minutes of the 2018 edition, a 10.9% increase from Brazil 2014. Meanwhile, 2.49 billion viewers watched for at least 30 minutes, up from 1.95 billion in 2014 (FIFA, 2018).

Structure

Members of the press are accredited by committees in each country two years in advance. The process is divided among print, photography, and radio/TV broadcasters, which also differs between those who hold broadcasting rights and those who do not. This differentiation of the accredited creates embarrassment for journalists, who are classified according to the level of their company's economic participation with the entities representing the events. Written and photographic press, including technical support and radio/TV reporters, called non-right holders, are accredited in a generic category called Category E. The number of accredited professionals is determined for each game, based on the previous edition. At the 2014 Olympics, the credentials for journalists were divided into the following categories: Journalist (E), Specialized Journalist (Es), Photographer (EP), Specialized Photographer (EPs), Technicians (ET), Support Team (EC), and Non-holders of Transmission Rights (ENR). These various categories predetermine the outcome of journalistic coverage:

> This latter group wears Olympic credentials marked 'ENR,' which is Olympic-ese for 'non-rights-holding broadcaster.' They are the untouchables of the Olympic press corps and they are barred from high-demand events (including swimming, opening and closing ceremonies, and basketball finals). That still leaves the bulk of competition for the scarlet lettered ENRs but they can't enter Olympic venues with recorders, microphones or video cameras. They can't record in 'mixed zones' where reporters encounter sweating or dripping athletes

as soon as the Olympians walk off the track, the pool deck, the beach volleyball sand, or the competition arena. And they can't record medal-winning athletes and coaches at their victory news conferences at Olympic venues.

(Berkes, 2012, p. 7)

For the 2016 Summer Olympics in Rio, Brazilian television channels Globo Network, Record Network, and Bandeirantes Network generated the international radio and TV signals. The accreditation of more than 25,100 official media professionals started three years before the event (Mioli, 2015). More than 7,000 hours of video and audio coverage were produced and distributed to an audience of six billion people in 220 countries (Long, 2016). Globo Network planned multiplatform coverage of the Games, including online streaming, social media networks, mobile applications, and websites. The websites remain live and are updated. Globo Network's journey toward the 2016 Rio Olympics began in August 2009, shortly before the Games were awarded to Brazil. The company, which aired its first Olympics coverage in 1992, secured the domestic rights to the event as the head of the consortium that included the other two Brazilian media companies (Record Network and Bandeirantes Network). Under the terms of the IOC contract, Globo Network was obligated to broadcast at least nine hours of free-to-air coverage per day. However, the network aired at least ten hours of programming per day, with comprehensive programming across cable, video-on-demand, and online services. The broadcaster's free-to-air offering included 160 hours of content throughout the Games, with more than 100 hours broadcasted live and in prime time. SporTV, Globo Network's cable sports channel, provided high-definition transmission on television, the Internet, and mobile platforms (SporTV, 2016). The around-the-clock on-demand service, SporTV Play, and a dedicated mobile application, SporTV Rio 2016, rounded out the free coverage (Long, 2016). During the Games, the company's technical workforce was increased by more than 2,000 individuals. The team was split into two groups: One group was positioned at Globo Network headquarters in Rio de Janeiro, and the other was based in a newsroom at the International Broadcast Center (IBC). The broadcaster's public operations took place inside the network's Olympic Studio facility in the heart of the Olympic Park. Constructed almost entirely out of glass, the 500-square-meter, three-story facility was the set for the many news shows and on-air interviews aired during the Games (Long, 2016). Anchoring the coverage was what the network called its "dream team": a dozen former star Olympic athletes. Globo Network allegedly invested around US$250 million in this coverage (Feltrin, 2016). This structure and large investment collaborated to effectively execute the planned transmedia strategies for the news coverage.

The broadcaster built the concept "we are all Olympians," on which the network based its actions to involve and engage the audience. The warm-up for the Games started in March 2016. About 2,500 news pieces on the subject were aired before the Opening Ceremony. Globo Group involved several of the group's content platforms in this coverage. This group coverage did not occur during the coverage of the 2014 FIFA World Cup (Gambarato et al., 2017). This time, Globo created different concepts for each media platform, a core characteristic of transmedia storytelling and journalism. Cable television, with more than 1,000 professionals involved in the coverage, provided a broad experience of the Games. Print media, under the premise "digital first," delivered material to websites, mobile applications, e-books, and special magazines. A free printed tabloid paper and a guide to the Olympics were published. A special digital environment was created to follow the competitions in real time and focus on user interactivity. Infographics, photo galleries, videos, quizzes, and minidocumentaries were also available. Specific actions were conducted on social media to encourage user involvement through posts and comments. The coverage also offered a competition-based game, divided into stages. Players scored points by answering questions related to the Games. The mobile application was developed to provide information, news about competitions, and itineraries for the event's day-to-day schedule. The application provided information about which bars broadcasted competitions, venues where fans from a certain country gathered, and other services. The newspapers focused on stories of citizenship, optimism, overcoming difficulties, inclusion, and other Olympic values. With information about and services for tourists on how to make the most of their stay in the city, Infoglobo served as an alternative for brands wanting to communicate directly with tourists. Radio operations concentrated on information, thrills, and humor throughout bulletins and programs, always striving to present the Olympic sports in an easier, more practical manner to the audience. The *Construindo Campeões* [Building Champions] project visited schools in Rio de Janeiro and neighboring municipalities, offering students the opportunity to experience the role of radio reporters and commentators through their schoolmates' games (Grupo Globo, 2016).

The broadcasting rights (TV, radio, Internet, and mobile coverage) for the tournaments are sold to media companies in each individual territory either directly by FIFA or the IOC or through licensed companies. The sale of these rights accounts for about 60% of FIFA's income from a World Cup. The International Broadcast Centre was situated at the Riocentro in the Barra da Tijuca neighborhood of Rio de Janeiro.

For special coverage of the World Cup in Russia, Globo involved 400 professionals, a panoramic studio in the Red Square, technological innovations, and distinct programming. Globo broadcasted all the tournament's matches, with 56 live transmissions. The space generated a 180-degree panorama of the postcard landscape. Augmented reality and artistic effects, like match schedules and player images, were displayed on LED screen walls and floor. In addition to the press coverage, Globo's international channels broadcasted the *Conexão Rússia* [Russia Connection] program to more than 3 million subscribers worldwide. The program was created to capture and transmit reports for the event.

In a nutshell, the news coverage of the 2014 and 2018 FIFA World Cups in Brazil and Russia, respectively, encompassed various media platforms and the flow of information in the intersection between mass media (especially TV) and social media (especially Twitter and Facebook). Our research findings demonstrate that the Globo Network coverage was modestly transmediatic in 2014 and 2018, presenting audience engagement methods and limited content expansion within technological advances. However, there was no solid transmedia plan aimed at articulating transmediality to build a universe designed for various integrated media platforms.

The fact that the 2016 Olympic Games were held in Rio had a huge impact on the investments made by Globo Network, which resulted in consolidated strategic transmedia planning for the coverage. News coverage of the 2016 Rio Olympics in Brazil encompassed multiple media platforms and the flow of information in the intersection between mass media (especially TV) and social media (especially Snapchat and Instagram). The 2016 Rio Olympics was the Games of Snapchat stories and filters and Instagram stories for news coverage. The findings show the coverage presented systematic content via various media platforms but involved limited audience engagement, particularly audience participation.

Closing thoughts

Transmedia journalism is an elastic term with various theoretical approaches (Dominguez, 2012). The conceptual confusion can eventually blur the real scope, practices, and principles. However, independently of the terminology and the elusive understanding that can be depicted, the multi-platform method of *produsage* (Bruns, 2008), which refers to the user-led content creation available in online environments, has a global perspective. Planned events can vary in scale (Bowdin et al., 2012) and function (Getz, 2012). News coverage of planned events can vary in all dimensions, including the size of the news company involved, the technological apparatus, the number and variety of professionals, and the strategies behind it. Large broadcasters and independent news companies are likely already aware of the developments of transmedia strategies in journalism and the spreadable core characteristics of transmedia journalism. Multiplatform news media production is already a reality that, although probably more modest than comprehensive, tends to grow and improve. "Actually, our brain is transmedia" (Renó, 2014, p. 8). The model of analysis of transmedia strategies for the news coverage of planned events we presented can contribute to this process of growth and improvement in transmedia journalism. Analysis potentially leads to synthesis (Liestøl, 2003) and could advance transmedia practices in journalism. The five dimensions of the model (story, premise, extensions, audience, and structure) specify the minutiae incorporated in transmedia strategies for journalism in applied research in the interest of the news media industry. The model exposes the transmedia features behind news media coverage, serving scholars' analysis and guiding journalists in the transmedia strategy praxis. Journalism is not isolated: It is in a symbiotic relationship with political, legal, economic, and technological structures. Understanding the structural context of journalism is important. Above all, in transmedia strategies of news coverage and news media practice, good journalism principles should prevail. "TS [transmedia storytelling] is both a reality and a tendency worldwide and the prospect of TS is to grow and to improve rapidly. TS analysis can help this process" (Gambarato, 2013, p. 98). Ultimately, "the purpose of a transmedia news story is to inform the readers in the best way possible" (Ford, 2007, para. 6).

References

Anderson, R., Dardenne, R. W., & Killenberg, G. M. (1994). *The conversation of journalism: Communication, community, and news.* Westport, CT: Praeger.

Bauman, Z. (2000). *Liquid modernity.* Cambridge, England: Polity Press.

BBC. (2013). *Annual report 2012/2013.* Retrieved from http://www.bbc.co.uk/annualreport/2013/executive

BBC. (2016, January 6). Who are the indicted Fifa officials? *BBC.* Retrieved from https://www.bbc.com/news/world-latin-america-32897171

Berkes, H. (2012, October 15). Inside the rings. *Nieman reports.* Retrieved from https://nieman.harvard.edu/articles/inside-the-rings

Bowdin, G. A. J., McDonnell, I., Allen, J., & O'Toole, W. (2012). *Events management.* London, England: Routledge.

Boyle, R. (2006). *Sports journalism: Context and issues.* London, England: Sage.

Bruns, A. (2008). *Blogs, Wikipedia, Second Life, and beyond: From production to produsage.* New York, NY: Peter Lang.

Canavilhas, J. (2014). Jornalismo transmídia: Um desafio ao velho ecossistema midiático [Transmedia journalism: A challenge to the old media ecosystem]. In D. Renó, S. Ruiz, C. Campalans, & V. Gosciola (Eds.), *Periodismo transmedia: Miradas múltiples* [Transmedia journalism: Multiple views] (pp. 53–68). Bogotá, Colombia: Editorial Universidad del Rosario.

Canavilhas, J. (2018). Journalism in the twenty-first century: To be or not to be transmedia? In R. Gambarato & G. Alzamora (Eds.), *Exploring transmedia journalism in the digital age* (pp. 1–14). Hershey, PA: IGI Global.

Carney, J., & Phelps, C. (2016, August 3). Welcome to the poo-lympics: Raw sewage pours into Rio's Guanabara Bay as athletes are warned to shower straight after leaving the water and paramedics wait on the shore to treat cuts. *Daily Mail.* Retrieved from https://www.dailymail.co.uk/news/article-3720802/Rio-Olympics-pollution-problem-worsens-raw-sewage-pours-Guanabara-Bay.html#ixzz4d87H9ETp

Caryl, C. (2014, February 5). Why Sochi? *The New York Review of Books.* Retrieved from https://www.nybooks.com/daily/2014/02/05/why-sochi-russia-olympics/

Craig, D. A. (2011). *Excellence in online journalism: Exploring current practices in an evolving environment.* Los Angeles, CA: Sage.

Dahlgren, P., & Carpentier, N. (2013). The social relevance of participatory theory. *Comunicazioni Sociali, 3,* 301–315.

Dayan, D., & Katz, E. (1992). *Media events: The live broadcasting of history.* Cambridge, MA: Harvard University Press.

Dominguez, E. (2012). Periodismo transmedia, ¿Nuevo o renovado? [Transmedia journalism, new or renewed?]. *Revista de los Estudios de Ciencias de la Informacion e Comunicacion, 13.* Retrieved from http://comein.uoc.edu/divulgacio/comein/es/numero13/articles/Article-Eva-Dominguez.html

DW. (2016, December 9). Timeline: Doping in Russia. *Deutsch Welle.* Retrieved from https://www.dw.com/en/timeline-doping-in-russia/a-19409797

ESPN. (2018, April 25). *Russia predicts World Cup will have $31 billion economic impact.* Retrieved from https://www.espn.com/soccer/fifa-world-cup/story/3471440/russia-predicts-world-cup-will-have-$31-billion-economic-impact

Esporte e Mídia. (2016, July 13). Globoesporte.com detalha cobertura dos Jogos Olímpicos; saiba mais [Globoesporte.com presents the details of the Olympic Games coverage; learn more]. *Esporte e Mídia.* Retrieved from http://www.esporteemidia.com/2016/07/globoesportecom-detalha-cobertura-dos.html

Feltrin, R. (2016, August 21). Exclusivo: Globo investiu US$ 250 milhões na Rio 2016 [Exclusive: Globo invested US$250 million on Rio 2016]. *UOL.* Retrieved from https://tvefamosos.uol.com.br/noticias/ooops/2016/08/21/exclusivo-globo-investiu-us-250-mi-na-rio-2016-veja-gastos-de-outras-tvs.htm?cmpid=copiaecola

FIFA. (2012). *Globo buys broadcast rights to 2018 and 2022 FIFA World Cups.* Retrieved from https://www.fifa.com/about-fifa/who-we-are/news/globo-buys-broadcast-rights-2018-and-2022-fifa-world-cupstm-1591131

FIFA. (2014a). *FIFA public guidelines for use of FIFA's official marks.* Retrieved from https://resources.fifa.com/mm/document/affederation/marketing/01/37/85/97/2014_fifapublicguidelines_eng_13032014_neutral.pdf

FIFA. (2014b). *Preliminary draw 2014 FIFA World Cup Brazil: Television audience report.* Retrieved from https://img.fifa.com/image/upload/n3z25ncdjj9qdwja1tet.pdf

FIFA. (2018). *More than half the world watched record-breaking 2018 World Cup.* Retrieved from https://www.fifa.com/worldcup/news/more-than-half-the-world-watched-record-breaking-2018-world-cup

Ford, S. (2007, April 5). Transmedia journalism: A story-based approach to convergence. *Futures of Entertainment.* Retrieved from http://www.convergenceculture.org/weblog/2007/04/transmedia_ journalism_a_storyb.php.

G1. (2016, August 22). Rio 2016 é evento mais "instagramado" da história; foto de Neymar bomba [Rio 2016 is the most "instagrammed" event in history; Neymar's photo pumps]. *G1.* Retrieved from http://g1.globo.com/tecnologia/noticia/2016/08/rio-2016-e-evento-mais-instagramado-da-historia-foto-de-neymar-bomba.html

Gambarato, R. R. (2012). Signs, systems and complexity of transmedia storytelling. *Communication Studies, 12,* 69–83.

Gambarato, R. R. (2013). Transmedia project design: Theoretical and analytical considerations. *Baltic Screen Media Review, 1,* 80–100.

Gambarato, R. R., & Alzamora, G. (2018). *Exploring transmedia journalism in the digital age.* Hershey, PA: IGI Global.

Gambarato, R. R., Alzamora, G., & Tárcia, L. (2016). Russian news coverage of 2014 Sochi Winter Olympic Games: A transmedia analysis. *International Journal of Communication, 10,* 1446–1469.

Gambarato, R. R., Alzamora, G., & Tárcia, L. (2018). Rio Summer Olympics and the transmedia journalism of planned events. In R. R. Gambarato & G. Alzamora (Eds.), *Exploring transmedia journalism in the digital age* (pp. 126–146). Hershey, PA: IGI Global.

Gambarato, R. R., Alzamora, G. C., Tárcia, L., & Jurno, A. (2017). 2016 FIFA World Cup on the Brazilian Globo Network: A transmedia dynamics? *Global Media and Communication, 13*(3), 283–301.

Gambarato, R. R., & Tárcia, L. (2017). Transmedia strategies in journalism: An analytical model for the coverage of planned events. *Journalism Studies, 18*(11), 1381–1399.

Getz, D. (2012). *Event studies: Theory, research and policy for planned events.* New York, NY: Routledge.

Globo TV. (2015, June 4). Ninguém pode dizer o que vai ser da Fifa depois do escândalo de corrupção [No one can say what FIFA will be after the corruption scandal]. *GloboPlay.* Retrieved from https://globoplay.globo.com/v/4231209/

Gomez, A. (2016, August 14). Muggings, violence during Olympics highlight Brazil's tourism woes. *USA Today.* Retrieved from https://eu.usatoday.com/story/sports/olympics/rio-2016/2016/08/14/rio-olympics-muggings-brazil-tourism-woes/88719804/

Gomez, J. (2010). Pergunta: Esse modelo de narrativa transmídia storytelling pode ser aplicado ao jornalismo? Você conhece algum caso? [Question: Can this transmedia storytelling narrative model be applied to journalism? Do you know any cases?]. *Rede Globo.* Retrieved from http://redeglobo.globo.com/platb/tarolando/2010/02/05/pergunta-pergunta-esse-modelo-de-narrativa-transmidia-storytelling-pode-ser-aplicado-ao-jornalismo-voce-conhece-algum-caso

Grupo Globo. (2016, June 22). Grupo Globo announces media sponsorship of the Rio 2016 Olympic Games. *Grupo Globo.* Retrieved from http://grupoglobo.globo.com/ingles/news/grupo_globo_sponsorship_olympic_games.php

Hayes, G. (2011). *How to write a transmedia production bible.* Sydney, Australia: Screen Australia.

Heinrich, A. (2011). *Network journalism: Journalistic practice in interactive spheres.* New York, NY: Routledge.

Hepp, A., & Couldry, N. (2010). Introduction: Media events in globalized media cultures. In N. Couldry, A. Hepp, & F. Krotz (Eds.), *Media events in a global age* (pp. 1–20). London, England: Routledge.

Herreros, M. C., & Vivar, J. M. F. (2011). *Periodismo en la telefonia móvil* [Journalism in the mobile telephony]. Madrid, Spain: Editorial Fragua.

Horne, J. (2012). The four 'cs' of sports mega-events: Capitalism, connections, citizenship and contradictions. In G. Hayes & J. Karamichas (Eds.), *Olympic Games, mega-events and civil societies: Globalization, environment, resistance* (pp. 31–45). New York, NY: Palgrave Macmillan.

Horne, J., & Whannel, G. (2012). *Understanding the Olympics.* London, England: Routledge.

IBM. (2016, September). *Globo TV scored huge audiences during the 2014 FIFA World Cup by teaming up with IBM analytics.* Retrieved from https://www-03.ibm.com/software/businesscasestudies/bg/bg/corp?synkey=W085221C53959R92

International Olympic Committee. (2014). *Sochi 2014 facts & figures*. Retrieved from https://stillmed.olympic.org/media/Document%20Library/OlympicOrg/Games/Winter-Games/Games-Sochi-2014-Winter-Olympic-Games/Facts-and-Figures/Factsheet-Facts-and-Figures-Sochi-2014.pdf

International Olympic Committee News. (2015). IOC reaches agreement for broadcast rights in Brazil with Grupo Globo through to 2032. *IOC News*. Retrieved from https://www.olympic.org/news/ioc-reaches-agreement-for-broadcast-rights-in-brazil-with-grupo-globo-through-to-2032

Jenkins, H. (2009a, December 12). Revenge of the origami unicorn: The remaining four principles of transmedia storytelling. *Confessions of an aca-fan*. Retrieved from http://henryjenkins.org/blog/2009/12/revenge_of_the_origami_unicorn.html

Jenkins, H. (2009b, December 12). The revenge of the origami unicorn: Seven principles of transmedia storytelling (Well, two actually. Five more on Friday). *Confessions of an aca-fan*. Retrieved from http://henryjenkins.org/2009/12/the_revenge_of_the_origami_uni.html

Jones, J., & Salter, L. (2012). *Digital journalism*. London, England: Sage.

Joven Pan. (2016, August 5). Rio 2016: Ex-BBB Ana Paula vence desafio e terá tweet projetado em monumento [Rio 2016: Ex-BBB Ana Paul won the challenge and her tweet will be projected onto monument]. *Joven Pan*. Retrieved from https://jovempan.com.br/esportes/rio-2016-ex-bbb-ana-paula-vence-desafio-e-tera-tweet-projetado-em-monumento.html

Kaiser, A. (2014, July 7). Brazil 2014: World Cup where politics and social media invaded the pitch. *The Guardian*. Retrieved from https://www.theguardian.com/football/2014/jul/07/brazil-world-cup-politics-social-media-debate-fifa-football

Kolodzy, J. (2012). *Convergence journalism: Writing and reporting across the news media*. London, England: Routledge.

Lessig, L. (2008). *Remix: Making art and commerce thrive in the hybrid economy*. New York, NY: Penguin Press.

Liestøl, G. (2003). Gameplay: From synthesis to analysis (and vice versa): Topics of conceptualization and construction in digital media. In G. Liestøl, A. Morrison, & T. Rasmussen (Eds.), *Digital media revisited* (pp. 389–413). Cambridge, MA: MIT Press.

Lewis, S. (2012). The tension between professional control and open participation. *Information, Communication & Society, 15*(6), 836–866.

Lobo, A. P. (2016, August 8). Globo usa DWDM nacional para transmitir em 8K na Rio 2016 [Globo uses national DWDM to broadcast in 8K in Rio 2016]. *Convergência Digital*. Retrieved from http://www.convergenciadigital.com.br/cgi/cgilua.exe/sys/start.htm?UserActiveTemplate=site&%25252525253Butm%252525252525252525255Fmedium=&UserActiveTemplate=site%252Csite&infoid=43182&sid=4

Long, M. (2016, August 4). Globo gathering: How Brazil's biggest broadcaster is tackling Rio 2016. *SportsPro*. Retrieved from http://www.sportspromedia.com/magazine_features/globo_gathering_how_brazils_biggest_broadcaster_is_gearing_up_for_rio_2016

Lovato, A. (2018). The transmedia script for nonfictional narratives. In R. R. Gambarato & G. Alzamora (Eds.), *Exploring transmedia journalism in the digital age* (pp. 235–254). Hershey, PA: IGI Global.

Looney, M. (2013, January 30). 5 tips for transmedia storytelling. *Media Shift*. Retrieved from http://www.pbs.org/mediashift/2013/01/5-tips-for-transmedia-storytelling030

Massiah, A. (2014). #BBCtrending: The World Cup in social media stats. *BBC*. Retrieved from http://www.bbc.com/news/blogs-trending-28295898

McLaughlin, E. C., & Botelho, G. (2015, May 28). FIFA corruption probe targets "World Cup of fraud," IRS chief says. *CNN*. Retrieved from https://edition.cnn.com/2015/05/27/football/fifa-corruption-charges-justice-department/index.html

Mermelstein, A. (2016, August 26). Olimpíada impulsionou Globo em diversas plataformas [Olympics boosted Globo Network in various platforms]. *Converge Comunicações*. Retrieved from http://convergecom.com.br/telaviva/paytv/26/08/2016/olimpiadas-impulsionaram-globo-em-diversas-plataformas

Mioli, T. (2015, October 26). Rio 2016 Olympic Games communications director explains how the city is getting ready for 30,000 journalists. *Journalism in the Americas*. Retrieved from https://knightcenter.utexas.edu/blog/00-16397-rio2016-olympic-games-communications-director-explains-how-city-gettingready-30000-jo

Moloney, K. T. (2011). *Porting transmedia storytelling to journalism* (Unpublished master's thesis). University of Denver, Denver, CO.

Moloney, K. T. (2018). Designing transmedia journalism projects. In R. R. Gambarato & G. Alzamora (Eds.), *Exploring transmedia journalism in the digital age* (pp. 83–103). Hershey, PA: IGI Global.

Moragas, M., Rivenburg, N., & Larson, J. (1995). *Television in the Olympics*. London, England: Libbey.

Panagiotopoulou, R. (2010). Sports events: The Olympics in Greece. In N. Couldry, A. Hepp, & F. Krotz (Eds.), *Media events in a global age* (pp. 233–249). London, England: Routledge.

Pase, A. F., Goss, B. M., & Tietzmann, R. A. (2018). Matter of time: Transmedia journalism challenges. In R. R. Gambarato & G. Alzamora (Eds.), *Exploring transmedia journalism in the digital age* (pp. 49–66). Hershey, PA: IGI Global.

Penteado, C. (2014). Globo e a estratégia para a Copa: Projeto é um dos maiores liderados por Sergio Valente desde sua chegada [Globo and the strategy for the World Cup: Project is one of the largest led by Sergio Valente since his arrival]. *Propmark*. Retrieved from http://propmark.com.br/midia/globo-e-a-estrategia-para-a-copa

Propmark. (2016, June 28). Infoglobo prepara ambiente digital para cobertura da Rio 2016 [Infoglobo prepares digital environment for coverage of Rio 2016]. *Propmark*. Retrieved from http://propmark.com.br/midia/infoglobo-prepara-ambiente-digital-para-cobertura-da-rio-2016

Pumerantz, Z. (2012). Ranking the biggest events in sports. *Bleacher Report*. Retrieved from https://bleacherreport.com/articles/1247928-ranking-the-biggest-events-in-sports#slide10

Rede Globo. (2016a, July 29). Aplicativo Globo Rio 2016: Guia de serviços e realidade aumentada; baixe [Rio 2016 Globo application: Service guide and augmented reality; download it]. *Rede Globo*. Retrieved from http://redeglobo.globo.com/novidades/noticia/2016/07/aplicativo-globo-rio-2016-guiade-servicos-e-realidade-aumentada-baixe.html

Rede Globo. (2016b, July 29). Globo estreia estúdio no coração dos Jogos Olímpicos no domingo, dia 31 [Globo launches studio in the heart of the Olympic

Games on Sunday, 31]. *Rede Globo*. Retrieved from http://redeglobo.globo.com/novidades/noticia/2016/07/globo-estreia-estudio-no-coracao-dos-jogosolimpicos-no-domingo-dia-31.html

Rede Globo. (2016c, August 3). Rio 2016: Globo e Snapchat fecham parceria para produção de conteúdo [Rio 2016: Globo and Snapchat agree on partnership for content production]. *Rede Globo*. Retrieved from http://redeglobo.globo.com/novidades/noticia/2016/08/rio-2016-globo-e-snapchat-fecham-parceriapara-producao-de-conteudo.html

Renó, D. (2014). Transmedia journalism and the new media ecology: Possible languages. In D. Renó, C. Campalans, & S. Ruiz (Eds), *Periodismo transmedia: Miradas múltiples* [Transmedia journalism: Multiple perspectives] (pp. 3–19). Barcelona, Spain: Editorial UOC.

Rivera, R. (2011, June 17). Connected storytelling: One service, ten products, four screens. *BBC*. Retrieved from https://www.bbc.co.uk/blogs/aboutthebbc/2011/06/connected-storytelling-one-service-ten-products-four-screens.shtml

Roche, M. (2000). *Mega-events and modernity: Olympics and expos in the growth of global culture*. London, England: Routledge.

Rosenberg, M., & Ingram, D. (2015, December 14). U.S. investigates broadcasters in widening FIFA case. *Reuters*. Retrieved from https://www.reuters.com/article/soccer-fifa-broadcasting-idUSKBN0TX06720151214

Scolari, C. A. (2013, May 15). *Transmídia para além da ficção* [Transmedia beyond fiction] [PowerPoint slides]. Lecture, Belo Horizonte, Brazil.

SporTV. (2016, July 8). SporTV entrega a maior cobertura dos Jogos Olímpicos Rio 2016 [SporTV delivers the biggest coverage of the 2016 Rio Olympic Games]. *SporTV*. Retrieved from http://sportv.globo.com/site/programas/rio-2016/noticia/2016/07/sportv-entrega-maior-cobertura-dos-jogos-olimpicos-rio-2016.html

Soutelo, N. (2016, August 26). O que as redes sociais fizeram pelas Olimpíadas e o que também podem fazer pela sua marca [What have social media networks done for the Olympics and what they can also do for your brand]. *SocialBrain*. Retrieved from http://www.socialbrain.com.br/inbound-marketing/oque-as-redes-sociais-fizeram-pelas-olimpiadas-e-que-tambem-podem-fazer-pela-sua-marca

Stycer, M. (2016, August 25). Audiência do SporTV na Rio-2016 foi maior que a soma de todos os concorrentes [SporTV's audience during the 2016 Rio Olympics was bigger than the sum of all other concurrents]. *Blog do Mauricio Stycer*. Retrieved from https://mauriciostycer.blogosfera.uol.com.br/2016/08/25/audiencia-do-sportv-na-rio-2016-foi-maior-que-a-soma-de-todos-concorrentes

Sun, L. H. (2016, May 27). 150 experts say Olympics must be moved or postponed because of Zika. *The Washington Post*. Retrieved from https://www.washingtonpost.com/gdpr-consent/?destination=%2fnews%2fto-your-health%2fwp%2f2016%2f05%2f27%2f125-experts-say-olympics-must-be-moved-or-postponed-because-of-zika%2f%3f

Tárcia, L. (2015). *Tramas da convergência: Cartografia de dispositivos acoplados na cobertura dos Jogos Olímpicos de Verão pela BBC em 2012* [Convergence plots: Cartography of coupled diapositives on BBC Summer Olympics coverage in 2012] (Unpublished doctoral dissertation). Federal University of Minas Gerais, Belo Horizonte, Brazil.

Tárcia, L. (2016). Tramas da convergência: Hiperdispositivo e a cobertura dos Jogos Olímpicos de Verão pela BBC em 2012 [Convergence plots: Hyperdispositif and BBC Summer Olympics coverage in 2012]. *Dispositiva, 5*(2), 15–30.

Tavares, O., & Mascarenhas, A. (2013). Jornalismo e convergência: Possibilidades transmidiáticas no jornalismo pós-massivo [Journalism and convergence: Transmedial possibilities in post mass journalism]. *Revista Famecos, 20*(1), 193–210.

The Guardian. (2015, December 9). IOC: Brazil's political turmoil will "inevitably" affect Rio 2016 Olympics. *The Guardian.* Retrieved from https://www.theguardian.com/sport/2015/dec/09/brazil-turmoil-rio-2016-olympics

Toffler, A. (1980). *The third wave: The classic study of tomorrow.* New York, NY: Bantam.

Vieira, B. (2014). The huge impact of the 2014 World Cup on Internet usage in Brazil. *Comscore.* Retrieved from http://www.comscore.com/Insights/Blog/The-Huge-Impact-of-the-2014World-Cup-on-Internet-Usage-in-Brazil

Wenner, L. A., & Billings, A. C. (2017). *Sport, media and mega-events.* New York, NY: Routledge.

Wüthrich, M. (2016, April). Protecting the Olympic properties. *WIPO magazine.* Retrieved from https://www.wipo.int/wipo_magazine/en/2016/04/article_0004.html

Part III
Strategic planning

5 Transmedia strategic planning for education[1]

About education, communication, and dialogues

The words *education* and *communication* are etymologically derived from the Latin word *ónis*, which specifically refers to human action. Scientifically, theorists on education and communication emphasize the social rules that guide such practices (Messias, 2011). For Charlot (1992) and Freire (1973), for instance, the historical social subject must be educated through a communication act. Likewise, communication is embedded in education and needs to be taught as a pedagogy of communication (Freire, 1976):

> Teaching and learning are thus moments of a larger process—that of knowing, of cognizing, which implies recognizing. At the bottom, what I mean is that the educand really becomes an educand when and to the extent that he or she knows, or comes to know, content, cognoscible objects and not in the measure that the educator is depositing in the educand a description of the objects or contents.
>
> (Freire, 2014, p. 38)

Freire emphasizes the mediating character of communication as process and act. When someone communicates, they do so not only because they have the intention but also because they act. Communication, whether through media or not, is an object of learning. Communicators and educators face great challenges, as their social roles are interconnected, even more so today. A key aspect of Freire's perspective is dialogue. According to him, dialogue presupposes intersubjectivity, exchange, and immersion in the cultural universe of others. From his viewpoint, dialogue is based on and transforms communication, as they are inseparable: "For humanism there is no path other than dialogue. To engage in dialogue is to be genuine. For true humanism, to engage in dialogue is not to engage without commitment. Humanism is to make dialogue live" (Freire, 1976, p. 108). As argued by Jenkins (see Chapter 1), horizontality is a key feature of communication, and one of the most relevant aspects of convergence culture, which means the possibility of giving voice to those who are "the most oppressed and most dispossessed to get their stories out and get their stories in circulation" (HCDMediaGroup, 2009).

The school community is immersed in the communication world and in a complex supersystem composed of collective and individual stories, experiences, and platforms, as discussed in Chapter 2. The classroom functions as a communication microenvironment in which teachers, students, staff, parents, and communities interact.

As a method of literacy for the world, Freire's pedagogy advocates in addition to technological skills the experience of life of historical subjects, in which "the act of studying, a curious act of the subject facing the world, is an expression of a form of existing" (Freire & Macedo, 2005, p. 53). Moreover, he believes that "since human beings are social, historical beings, they are doers, they are transformers, they not only know, but know that they know" (Freire & Macedo, 2005, p. 60).

Freire examined the ability of media culture to mobilize and raise awareness of themes that are underexplored or ignored by schools. These mobilizations from a participatory culture (see Chapter 1) are independent of the technologies themselves and relate to the idea that students become producers of valuable knowledge, exploring analog and/or digital platforms. This perspective emerges at the heart of educommunication, a theoretical field of study founded by the Latin American theoretical currents of liberating pedagogy, popular communication, and cultural studies during the mid-1980s. According to Mateus and Quiroz-Velasco (2017, p. 53), educommunication "currently constitutes a dynamic line of research with a life of its own." Educommunication is interested in the dialogic relationship between media and its impact on the educational environment and its main actors—students, teachers, and parents. Concepts such as media education and media pedagogy; media, visual, and informational literacy; new literacies; and digital and informational skills appear in the literature on educommunication, sometimes as synonyms for or as different models of it (Mateus & Quiroz-Velasco, 2017):

> Since there is evidence regarding educommunication from the first half of the twentieth century in terms of initiatives and projects in different parts of the world, it is impossible to attribute a specific nationality to this concept. For political and idiomatic reasons, the Anglo-Saxon concept of 'Media Literacy' became the most widespread. Even today, it is almost impossible to find publications in English related to Latin American authors—including Mario Kaplún, Francisco Gutiérrez, or Daniel Prieto Castillo—who began developing the concept of educommunication during the 1960s. Other Southern authors, such as Paulo Freire, Luis Ramiro Beltrán, Jesús Martín-Barbero, or Néstor Garcia-Canclini, have achieved more recognition, albeit delayed.
>
> (Mateus & Quiroz-Velasco, 2017, p. 154)

Ismar de Oliveira Soares (2009), a seminal Brazilian author, defines educommunication as a dialogical field comprising four issues: (1) qualified reception, (2) popular education, (3) collective articulation for social change, and (4) its recognition as a right that must be included in public policies. Paulo Freire is considered a theoretical reference for the field due to his rescue of the political dimension of social change-oriented education and its liberating function, which enables students to produce and construct knowledge related to their environment through dialogue.

Freire (1970) also proposes the construction of a dialogue based on students' experiences and their ways of viewing the world as a mode of overcoming the vertical and authoritarian aspects of the traditional education system. Likewise, he highlighted orality as the link between the written word and the learner's emotions by introducing new types of textuality beyond the canonical: "In this proposal, communication is not limited to the printed culture, but includes all the orality and media that allows free expression for individuals" (Mateus & Quiroz-Velasco, 2017, p. 155).

Soares (2019, p. 15) proposes the educommunication paradigm as a path to a communication process "at the service of meaningful learning about the multiple spheres of knowledge and action inherent in a human rights education program." Students with access to critical media training recognize communication as a tool for "mobilizing and engaging their energies in causes they deem fair and of interest to the entire community" (p. 16). This communication is integral and integrative, focusing mainly on human coexistence and collective commitment.

To summarize, educommunication proposes a model based on dialogue and horizontal communication along with the recognition that knowledge is a collective creation that arises from cultural contexts. Thus, this theoretical perspective assumes that technology is never an end in itself and proposes a dialogic approach based on communication as a tool for expression and not just for the transmission of content. Educommunication promotes citizenship in its fullness, strengthens living spaces, expands the communicative potential of individuals and groups, educates through communication, and favors the communicative protagonism of children and youth. Educommunication is about planning and implementing practices designed to create and develop open and creative systems in educational spaces, thus increasing the possibilities of expression for all members of the educational community. It offers three fundamental insights for our study: (1) the recognition of intersubjectivity as a critical element for understanding the interactions between individuals and media, (2) the attention assigned to cultural communicative practices and political dimensions, and (3) the focus on the individual rather than on the technological devices available, deviating from instrumental theoretical perspectives (Mateus & Quiroz-Velasco, 2017).

Transmedia dynamics and educommunication

The transmedia dynamics in education configures a layered narrative to promote learning experiences, extending interactions across multiple media channels and promoting students' involvement, engagement, and participation (see Chapter 2) in the process (Carpentier, 2015).

Transmedia education is a response to the demands of students' behavior today, with a focus on improving the teaching experience inside and outside the classroom (Coiro, 2003; Jenkins, Ford, & Green, 2013). Understanding transmedia dynamics applied to education involves considering, relating, and articulating learning practices permeated by emotional connections, strategies, and mediations. The learner's engagement and empowerment are permeated by purpose-based stories, experiences, coexistence, and passion. This experience is about reporting and building knowledge in collaboration with schools, communities, students, and teachers; learning together through affection; and considering blended cultures and different local realities.

For many years, transmedia strategies have been conceived from grandiose projects anchored in understanding the uses of new technologies and digital knowledge embedded in the baggage of actors immersed in binary networks. In the educational field, large studies such as the Transmedia Literacy Project (Scolari, 2018) have sought to map students' digital repertoires and skills to narrow the gap between connected teachers and students. According to Scolari (2016), these digital repertories and skills are still poorly defined involving games, social networking, browsing in interactive environments, and the creation and diffusion of all types of content across different media and platforms. "Many teenagers are experienced players, others actively participate in social networks, while some produce content of all kinds and participate in social networks" (p. 7).

Experience reports (Castells & Illera, 2017; Favrin, Gola, & Ilardi, 2015), case studies (Scolari, Lugo, & Masanet, 2019), participatory research (Moreira & Mattos, 2019), dedicated platforms (Pratten, 2019), and some experimental projects connect efforts to cope with this hectic pace of new tools designed to bridge the gap between so many different learning environments inside and outside schools. Contemporary literacy includes concepts such as media and information literacy (UNESCO, 2009), transliteracy (Fraug-Meigs, 2012; Lugo, 2016; Thomas et al., 2007), new media literacies (Jenkins et al., 2006), media competencies (Ferrés & Piscitelli, 2012), new literacies, multiliteracies (Cope & Kalantzis, 2009), transmedia literacy (Scolari, 2016), ludoliteracy (Zagal, 2010), multimodal literacy (Jewitt & Kress, 2003), and transmedia edutainment (Kalogeras, 2014).

In this environment, digital platforms have been acclaimed for establishing a space for autonomy and participation in transmedia dynamics. However, Srinivasan and Fish (2017) question the existence of a digital revolution and signal the importance of attributing value to these tools as precursors of new social behavior. For them, the process is primarily cultural and cognitive, comprising the marks of a collective and heterogeneous articulation that connects online and off-line dynamics. This process is in line with the precepts of convergence culture, a theme explored by Jenkins (2006) in the early 2000s, which encompasses not only the technological dimension but also the social and cultural transformation centered on the transmedia experience.

Based on the same perspective of dialogical education, UNESCO proposes media and information literacy (MIL) that brings together the three distinct dimensions of information literacy, media literacy, and information and communications technology (ICT) or digital literacy. Acting as an umbrella concept, it is "a new literacy construct that helps empower people, communities and nations to participate in and contribute to global knowledge societies" (UNESCO, 2009, para. 3). It encompasses,

> the full range of cognitive, emotional, and social competencies that include the use of text, tools and technologies; the skills of critical thinking and analysis; the practice of messaging composition and creativity; the ability to engage in reflection and ethical thinking; as well as active participation through teamwork and collaboration.
>
> (Hobbs, 2010, p. 17)

According to Jenkins et al. (2006),

> Participatory culture shifts the focus from literacy to an individual's expression to community involvement. New literacy involves social skills developed through collaboration and networking. These skills are built on the foundation of traditional literacy, research skills, technical and analytical-critical skills taught in the classroom.
>
> (p. 4)

In that context, ideas from the field of educommunication in a transmediatic perspective encompass interest in knowing the voice of the actors as a basic notion for engaging students in a meaningful learning environment. In addition to the functionalist sense of content transmission, the transmedia education encompasses the emotions and the particular views of each individual as proposed by Freire. Educommunication accords priority to the human being as an objective and thus ensures that the human being is important not only as a consumer but also as a citizen; further, educommunication seeks empowerment rather than protectionism.

In our research, we contemplate educommunication from the transmedia perspective, as the "critical formation to read and to appropriate the rich multiplatform and multimodal narratives focusing on dialogic relations, by understanding the fluid communication system and using diverse tools to strengthening polyphonic communicative ecosystems in educational spaces" (Tárcia, 2017, p. 63). Above all, transmedia education should facilitate human interaction and help students participate in and create their own learning processes by developing stories, games, and relevant activities within a community of people. Transmedia education is about connecting people to learn through narratives, creativity, engagement, and sustainability, creating and enhancing critical learning experiences.

Citizenship, as a mediating instance of the relationship between communication and education, is characterized not by the quantity or conveyance of content but by the quality of the communication and involvement of the agents of interest. Diverse content and available platforms require complex planning for effective results.

Transmedia strategic planning for education initiatives

Revisiting the seven principles (spreadability vs. drillability, continuity vs. multiplicity, immersion vs. extractability, worldbuilding, seriality, subjectivity, and performance) of transmedia storytelling as they apply to education, Jenkins (2010) challenges teachers to involve students and to encourage them to utilize what they see, hear, and read. In such a system, students are urged to seek out content, explore different pieces of information in various contexts, interact easily with other readers, and evaluate ideas across formats. In this sense, students should be allowed to seek out information related to their interests across the broadest possible range of terrains while also drilling deep into what matters to them as individuals. Educators should think more about what motivates students to go deeper and consider how they can facilitate students' capacity to delve into a topic that they have deemed important. By asking "what if" questions, students should be able to think beyond established canons and explore multiple possibilities, various factors, different values, and diverse cultures. Transmedia education should provide "activities where students build their own virtual worlds—deciding what details need to be included, mapping their relationship to each other, guiding visitors through their worlds, and explaining the significance of what they contain" (Jenkins, 2010, para. 17).

Hovious (2013) proposes the use of transmedia projects to develop seven literacies: (1) multimodal because it is necessary to make meaning across all the elements in the story to fully understand it; (2) critical, as de-structuring and restructuring of multiple modes of text can be a very complex task; (3) digital, to be able to evaluate the digital elements in the story; (4) media because transmedia storytelling exists across multiple forms of media, and each media element must be evaluated separately before multimodal meaning-—making can take place; (5) visual, providing a visually rich experience, in which images play a significant role in the narrative; (6) information, enhanced by information literacy skills; and (7) gaming, which requires the use of logical and strategic thinking.

The power of the transmedia approach was recognized by the U.S. Department of Education in 2011. According to the Office of Innovation and Improvement (ED Innovation, 2011, para. 6) "the rich, fictional worlds of transmedia tend to create a greater level of social interaction that can inspire children to create their own stories and media products and to share them with each other." We argue that not only fictional worlds but also nonfictional worlds can contribute to effective transmedia education.

Between 2010 and 2015, the U.S. Department of Education's Ready to Learn (RTL) television program supported three large national projects that attempted to create educational television and digital media products for young children between the ages of two and eight to support their development of math learning and literacy skills. These programs explored whether "a transmedia approach would result in increased educational effectiveness when used with learners from low-income backgrounds" (ED Innovation, 2016, para. 19).

The review findings reveal that the three educational transmedia experiences developed as a result of RTL funding not only were effective mechanisms by which young children were taught academic skills pertaining to math and literacy but also functioned as support systems for parents and educators. The report includes the following major conclusions:

(1) Positive associations between at-home transmedia engagement and children's math learning; (2) home study intervention parents' increased awareness of and engagement in their children's math learning; and (3) positive associations for at least some students in the intervention groups for the school-based evaluations.

(Wartella, Luricella & Blackwell, 2016, p. 1)

The authors concluded that federal investment in public media and broadband infrastructure is important and should be a national educational priority when seeking to decrease the gap between rich and poor preschoolers.

In 2017, we started the Transmedia Education Project focused on theoretical, empirical, and methodological aspects of transmedia education. The project's aim is to study and develop communication planning for public schools in the member countries of the Community of Portuguese Speaking Countries (CPLP). The primary focus is public schools located in low-income communities, typically marked by limited access to digital technologies considering the social, political, and economic contexts, as well as the students' average media consumption habits. Thus far, our research project has developed transmedia educational solutions in Brazil, East Timor, and Mozambique.

To achieve our transmedia educational goals in these countries, we developed a methodology encompassing the reasoning of transmedia and educommunication strategies to produce collaborative knowledge in school settings, which we discuss later in the chapter. In addition, we implemented the theoretical and methodological assumptions from Charles Sanders Peirce's semiotics to verify the improvement in communication within the multiplatform narrative flow to generate new learning processes, intensify social engagement in the classroom, and potentially transform the local community. Our research project is grounded on the interlocution between communication of public interest and transmediality as a nonfictional and educational phenomenon, aiming to promote social innovation in communities, with limited human, financial, and technological resources.

Transmedia educommunication methodology

The reality of the low-income communities involved in our research project, which implies scarcity of digital resources, encouraged the creation of a different methodology for developing transmedia dynamics in such conditions. In addition, another recurring concern of our research project was to add playful elements that would immerse students and teachers within the narrative created. To understand this reality, the methodology is anchored in a social perspective to actively promote citizen formation. For this reason, we used the concept of transmedia activism proposed by Srivastava (2009)—and discussed in Chapter 1—to designate collective and creative processes that coordinate an expanding transmedia cultural narrative. In this context, transmedia dynamics emerges as a strong social innovation capable of creating the necessary involvement of the interested actors through a narrative that covers and encompasses the central theme. The complex production of content triggers small fragments of this story from a collaborative work that aims to generate awareness, engagement, action, and change among participants, and the social contexts in which they are inserted. According to Srivastava (2009), this type of activism uses local voices as its core aspect, aiming at generating participation focused on mobilization points to connect the agents of societal change across multiplatform media.

In this context, any kind of communication platform can be incorporated into transmedia strategies as long as the platform works to expand the narrative. Thus, digital environments, interpersonal communication, newspapers, radio, posters, public assemblies, and so forth are at the heart of transmedia dynamics. According to Jenkins et al. (2018), this happens mainly in relation to younger audiences, who seek greater dynamism between practices and communication rituals.

> Many groups are now experimenting with what alternative media strategies that empower their supporters to take a more active role in shaping communication flows might look like. Transmedia mobilization is unstable and fluid, shifting tactically in response to changing conditions on the ground.
>
> (Jenkins et al., 2018, p. 27)

Thus, transmedia educommunication projects developed for low-income communities use a multitude of platforms, especially analogical, to promote an activist stance in the classroom. This variety of tools shapes the social agenda and reaches stakeholders through incentives to participate. Cultural behavior shapes the creative use of media platforms and change in behavior is achieved through social engagement. To stimulate the creative potential and appropriate approach, the methodology we developed is divided into five complementary steps: (1) diagnosis, (2) planning, (3) product development, (4) execution of planned actions, and (5) evaluation of the results achieved. The concrete objective is to awaken citizen awareness, generate engagement through action, and achieve effective changes in educational processes through communication.

The diagnosis phase involves the following methodological procedures: (1) conducting in-depth interviews with teachers and principals of the partner school, (2) forming focus groups with students, (3) conducting a design thinking workshop for constructing personas to better understand our target group, and (4) performing subsequent script definition for multiplatform proposition of the projected canon narrative. The planning phase corresponds to the strategic and tactical stage of the elaboration of actions and prototypes that would be used in the school based on the communication problem identified after the diagnosis. From the multiplatform roadmap created, the products that would configure the transmedia educational kit (a set of transmedia educational products), as well as manuals to assist teachers in the classroom, are developed. The execution of planned actions phase is then carried out by the support team, which involves companies and partners, teachers and students from the chosen school, project coordinators, and teachers and students from Brazilian and local universities. In the evaluation of the results achieved phase, to track project development in the school community and transnational reverberation, appropriate metrics are chosen to analyze whether the goals have been met.

The planning phase comprises sub-procedures that observe the following dynamics: (1) the immersion phase in the participating school, (2) identification of the problem, (3) creation of the project purpose, (4) creation of personas, (5) construction of the central theme, (6) construction of the background and context story, (7) design thinking workshop for gathering ideas, (8) construction of the synopsis of the main narrative, (9) definition of platforms and insertion points, (10) search for partnerships for product realization, (11) definition of required channels and resources, (12) creation of the script, (13) creation of the user journey, (14) definition of engagement triggers, (15) definition of the main events and actions, and (16) definition of the execution schedule.

The methodology is anchored in the theoretical framework of Peirce's semiotics (see Chapter 1) to accompany the semiosis that arises with the creative use of multiple media platforms in the classroom. This methodology operates under various aspects of mediation that are related to each other: communication, education, culture, Portuguese language, literature, and activism. As we discussed in Chapter 1, according to Peirce (CP 2.308), the notion of mediation is linked to the idea of semiosis, which constitutes a triadic logical model composed of the connections among the sign (representamen), object, and interpretant. This complex process involves the determination of a preceding sign (object) and the representation of a later sign (interpretant). The sign (representamen) establishes mediation between the object and the interpretant, with the latter becoming a mediating element of the subsequent sign triad and thus is successive. The interpretant has the nature of a new sign, so it is considered the mediating element that guarantees the vitality of semiosis.

As developed in Chapter 1, for Peirce (CP 2.227), semiotics is synonymous with logic as a science that deals with the laws of evolution of thought in the production and transmission of meaning. Semiotics or logic is a science founded on the principles of ethics, focusing on aesthetics. Peirce believed that these three instances are guided by ideal norms, which constitute the field of normative sciences (EP 2.371). Within Peirce's pragmatism, ethics qualifies action, continually modified by logic, in search of the ideal of perfection of aesthetics. The diagram of normative sciences is organized by Peirce through three phenomenological categories, which are omnipresent in all that appears to the mind (EP 2.177): For *firstness*, the phenomenon emerges as a mere possibility, revealing a quality of feeling—a sensation (CP 8.329). *Secondness* refers to existence, which produces the flow between cause and effect. It is the dichotomous update between two phenomenological fields, from which the fact emerges. When the process between the causal act and the effect is revealed, the presence of a third (*thirdness*), which refers to mediation, is identified.

There is a connection between the phenomenological categories that establishes the sign action (CP 2.274). This shows that one category is linked to another, forming Peirce's concept of mediation, which is empirically linked to his notion of sign. For Peirce (CP 2.228), a sign is—in a way—that which represents something to someone, understanding semiosis as a process of interpretation *ad infinitum* because the meaning of a sign is always another sign, and so on. Therefore, the process of semiosis is also a process of mediation (CP 2.308) because a sign always produces an effect on the mind, whether human or not, to represent the object that determined it.

The prism mediation of Peirce's semiosis reverberates in the way the creative extensions of the transmedia project are conceived through the proliferation of interpretants. Semiosis is the result of a network of changing meanings that forms through the narrative flow across various media platforms. These changes in meaning occur because the representative capacity of the sign is limited by the impossibility of it embracing the whole object that determined it, which demands the association of other signs in the formation of the interpretant through collateral experience. Collateral experience concerns the previous familiarity with the object that denotes the sign—a necessary condition for semiosis that operates by proximity and otherness with the object. According to Bergman (2010), Peirce's notion of collateral experience describes the impossibility of any contact with the object of representation, or references, except through sign mediations. Moreover, as this process depends on social engagement, the creation of interpretants is incomplete, as it always points to new signs. Therefore, semiosis is composed of a series of successive interpretants, which prevent its closure.

In this sense, in the proposed methodology, the object is related to the cultural reality established in public schools of Portuguese-speaking countries, whose communication problem is defined and worked in a particular manner in each elaborated planning. The elements described previously (communication, education, culture, Portuguese language, literature, and activism) promote the mediation between cultural reality and creative extensions that emerge from the created products, which result in new signs through collateral experience. This proliferation of interpretants is a result of the way each individual or community adds their own content based on their local experiences (collateral experience), which contributes to the creative expansion (semiosis) of communication planning in transmedia education.

Peirce presents the interpretant's trichotomy to classify the meaning effect of the sign, which may be a feeling, effort, or thought (habit). Using the three phenomenological categories listed previously, he defines the emotional (*firstness*), energetic (*secondness*), and logical (*thirdness*) interpretants. In the first effect, the feeling appears as proof of the understanding of the specific effect of the sign and may be the only meaning produced. This feeling is not governed by emotional charge, but it is a quality of feeling that is difficult to translate. The second effect indicates a continuous and persistent effort, whether physical or mental, and is a singular act. It involves the use of energy to generate acts of imagination. The third effect brings the interpretation of the sign through a rule adopted by the interpreter. It leads to a change of habit that reveals a change in action trends. They are voluntary acts that point to a pattern, producing a predictive outcome.

Engaging with these mediation processes points to a communication experience that expands locally through identification (emotional interpretant), mobilization (energetic interpretant), and activism (logical interpretant), which is understood as change-oriented action. The first signals a quality of feeling; the second, a continuous and persistent effort; and the third, the formation of a thought to the constitution of a provisional habit of action. This local interest gains global contours because of the narrative expansion (semiosis) and forms a network that goes beyond its radius through the intercultural, transmedial, and transnational nature of the project.

From these characteristics, Peirce's semiotics also assists in the procedural evaluation of the project. Because transmedia dynamics is a result of the content flow that runs through multiple media platforms, this process concerns the sign and should be investigated as a system of meaning (Alzamora, 2019). Thus, transmedia dynamics can be considered a pragmatic[2] branch of semiosis in the media—a perspective that explains the interpretant's incompleteness in forming temporary action habits (Alzamora & Gambarato, 2014). Consequently, Peirce's semiotics can contribute to describing the pragmatic improvement of this dynamic and the resulting communication logic (Alzamora, 2019).

Case study: East Timor, Mozambique, and Brazil

Based on the methodology created, communication planning in transmedia education can contribute to improving teaching and learning conditions in each cultural, social, political, and economic context, taking into account the media consumption habits of the students of each school and their — information-gathering and media entertainment preferences (Alzamora & Tárcia, 2018). Since 2016, our research dedicated to communication planning in transmedia education has taken place in an international context, encompassing research, teaching, and service actions in Brazil and abroad.[3]

We conducted research in a continuous discussion of the theoretical-methodological and empirical-conceptual precepts of the projects that were developed. The knowledge production involves international cooperation research between the Department of Social Communication of Federal University of Minas Gerais (UFMG), University Center of Belo Horizonte (UniBH), and the School of Education and Communication of Jönköping University (Sweden).[4] In addition to this collective research, several individual research projects were carried out within the scope of this project, such as postdoctoral,[5] doctoral,[6] and undergraduate work.[7] The knowledge produced in each related research project was shared in regular team meetings to unify the transmedia educational communication plans that the group developed in this area.

The teaching dimension of the project involves the participation of communication students from UFMG through the undergraduate discipline media and languages laboratory.[8] Enrolled students participate in the production of communication planning in transmedia education for public schools and communication planning for disseminating the transmedia project. One of the objectives of this research project is to enable researchers, students, and communication professionals to develop communication plans in transmedia education. Thus, we seek to multiply this knowledge in Portuguese-speaking countries, with the aim of promoting and improving intercultural relations among public schools. Therefore, the research team ideally visits the locality of the public school with the local university partner of the project, preferably before the diagnosis stage and after the selection of the public school and the media institutions involved in the transmedia experiment.

These visits aim to (1) present the project to the local academic community and other partners, such as representatives of the selected public school and media institutions interested in participating in the project; (2) offer a communication planning workshop on transmedia education at the affiliated university, which is open to representatives of the public school and participating media institutions; (3) enable teachers and students to work on the development of the diagnosis, the critical analysis of planning throughout its development (via email, closed Facebook groups, WhatsApp, Telegram, and Skype), product reviews, proposal execution, and evaluation of results; (4) get to know the selected public school and communication outlets involved, to strengthen the social ties among the participants and refine the communication planning to be proposed; and (5) establish links among institutions to improve the communication planning in transmedia education in light of the local reality, as well as to promote the exchange of academic, social, and cultural activities.

The service dimension of the research project comprises the development of communication planning for public schools in Portuguese-speaking countries. Service actions are officially registered at UFMG, ensuring that the developed projects have academic support from the university. In an integrated way, these three dimensions (research, teaching, and service) help develop our communication planning approach in transmedia education.

As outlined, the primary focus of our research project is public schools located in low-income communities, usually characterized by limited access to digital technologies, which requires thinking about transmedia dynamics outside the normative digital media configurations. Transmedia dynamics involves any media formats and channels, online and/or off-line, that establish "dispositions and configures ways of acting through the network that constitutes it" (Alzamora, Tárcia, Bicalho, & Oliveira, 2019, p. 69). In this light, transmedia dynamics is not restricted to multiplatform narratives outlined by media industries but also encompasses alternative and circumstantial media configurations. This understanding affects the empirical–conceptual singularities of the research we conducted, in which hegemonic media arrangements are varied, and digital connections are not always the most influential.

The Portuguese language acts as a linguistic process mediating our experiments in transmedia education, favoring the development of transmedia communication dynamics that brings students and teachers to participate in the project, in each country enrolled, in a constantly expanding transnational, intercultural, and transmedia network. This creative expansion of transmedia narratives is proposed in each school through planned collective actions, as it is the necessary condition for the vitality of the proposed transmedia network.

To stimulate engagement in the transmedia dynamics, the Portuguese language literature was used as a prevailing mediator in the projects. Thus, in the communication planning in transmedia education created for the

June 25th Primary School in Maputo (Mozambique),[9] the Brazilian author of children's literature Leo Cunha[10] reformulated the narrative *Adventures of the Imagination Class*—originally proposed by students from social communication enrolled in the Media and Languages Laboratory course offered at UFMG under the scope of this research project.[11]

For the public school in Dili, the capital of East Timor, the diagnosis made with children aged seven to nine years pointed to the need to create good hygiene habits, which could affect the community more broadly, as each child becomes a knowledge multiplier in their families. Consequently, the transmedia narrative *The Hygiene League* was created, which involved the production of comic books, TV animation, board games, memory games, puppets, and theater. Our local partners were the Timor Lorosa'e National University, East Timor Educational Television, and a local health clinic.[12]

East Timor is one of the youngest countries in the world. The country gained independence less than two decades ago in 2002. With a very ethnically and culturally diverse population, there are more than 30 languages and dialects in this small country. During the Indonesian occupation, the most commonly spoken language was Indonesian. Today, according to the Constitution, Tetum and Portuguese are the two official languages, while Indonesian and English are working languages. Our great difficulty in working on the project narrative was dealing with the low knowledge of the Portuguese language. We chose to use more images and simple phrases to minimize the possible noise in communication.

In Belo Horizonte, Brazil, the communication planning in transmedia education developed for the Belo Horizonte Municipal School, in partnership with UFMG and UniBH, was based on the idea of entrepreneurship, according to the diagnosis. We worked with 12- to 14-year-old full-time students. The problem we encountered was the parents' lack of interest in their children's school lives. To solve this problem, we held several meetings and interviews with the school's principal and teachers, aiming to understand the students' reality. Because the school is in a suburban neighborhood, and there are social problems such as unemployment and poverty, UFMG students performed a local immersion process to investigate the impact of the community on the school and vice versa. Through focus groups with the children, two personas were created to represent parents and students. The transmedia narrative generated was based on the theme of entrepreneurship, as we detected that most parents were self-employed, with no fixed jobs. We then chose to engage the students in professional development–focused activities to attract their parents' attention to the school context.

The execution involved two steps. In the first step, mediated by the hashtag *#EuQueFaçoBH* [#IDoItBH], we held entrepreneurship, photography, and video workshops, and created a Facebook page. Our partner, at this stage, was the Brazilian Micro and Small Business Support Service (SEBRAE), which aims to promote the economic development and competitiveness of micro and small businesses, stimulating entrepreneurship in Brazil. The students of the SEBRAE school conducted workshops for the school's students, who carried out research on the subject with the help of teachers. After the theoretical foundation, the students participated in two workshops on photography and video at a private university (UniBH) to see the possibilities in producing professional content for the Internet, aiming to strengthen autonomous business. A Facebook page was created to give visibility to these actions, as we discovered that the parents' media consumption habits were related to this platform. In the second step, the students participated in creative workshops for YouTube and Instagram and a presentation of the actions developed at the school's Science Fair, which was open to families.[13]

All the educational products developed within the scope of our research project paid special attention to the language used, considering the local reality and particularities of the Portuguese language in each country. Portuguese is an official language in 10 countries worldwide: Portugal, Brazil, Mozambique, East Timor, Angola, Guinea-Bissau, Equatorial Guinea, Macau, Cape Verde, and São Tomé and Príncipe. Although Portuguese orthography is unified (the Portuguese Language Orthographic Agreement was signed in 1990 and implemented in 2009), we incorporated the differences in pronunciation, vocabulary, and formal and informal speech in our transmedia educational projects. All materials underwent a thorough language review by students at local universities, including the contribution to the recording of audio for animations and radio programs, keeping the specific accent of each locality. Another important aspect is that the characters created for each project were representations of children to bring the narrative closer to the daily life of the participating students. We were also concerned about ensuring the protagonism of children during the execution of projects, encouraging creativity through collaborative work. In addition, the teachers received training and manuals to conduct classroom processes, leaving gaps in the stories to be filled throughout the learning process experience in the classroom. Importantly, all products generated could be modified and adapted according to the demands that arose in the classroom.[14]

Mozambique: diary of an experience[15]

The entire process in Maputo, Mozambique, was made possible through a partnership established between UFMG and the Higher School of Journalism (Mozambique). Under the supervision of the teachers of the Higher School of Journalism, Mozambican students from the social communication course (1) selected the project's participating public school, (2) carried out the diagnostic methodological phase and reviewed the products developed in Brazil, (3) worked with the Brazilian team in the planning execution phase in Maputo, and (4) were responsible for conducting the evaluation phase as planned by the Brazilian team. In total, about 30 people, including students, teachers, partners, and developers, were involved in the project, between March 2018 and November 2019.

A former colony of Portugal, Mozambique is one of the 10 poorest nations in the world with 48.3% of its population below the poverty line (World Bank, 2018). Following independence in 1975, Mozambique was torn by internal conflict, marked by countless acts of terror, that displaced at least four million people and resulted in the death of many more as a result of violence, famine, and disease (Penvenne, 1996). Violence and disunity hindered economic development, especially expansion of tourism, and discouraged foreign investment. The conflict formally ended in 1992, but there are many lingering effects: In the early 2000s, as many as one million unexploded land mines remained along the country's trails and roads, and much political strife continued between the major opposition forces and the central government (Penvenne, 1996).

Today, the country's main challenges, according to the World Bank (2019), include maintaining macroeconomic stability considering exposure to commodity price fluctuations and general elections, and reestablishing confidence through improved economic governance and increased transparency, including transparent handling of hidden debt investigations. Moreover, structural reforms are needed for the struggling private sector (World Bank, 2019).

Another major challenge for the economy is to diversify from the current focus on capital-intensive projects and low-productivity subsistence agriculture to a more diverse and competitive economy, while strengthening the key drivers of inclusion, such as improved quality education and health service delivery, which could, in turn, improve social indicators (World Bank, 2019).

Mozambique is culturally heterogeneous with patrilineal and matrilineal systems of social organization. The people are ethnically diverse, but the ethnic categories are fluid and reflect the country's colonial history. All inhabitants of the country were designated Portuguese in 1961, and some classifications such as Makua-Lomwe were created by colonial Portuguese officials. Within the country, in addition to Makua-Lomwe, live Tsonga, Sena, Ndau, Chopi, Chewa, Yao, Makonde, and Ngoni. Although Portuguese, the official language, is the main language of only a tiny fraction of the population, it is spoken as a *lingua franca* by some two-fifths of the country's inhabitants. Portuguese speakers are strongly concentrated in the capital of Maputo and other urban areas.

Within Mozambique's media system and infrastructure, the telecommunication market is changing very quickly. The fixed market has been losing ground to mobile due to underinvestment in infrastructure. However, only 18% of Mozambicans have access to the Internet. Most Internet users live in urban areas, and only 8.1% of the population are active social media users; 94% of them access the Internet via mobile media on prepaid connections (DataReportal, 2019).

According to the Alliance for Affordable Internet (2017), Mozambique has a long way to go to ensure affordable Internet access for its citizens. Although the government and regulator have introduced much needed reforms, further efforts to reduce the price of broadband for all—especially for the significant number of citizens living under the poverty line—are needed. Mozambique ranks 45th (out of 58 countries surveyed) on the 2017 Affordability Drivers Index (ADI). This is a decrease from Mozambique's 43rd place ranking in the 2015–16 Affordability Drivers Index, indicating the slow pace of the policy and regulatory progress.

Socially, the region experiences great challenges. Maputo province is the most heavily populated province in the south of the country, with more than 2.5 million inhabitants. The city of Maputo is a commercial and cultural center of the country, but it faces many challenges, such as a poor transportation system and drainage infrastructure, which have profound implications for people's livelihoods, particularly in informal settlements. Maputo has 1.08 million inhabitants, according to 2018 data from the National Institute of Statistics (INE), and is the most populous city in the country (National Institute of Statistics, 2019).

Although the country inherited a near 97% literacy rate at the time of its independence a quarter of a century ago, the overall literacy rate has decreased to 47% (USAID, 2019). However, according to UNICEF (2019), Mozambique has shown its commitment to education. The country has abolished school fees, provided direct support to schools and free textbooks at the primary level, as well as made investments in classroom construction. The sector receives the highest share of the state budget, more than 15%. As a result, there has been a significant rise in primary school enrollment over the past decade (UNICEF, 2019).

Yet quality and improvement in learning have lagged. In addition, enrollment in upper primary and secondary schools has stagnated despite increased provision. About 1.2 million children are not in school, more girls than boys, particularly in the secondary age group (UNICEF, 2019).

A recent USAID (2019) study showed that although 94% of girls in Mozambique enroll in primary school, more than 50% drop out by the fifth grade, only 11% continue on to study at the secondary level, and just 1% continue on to college. Among children who finish primary school, nearly two-thirds leave the system without basic reading, writing, and math skills.

The 2013 national learning assessment found that only 6.3% of third graders had basic reading competencies. A 2014 World Bank survey showed that only 1% of primary school teachers have the minimum expected knowledge, and only one in four teachers achieves two-digit subtraction. Absenteeism among teachers is high at 45%, and principals at 44%. About half of enrolled students are absent on any given day (UNICEF, 2019).

Another huge challenge according to UNICEF (2019) is the lack of early childhood learning services. Only an estimated 5% of children between three and five years benefit from them, and most services are located only in urban areas.

The government's capacity to enhance school access has not kept up with its ability to improve quality, according to USAID (2019). The rapid expansion has placed intense pressure on school management, teaching personnel, and the overall quantity and quality of effective classroom instruction, resulting in a large number of overcrowded multi-shift schools, growing student/teacher ratios, and plummeting reading and math test scores.

The USAID-funded study (USAID, 2019) on school effectiveness found that due to teacher absenteeism, limited instructional time, and other factors negatively affecting educational quality, Mozambican schools were limited to, on average, 30 days of actual instructional time per 193-day school year in 2010. Furthermore, the study found that 59% of third graders in the 49 schools studied could not read a single word per minute or recognize letters, and those students who could read only, on average, five words per minute. The Ministry of Education reported that less than half of the population finishes primary school, and of those who do finish, only 8% transition to secondary school. Mozambique's overall literacy rate is 47%; female literacy (28%) lags far behind that of male literacy (60%; USAID, 2019).

According to the last national reading assessment from 2016, only 4.9% of third graders can read at the expected level (UNICEF, 2016). The World Bank survey discovered that, of the seven African countries studied, Mozambican student outcomes ranked lowest, with an average score of 26 points on the math test and 23 on the language (Portuguese in Mozambique) test, in contrast to the highest scores from Kenya, which were 62 and 80, respectively (World Bank, 2018).

A total of 15.1% of Maputo's population, or about 163,000 people, have never attended school, according to the National Institute of Statistics (2019). Ten thousand young people age 10 to 15 years (6.1% of the city's population) are in this category, although Maputo is considered the most developed in the country, with the best socioeconomic indicators and one of the lowest rates of illiteracy. The poverty and vulnerability in Maputo are heterogeneous, varying according to socioeconomic factors and between the municipal districts. In this reality, in partnership with the Higher School of Journalism, we sought to identify how, from our methodological perspective, we could operate in Mozambique. This previous diagnosis was based on a mapping process carried out by partner teachers and students in Maputo's public relations and journalism programs.

Our identified partner school, June 25th Primary School, is located in KaMubukwani, the second most populous district in the city, considered peri-urban, with poor sanitary infrastructure. According to the National Institute of Statistics (2019), the district is home to approximately 320,000 people. It has 23 second-level primary schools, 14,033 students, and 333 teachers in service.

After conducting in-depth interviews with teachers and principals of the partner school, the major problem we identified among students was the lack of adequate competencies and skills in reading and writing not only among students but also among teachers. This problem was sent to the students in Brazil. After conducting focus groups in Brazil and using design thinking methodology, the Brazilian students created the script for the transmedia narrative and planned the actions to be implemented at the school in Maputo.

The transmedia storyworld was based on the story of a magic pencil and the imagination gang, composed of four friends. The more they used the pencil, the more beautiful stories and adventures were created. This premise lead to the formation of the Imagination Club, guided by three principles: (1) to enjoy reading, (2) to enjoy writing, and (3) to invite new friends to join. The transmedia extensions used were (1) reading and writing workshops, (2) board games, (3) comics, (4) animations, (5) an activity book, (6) a short story contest, and (7) a talent show.

In August 2019 in Maputo, a partnership was established with the Fernando Leite Couto Foundation[16] of the Mozambican author Mia Couto to offer a text production workshop to teachers of the school during the planning phase. In September 2019, at the June 25th Primary School, actions involving gamification practices, which were planned in association with the research team of the UFMG School of Letters, *Redigir*,[17] and the creation of a physical space for the Imagination Club were implemented. The Imagination Club was materialized in a room provided by the public school to stimulate students' creativity around the proposed transmedia narrative beyond the project execution phase. The whole experience can be seen on our website, www.educacaotransmidia.com.

Further reflections

These methodological procedures are common to all transmedia educational projects conducted by our research team, but each experiment involves a unique diagnosis, which also requires unique actions and country-specific partners. Thus, the exchange of experiences is made possible among the projects in Brazil, East Timor, and Mozambique because the specificities of each school context are outlined by common methodological procedures. The findings of the in-depth interviews with teachers, principals, students, and other actors involved in the projects in these three countries point in the direction of the following forces within educommunication transmedia projects:

1 *Narrative*: Local stories are strong drivers for learning and encouraging reading and writing, allowing for the identification and empowerment of actors.
2 *Connections*: Gamification presents itself as an aggregating agent for planned actions and transmedia extensions, constituting an important element for connection and meaningful relationships.

3 *Engagement*: Knowledge sharing, and networking enables broad cross-border participation and encourages intercultural reading and writing.

4 *Immersion*: Connecting through emotions alters the place of formal learning and enables immersion in universes that expand the classroom.

5 *Enthusiasm*: The playful aspect of transmedia interventions brings actors into expanded states of availability and interested in learning objects.

6 *Expansion*: The literature opens infinite possibilities for narrative expansion in diverse formats, including artistic expression, such as dance, singing, poetry, and drawing.

7 *Activism*: By embracing and appreciating local stories, transmedia actions can use call to action to raise awareness about relevant community causes.

8 *Multimodality*: Students can use their talents to share their experiences and voice their feelings.

9 *Continuity*: As ambassadors of a cause, students can bring other actors into the learning process within the developed transmedia storyworld.

10 *Sustainability*: It is not about digital technology but every technology that can be used to write, tell, and share stories to promote learning and citizenship.

In all projects, students were encouraged to be multipliers of the knowledge produced in transmedia dynamics in their communities. The purpose of exchanging experiences aimed at a collective transmedia, intercultural, and transnational network of public schools in Portuguese-speaking countries is to stimulate the creative expansion of the narratives initiated in our research project, unfolding them and subsequently the penetration of project.

Above all, transmedia dynamics in an educommunication perspective facilitates human interaction and helps students to participate in and create their own learning processes by generating stories, sharing play experiences, participating in relevant activities, and having fun. Developing a narrative over multiple platforms, either analog or digital, while interweaving learning outcomes has the potential to orchestrate transformational learning experiences as proposed by Paulo Freire. Our practice has shown that off-line extensions are a relevant part of transmedia educational projects, as they have the possibility to enhance the learning process independently of the availability of digital technology within the community.

Following the guidelines of transmedia activism (Srivastava, 2009), we sought to structure strategic actions for (1) generating awareness through the narratives created for each planning, involving the detection of a real student problem; (2) promoting engagement through products created and used inside and outside the classroom, especially with off-line extensions; and (3) structuring changes through sharing experiences among students affected by the project, promoting a cross-cultural exchange.

As proposed by Peircean semiotics, this process concerns the sign and should be investigated as a system of meaning (Alzamora, 2019). Thus, transmedia dynamics can be considered a pragmatic branch of semiosis in the media—a perspective that explains the interpretant's incompleteness in forming temporary action habits (Alzamora & Gambarato, 2014). Consequently, Peirce's semiotics contribute to describing the pragmatic improvement of this dynamics and the resulting communication logic (Alzamora, 2019). Our next step is to promote the exchange of experiences among children participating in the projects in each country by sending letters. This would contribute to the creative expansion of the intercultural and transnational network.

Notes

1 Luciana Andrade Gomes Bicalho contributed to this chapter.
2 Peirce's pragmatism, also called pragmaticism, examines the formation of provisional habits of action, relating to the action of thought.
3 For further information on this project, see http://transmediaeducation.com.br.
4 This international cooperation research is based on the project Transmedia Communication Methods and Strategies: Education for Sustainability, coordinated by Associate Professors Geane Alzamora (UFMG, Brazil) and Renira Rampazzo Gambarato (Jönköping University, Sweden) between 2019 and 2021.
5 *Transmedia communication strategies of public interest in the field of education: Network mediations* (Lorena Tárcia's postdoctoral research, under the supervision of Geane Alzamora, conducted at the UFMG Postgraduate Program in Social Communication, Brazil, between March 2017 and April 2018).
6 *Digital communication: Language, literacy and participation in Mozambique* (PhD research under development since 2019 at UFMG by Mozambican student Jane Alexandre Zefanias Mutsuque, with a PEC-PG/Capes scholarship, under the supervision of Geane Alzamora).
7 *Transmedia education: A planning study for public schools in Brazil and Timor-Leste* (undergraduate thesis in journalism defended in 2018 at the Department of Social Communication of UFMG, Brazil, by João Paulo Alves Soares, under the supervision of Geane Alzamora and co-supervision of Luciana Andrade Gomes Bicalho). In addition, the project yielded a work of scientific initiation, developed by undergraduate student Carmem Pimenta, with a PROEX/UFMG scholarship, under the supervision of Geane Alzamora.
8 The course is offered in the Department of Social Communication of UFMG by associate professor Geane Alzamora, with teaching interns Luciana Andrade Gomes Bicalho (between 2017 and 2018) and Ana Carolina Almeida Souza (since 2019).
9 See more information about the project's partners at www.educacaotransmidia.com.
10 Available at https://www.escritorleocunha.com/.
11 The communicative planning proposed by UFMG students for the Maputo public school (Mozambique) is available at http://labcon.fafich.ufmg.br/planejado-transmidia-maputo2/.
12 The communication planning developed by the communication students in the Media and Languages Laboratory course (UFMG) is available at http://labcon.fafich.ufmg.br/planejection-transmidia-timor/.

13 Planning is available at http://labcon.fafich.ufmg.br/planning-transmidia-bh/.
14 For example, in Mozambique, activity books can be modified (remixed) and reprinted on demand.
15 At the time of this writing, Mozambique was the first experience completed within the Transmedia Education project.
16 Available at https://www.fflc.org.mz/.
17 Available at http://www.redigirufmg.org/.

References

Alliance for Affordable Internet. (2017). *World Wide Web Foundation*. Retrieved from https://1e8q3q16vyc81g8l3h3md6q5f5e-wpengine.netdna-ssl.com/wp-content/uploads/2017/04/A4AI_2017_AR_Mozam_Screen_AW.pdf

Alzamora, G. (2019). A semiotic approach to transmedia storytelling. In M. Freeman & R. Gambarato (Eds.), *The Routledge companion to transmedia studies* (pp. 438–446). New York, NY: Routledge.

Alzamora, G., & Gambarato, R. R. (2014). Peircean semiotics and transmedia dynamics: Communication potentiality of the model of semiosis. *Ocula: Semiotic eye on media*, 15, 1–13. Retrieved from http://www.ocula.it/files/OCULA-15-CARVALHOALZAMORA-RAMPAZZOGAMBARATO-Peircean-semiotics-and-transmedia-dynamics.pdf

Alzamora, G., & Tárcia, L. (2018). Diálogos entre transativismo, comunicação de interesse público e educomunicação [Dialogue between transmedia activism, public interest communication, and educommunication]. In A. A. Braighi, C. Lessa, & M. T. Câmara (Eds.), *Interfaces do midiativismo: Do conceito à prática* [Interfaces of media activism: From concept to practice] (pp. 245–257). Belo Horizonte, Brazil: CEFET-MG.

Alzamora, G., Tárcia, L., Bicalho, L. A. G., & Oliveira, V. B. (2019). Percursos teórico-metodológicos em dinâmica transmídia: Jornalismo, educação, ativismo e entretenimento [Theoretical-methodological paths in transmedia dynamics: Journalism, education, activism and entertainment]. In B. G. Martins, M. A. Moura, & S. C. Pessoa (Eds.), *Experiências metodológicas em textualidades midiáticas* [Methodological experiences in media textualities] (pp. 115–140). Belo Horizonte, Brazil: Relicário.

Aparici, R. (2011). *Educomunicación: Más allá del 2.0* [Educommunication: Beyond 2.0]. Barcelona, Spain: Gedisa.

Bergman, M. (2010). C.S. Peirce on interpretation and collateral experience. *Signs*, 4, 134–161.

Carpentier, N. (2015). Differentiating between access, interaction and participation. *Conjunctions: Transdisciplinary Journal of Cultural Participation*, 2, 9–28.

Castells, N., & Illera, R. (2017). *La narrativa transmedia: La carta ancestral en educación secundaria* [Transmedia narrative: The ancestral card in secondary education]. Barcelona, Spain: Razón y Palabra.

Charlot, B. (1992). Rapport au savoir et rapport à l'école dans deux collèges de banlieue [Relationship with knowledge and relationship with school in two suburban colleges]. *Sociétés Contemporaines*, 11(12), 119–147.

Coiro, J. (2003). Reading comprehension on the Internet: Expanding our understanding of reading comprehension to encompass new literacies. *The Reading Teacher*, 56, 458–464.

Cope, B., & Kalantzis, M. (2009). Multiliteracies: New literacies, new learning. *Pedagogies, 4*(3), 164–195.

DataReportal. (2019, February 9). *Digital 2019 Mozambique v01*. Retrieved from https://pt.slideshare.net/DataReportal/digital-2019-mozambique-january-2019-v01

ED Innovation. (2011). *Why use transmedia in early learning?* Retrieved from https://sites.ed.gov/oii/2011/04/why-use-transmedia-in-early-learning/

ED Innovation. (2016). *What does a cartoon cat have to do with learning math? New reports highlight the impact of ready to learn television (2010–2015)*. U.S. Department of Education, Office of Elementary and Secondary Education. Retrieved from https://innovation.ed.gov/2016/04/13/what-does-a-cartoon-cat-have-to-do-with-learning-math-new-reports-highlight-the-impact-of-ready-to-learn-television-2010-2015/

Favrin, V., Gola, E., & Ilardi, E. (2015). Beyond e-learning: From blended methodology to transmedia education. *Research on Education and Media, 7*(1). https://doi.org/10.1515/rem-2015-0007

Ferrés, J., & Piscitelli, A. (2012). La competencia mediática: Propuesta articulada de dimensiones e indicadores [The media competition: Articulated proposal of dimensions and indicators]. *Comunicar, 38*(19), 75–82.

Fleming, L. (2013). Expanding learning opportunities with transmedia practices: Inanimate Alice as an exemplar. *Journal of Media Literacy Education, 5,* 370–377.

Fraug-Meigs, D. (2012). Transliteracy as the new research horizon for media and information literacy. *Medijske studije, 3*(6), 14–26.

Freire, P. (1970). *Pedagogy of the oppressed.* New York, NY: Seabury Press.

Freire, P. (1973). *Education for critical consciousness.* New York, NY: Continuum.

Freire, P. (1976). *Education: The practice of freedom.* London, England: Writers and Readers.

Freire, P. (2014). *Pedagogy of hope: Reliving pedagogy of oppressed.* London, England: Bloomsbury Academic.

Freire, P., & Macedo, D. (2005). *Literacy: Reading the word and the world.* New York, NY: Routledge.

Gambarato, R. R., & Debagian, L. (2016). Transmedia dynamics in education: The case of Robot Heart Stories. *Educational Media International, 53*(4), 229–243.

HCDMediaGroup. (2009, September 21). *Henry Jenkins* [Video]. YouTube. Retrieved from https://www.youtube.com/watch?v=ibJaqXVaOaI

Hobbs, R. (2010). *Digital and media literacy: A plan of action. a white paper on the digital and media literacy recommendations of the Knight Commission on the information needs of communities in a democracy.* Washington, DC: The Aspen Institute. Retrieved from https://www.knightfoundation.org/media/uploads/publication_pdfs/Digital_and_Media_Literacy_A_Plan_of_Action.pdf

Hovious, A. (2013, November 21). The 7 literacies of transmedia storytelling. *Designer Librarian.* Retrieved from https://designerlibrarian.wordpress.com/2013/11/21/the-7-literacies-of-transmedia-storytelling

Jenkins, H. (2006). *Convergence culture: Where old and new media collide.* New York: New York University Press.

Jenkins, H. (2010). Transmedia education: The 7 principles revisited. *Confessions of an aca-fan.* Retrieved from http://henryjenkins.org/blog/2010/06/transmedia_education_the_7_pri.html

Jenkins, H., Clinton, K., Purushotma, R., Robison, A. J., & Weigel, M. (2006). *Confronting the challenges of participatory culture: Media education for the 21st Century*. Chicago, IL: The MacArthur Foundation. Retrieved from http://www.newmedialiteracies.org/files/working/NMLWhitePaper.pdf

Jenkins, H., Ford, S., & Green, J. (2013). *Spreadable media: Creating value and meaning in a networked culture*. New York: New York University Press.

Jenkins, H., Shresthova, S., Gamber-Thompson, L., Kligler-Vilenchik, N., & Zimmerman, A. (2018). *By any media necessary: The new youth activism*. New York: New York University Press.

Jewitt, C., & Kress, G. (2003). *Multimodal literacy*. New York, NY: Peter Lang.

Kalogeras, S. (2014). *Transmedia storytelling and the new era of media convergence in higher education*. New York, NY: Palgrave Macmillan.

Lugo, N. (2016). *Diseño de narrativas transmedia para la transalfabetización* [Design of transmedia narratives for transliteracy] (Unpublished doctoral dissertation). Universidad Pompeu Fabra, Barcelona, Spain.

Mateus, J. C., & Quiroz-Velasco, M. T. (2017). Educommunication: A theoretical approach of studying media in school environments. *Dialogos, 14*, 152–163.

Messias, C. (2011). *Duas décadas de educomunicação: Da crítica ao espetáculo* [Two decades of educommunication: From critique to spectacle] (Unpublished master's thesis). São Paulo University, São Paulo, Brazil.

Moreira, B. D., & Mattos, A. (2019). *Educomunicação e transmídia: Um encontro na escola dos media, ciência e saberes populares* [Educommunication and transmedia: A meeting at the school of media, science and popular knowledge]. Cuiabá, Brazil: Editora Sustentável.

National Institute of Statistics. (2019). Instituto Nacional de Estatísticas [National Institute of Statistics]. Retrieved from http://www.ine.gov.mz/

Peirce, C. S. (1931–1958). *Collected papers of Charles Sanders Peirce*. C. Hartshorne, P. Weiss, & A. Burks (Eds.). 8 volumes. Cambridge, MA: Harvard University Press. (In-text references cite CP, followed by the volume number and paragraph number.)

Peirce, C. S. (1992–1998). *The essential Peirce: Selected philosophical writings*. 2 volumes. The Peirce Edition Project (Ed.). Bloomington, IN: Indiana University Press. (In-text references cite EP, followed by the volume number and page number.)

Penvenne, J. M. (1996). João dos Santos Albasini (1876–1922): The contradictions of politics and identity in colonial Mozambique. *The Journal of African History, 37*(3), 419–464.

Pratten, R. (2019). Transmedia production: Embracing change. In M. Freeman & R. R. Gambarato (Eds.), *The Routledge companion to transmedia studies* (pp. 214–222). New York, NY: Routledge.

Scolari, C. (2016). ¿Qué están haciendo los adolescentes con los medios fuera de la escuela? [What are the teenagers doing with the media outside school?]. *RELPE – Red Latinoamericana de Portales Educativos*. Retrieved from: http://www.relpe.org

Scolari, C. A. (2018). *Teens, media and collaborative cultures: Exploiting teens' transmedia skills in the classroom*. Barcelona, Spain: Universitat Pompeu Fabra.

Scolari, C. A., Lugo, N., & Masanet, M. J. (2019). Educación transmedia: De los contenidos generados por los usuarios a los contenidos generados por los estudiantes [Transmedia education: From the contents generated by the users to the contents generated by the students]. *Revista Latina de Comunicación Social*, 74, 116–132.

Soares, I. O. (2000). Educomunicação: Um campo de mediações [Educommunication: A field of mediation]. *Comunicação & Educação, 19*, 12–24.

Soares, I. O. (2009). Caminos de la educomunicación: Utopias, confrontaciones, reconocimientos [Pathways of educommunication: Utopias, confrontations, recognitions]. *Revista nómades. Nómadas, 30*, 194–207.

Soares, I. O. (2019). A educomunicação a serviço dos planos estaduais de educação para os direitos humanos [Educommunication at the service of state human rights education plans]. In B. D. Moreira & A. Mattos (Eds.), *Educomunicação e transmídia: Um encontro na escola dos media, ciência e saberes populares* [Educommunication and transmedia: A meeting at the school of media, science and popular knowledge] (pp. 17–27). Cuiabá, Brazil: Editora Sustentável.

Srinivasan, R., & Fish, A. (2017). *After the Internet.* Cambridge, England: Polity.

Srivastava, L. (2009, March 4). Transmedia activism: Telling your story across media platforms to create effective social change. *Namac.* Retrieved from http://archive.li/8O1Rd

Tárcia, L. (2017). Transmídia, multimodalidades e educomunicação: O protagonismo infanto-juvenil no processo de convergência de mídias [Transmedia, multimodalities and educommunication: Children's leading role in the process of media convergence]. *E-Com: Revista Científica de Comunicação Social do Centro Universitário de Belo Horizonte (UniBH), 10*(2), 60–71.

Tárcia, L. (2019). Transmedia education: Changing the learning landscape. In M. Freeman & R. R. Gambarato (Eds.), *The Routledge companion to transmedia studies* (pp. 314–322). New York, NY: Routledge.

Thomas, S., Joseph, C., Laccetti, J., Mason, B., Mills, S., Perril, S., & Pullinger, K. (2007). Transliteracy: Crossing divides. *First Monday, 12*(12). Retrieved from https://firstmonday.org/article/view/2060/1908

UNESCO. (2009). *Media and information literacy.* Retrieved from https://en.unesco.org/themes/media-and-information-literacy

UNICEF. (2016). *Mozambique strategy note: Education in the new country program.* Retrieved from http://files.unicef.org/transparency/documents/Mozambique%20CPD%20-%20Education%20Strategy%20Note%20%20 20-%2028%20March%202016.pdf

UNICEF. (2019). *Mozambique for every child research and reports.* Retrieved from https://www.unicef.org/mozambique/en/research-and-reports

USAID. (2019). *Mozambique report.* Retrieved from https://www.usaid.gov/mozambique/history

Warren, S., Wakefield, J., & Mills, L. (2013). Learning and teaching as communicative actions: Transmedia storytelling. In L. Wankel, P. Blessinger, & J. Stanaityte (Eds.), *Increasing student engagement and retention using multimedia technologies: Video annotation, multimedia applications, videoconferencing and transmedia storytelling* (pp. 67–94). Bingley, England: Emerald.

Wartella, E., Luricella, A., & Blackwell, C. (2016). *The ready to learn program: 2010–2015 policy brief.* Evanston, IL: Northwestern University. Retrieved from http://cmhd.northwestern.edu/wp-content/uploads/2016/04/RTL-Policy-Brief-2010-2015-Wartella-et-al-FINAL-March-2016.pdf

World Bank. (2018, April). Strong but not broadly shared growth: Mozambique - poverty assessment. Poverty and equity global practice Africa region. *World Bank.*

Retrieved from http://documents.worldbank.org/curated/en/248561541165040969/pdf/Mozambique-Poverty-Assessment-Strong-But-Not-Broadly-Shared-Growth.pdf

World Bank. (2019). *The World Bank in Mozambique.* Retrieved from https://www.worldbank.org/en/country/mozambique/overview

Zagal, J. P. (2010). *Ludoliteracy: Defining understanding and supporting games education.* Pittsburgh, PA: ETC Press. Retrieved from http://press.etc.cmu.edu/content/ludoliteracy-defining-understanding-and-supporting-games-education

Final considerations

What characterizes transmedia dynamics, and to what extent can this approach clarify relevant aspects of contemporary communication phenomena? This question, which is general and normative, permeates the set of investigations of transmedia dynamics in activism, entertainment, journalism, and education presented in this book. The theoretical-methodological parameters adopted are the basis for the case studies reported, constituting our perspective on analysis and strategic communication planning in transmedia dynamics.

The book's premise is an up-to-date recollection of our original research on various facets of fictional and nonfictional transmedia studies, especially the theoretical approach in conjunction with Peircean semiotics and the methodological development of specific analytical models for transmedia dynamics. We consider transmedia dynamics as a manifestation of a contemporary communication logic. For this reason, we sought first to characterize the transmedia communication logic from a Peircean theoretical and methodological point of view. Subsequently, we reported empirical cases related to transmedia analysis and strategic communication planning in fictional and nonfictional transmedia dynamics.

The distinctive characteristics of transmedia dynamics are presented in the introduction. There, we discussed the notion of transmedia dynamics as a trajectory, that is, the way in which strategic communication planning and collective tactics actions delineate the path of transmedia dynamics. In our view, transmedia dynamics is also a semiosis, or a sign mediation trajectory. In addition, we highlighted how the prefix "trans-" specifically delineates the transmedia dynamics based on a broad media conception, which is conducive to language experimentation, to deviations from original functions, and to resignifications arising from social uses.

To characterize transmedia dynamics as transmedia communication logic, we presented the Peircean pragmatic view in Chapter 1. Based on pragmatic and semiotic foundations, our description of transmedia dynamics defines it as a communication model that outlines the systems of transmediality from aesthetic, ethical, and logical perspectives. We took Peirce's idea of the productive incompleteness of the interpretant as a conceptual parameter for understanding the way in which media consumption regulates habits and delineates the transmedia narrative in the sign process and its correlated associations.

According to this approach, transmedia dynamics involves all media environments, from digital to analog, online to off-line. In this sense, transmedia dynamics are not restricted to the multiplatform narratives guided by media industries because they also encompass alternative media configurations. Thus, any mediacentric connotation of transmedia dynamics was removed. We demonstrated our approach by analyzing the context of transmedia mobilization mediated by hashtags used in Brazil.

We further developed the theoretical discussion of Chapter 1 in Chapter 2. We understand transmedia dynamics as a system of signs, in an approach that combines contributions from Peircean semiotics and systems theory. The complexity of transmedia dynamics also refers to the complexity of the dispositions of users/consumers/players as interpreters of semiotic elements present in transmedia stories. Transmedia dynamics extends further to the complexity of social, cultural, economic, and political constructs around transmedia experiences. This perspective of complexity falls within the scope of what we call the transmedia effect: the expansion of storyworlds that are robust and exciting enough to function across multiple levels of interest, from audiences to producers to authors to financiers. We presented several audiovisual examples of this transmedia scenario.

In Chapter 3, we developed our own transmedia design analytical and operational model, based on theoretical-methodological discussions in Chapters 1 and 2. Transmedia projects are complex phenomena involving multiple dimensions, such as narrative, cultural context, marketing, business model, and audience engagement. We consider all these aspects to better analyze an entire transmedia project. In this sense, we discussed the essential features of the design process of transmedia projects, contributing to support the analytical needs of transmedia designers and the applied research for media industries. We applied the proposed analytical model to the case of *The Handmaid's Tale*, a fictional transmedia project that represents the idea of the transmedia effect discussed in Chapter 2.

We used the same structure of this model to analyze a nonfictional context in Chapter 4. We applied the same structure and presented a specific version of the model dedicated to analyzing how transmedia features are structured and implemented in the news coverage of mega events. The cases analyzed relate to mega sporting events: the Olympic Games (Sochi and Rio) and the Fédération Internationale de Football Association (FIFA) World Cup (in Brazil and Russia). The case studies reported summarize the authors' investigative path, between 2014 and 2018, in the transmedia journalism dimension of global sporting events.

In Chapter 5, we presented our own proposal for transmedia education communication planning elaborated and applied to public schools in Portuguese-speaking countries, especially those located in low-income communities. Since 2016, we have carried out experiments in transmedia education for public schools in East Timor, Brazil, and Mozambique. The methodology we developed is anchored on Peircean semiotics. Based on the Peircean pragmatic model of semiosis, we followed the trajectory of collective actions that arise with the creative use of multiple media platforms in the classroom.

Our methodology, which encompasses five steps, operates under various aspects of mediation that are related to each other, such as communication, education, culture, Portuguese language, literature, and activism. Thus, our communication planning in transmedia education aims to contribute to improving teaching and learning conditions in diverse cultural, social, political, and economic contexts, taking into account the media consumption habits of students of each school and their preferences in terms of media content.

The case studies reported throughout this book have in common experimental empiricism, as they all seek to verify the analytical potential of our theoretical and methodological proposals for varied transmedia dynamics. Subsequently, the reported case studies have the potential to present an original contribution to the area, resulting in innovation and improvement of the actions developed in transmedia studies. Nonetheless, the case studies also involve typical risks of experimental methodologies, such as (1) a reduced empirical dimension, which impairs their practical evaluation, and (2) small academic insertion, which restricts their peer evaluation.

Despite these risks, which are important limits of our theoretical-methodological and empirical-conceptual proposal, we are convinced of the potential of our proposed approach. For this reason, we always seek to send the results of our research to peer review. In addition, we invest in improving our proposal with each assessment of practical development and in diversifying the empirical dimension of the transmedia dynamics that we investigate.

In this regard, we are expanding our research interests in transmedia dynamics in two empirical contexts based on the similar theoretical and methodological approach: (1) the spreadability of fake news on online social network connections and (2) communication planning in transmedia education for sustainability. Both configure our future realm of research in which we would like to improve our theoretical and methodological proposal in transmedia dynamics.

To improve our studies on these subjects, we have started researching. Some results of our investigations in the realm of the propagation of fake news in online social networks have been published, such as in the *Brazilian Journalism Research* special issue on *Fake News: Challenges and risks for contemporary journalism*, edited by Salomão Bruck, Lorena Tárcia, and Renira Gambarato in December 2019. In this special issue, the authors stress that the discussion on fake news requires "the careful examination of complex processes of contemporary mediation through which interconnected and globalized societies circulate fierce positions, speeches regarding intolerance and hatred, and intentional dishonesty" (Bruck et al., 2019, p. 426).

From a Peircean semiotic perspective, Borges and Gambarato (2019) discussed the logic of algorithms employed by Facebook to foster audience engagement as it relates to the spreadability of fake news in the context of transmedia journalism. Based on a theoretical and methodological semiotic approach, they also discussed how Peirce's methods of fixation of beliefs influence the process by which fake news is spread. In the same pragmatic semiotic view, Alzamora and Andrade (2019) analyzed the spreading of fake news on social media surrounding the trial of former Brazil President Luiz Inácio Lula da Silva in January 2018. The findings indicate that the dispute for the semiotic value of truth fostered the transmedia expansion of fake news and, paradoxically, of verified news as well. The collective effort to establish competing beliefs was characterized by the Peircean methods of tenacity and authority.

In the realm of transmedia education for sustainability, we recently started an international research collaboration between Federal University of Minas Gerais (Brazil) and Jönköping University (Sweden) to develop further our research in transmedia education. In this project, we invest in the development of a transmedia educommunication methodology. The premise is that the processes involved in the transmedia education sphere, especially in connection with notions of transmedia activism, can contribute to the development of actions promoting sustainability, cultural diversity, social responsibility, and environmental awareness.

With this project, we aim to develop and apply original transmedia communication and education for sustainability methodologies to stimulate the formation of an international research network on transmedia communication. We believe, however, that the collective effort of transmedia researchers is fundamentally important for the improvement of methods and theoretical approaches of transmedia communication in its most varied empirical facets. We would like this book to be read as an invitation to everyone to face this challenge.

References

Alzamora, G., & Andrade, L. (2019). The transmedia dynamics of fake news by the pragmatic conception of truth. *Matrizes, 13*(1), 109–131. Retrieved from http://www.revistas.usp.br/matrizes/article/view/149592/152964

Borges, P., & Gambarato, R. R. (2019). The role of beliefs and behavior on Facebook: A semiotic approach to algorithm, fake news and transmedia journalism. *International Journal of Communication, 13*, 603–618.

Bruck, M. S., Tárcia, L., & Gambarato, R. R. (2019). Introduction: Special issue fake news: Challenges and risks for contemporary journalism. *Brazilian Journalism Research, 15*(3), 426–429.

Index

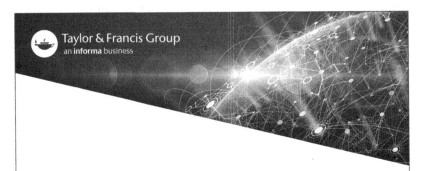

Printed in the United States
by Baker & Taylor Publisher Services